Writers' Workshops
& the Work of
Making Things

Writers' Workshops & the Work of Making Things

Patterns, Poetry . . .

Richard P. Gabriel

∼

★Addison-Wesley

Boston • San Francisco • New York • Toronto • Montreal
London • Munich • Paris • Madrid
Capetown • Sydney • Tokyo • Singapore • Mexico City

Many of the designations used by manufacturers and sellers to distinguish their products are claimed as trademarks. Where those designations appear in this book, and Addison-Wesley, Inc. was aware of a trademark claim, the designations have been printed with initial capital letters or in all capitals.

The author and publisher have taken care in the preparation of this book, but make no expressed or implied warranty of any kind and assume no responsibility for errors or omissions. No liability is assumed for incidental or consequential damages in connection with or arising out of the use of the information or programs contained herein.

The publisher offers discounts on this book when ordered in quantity for special sales. For more information, please contact:

Pearson Education Corporate Sales Division
201 W. 103rd Street
Indianapolis, IN 46290
(800) 428-5331
corpsales@pearsoned.com

Visit A–W on the Web: www.awprofessional.com

Library of Congress Cataloging-in-Publication Data
Gabriel, Richard P.
Writer's workshops & the work of making things : patterns, poetry .../
Richard P. Gabriel.
  p.   cm.
Includes bibliographical references and index.
ISBN 0-201-72183-X
1. Computer software—Development.   1. Title: Writers' workshops and the work of making things.   II. Title.
QA76.76.D47 G34 2002
005.3—dc21   2002003778

Copyright © 2002 Richard P. Gabriel

All rights reserved. No part of this publication may be reproduced, stored in a retrieval system, or transmitted, in any form, or by any means, electronic, mechanical, photocopying, recording, or otherwise, without the prior consent of the publisher. Printed in the United States of America. Published simultaneously in Canada.

For information on obtaining permission for use of material from this work, please submit a written request to:

Pearson Education, Inc.
Rights and Contracts Department
75 Arlington Street, Suite 300
Boston, MA 02116
Fax: (617) 848-7047

ISBN 0-201-72183-X
Text printed on recycled paper
1 2 3 4 5 6 7 8 9 10—CRS—0605040302
First printing, June 2002

FOR JOHN P. GABRIEL
*builder and inventor, who gave up ambition
to concentrate on life*

Contents

	Preface	ix
	Acknowledgments	xi
	Introduction	xiii
ONE	Writers' Workshop Overview	1
TWO	Crowd	11

PART ONE
The Work of Making Things

THREE	Triggers and Practice	25
FOUR	Work in Progress	33
FIVE	The Gift	41

PART TWO
Writers' Workshop

SIX	The Players	53
SEVEN	The Setting	69
EIGHT	In Situ	77
NINE	Preparing for the Workshop	85
TEN	Shepherds	97

ELEVEN	The Author Reads	101
TWELVE	Fly on the Wall	109
THIRTEEN	Summarize the Work	115
FOURTEEN	Positive Feedback	127
FIFTEEN	Suggestions for Improvement	135
SIXTEEN	Clarifications	147
SEVENTEEN	Wrapping Up	151
EIGHTEEN	Revising the Work	155
	Coda: The Work of Making Things	167
	Notes	175
	Appendix A: Examples	187
	Appendix B: Writing Workshops Guidelines for Feedback	201
	References	205
	Index	209
	About the Author	269

Preface

In November 1999, Paul Becker of Addison-Wesley approached me at a conference in Denver and told me I was the perfect person to write a book on the writers' workshop. I thought he was nuts. He thought I was nuts back. We were both right. He was thinking of a book only for the software world—a primer on the writers' workshop as I had introduced it there. I was thinking of a book for both software people and "real" writers. I was sure there were plenty of books about the writers' workshop: There are books about every aspect of writing except maybe how to sharpen pencils. But not so—I couldn't find much that talked about the writers' workshop and how it worked.[1]

I told him to forget it anyway.

He emailed me a few times.

Forget it.

After the third or fourth email, I was starting to believe it might be fun since I had been thinking about how to address both audiences at once. I finally agreed.

But I missed all his deadlines, and the draft I sent him in July 2001 was OK, but minimal. We had agreed on a short book, but I had sent him a chapbook.

Then I asked the two writing communities I am in—the alumni of the Warren Wilson College MFA Program for Writers and the design patterns community—to tell me what they knew about the writers' workshop, and I was hit by a tsunami of stories, advice, and ideas. Many of them were so good that I left them mostly in their words. It's part of the writers' tradition of stealing (but I did ask if it was OK).

Writing a book on writers' workshop brings one dangerously close to the possibility of writing about writing and creativity in general. There are already many books on those two topics. I am an expert in neither, certainly not as measured by education and research. I am a practitioner of both, though, and I've approached this book from the outlook of a simple laborer in those areas. There are theories of learning, ideas developed by composition theorists—I could have looked into how theories of creativity and selfhood play into the workshop, or how to apply stage-development theory and philosophy to the problem of how to help a writer become autonomous. I could have delved more deeply into cultural, racial, and gender issues in the workshop. These would be good things to do, but they are not the good things I am able to do well.

I know what it feels like to try to learn how to write, how to be a musician, how to create new ideas. Not being blessed with much talent to begin with, I think I've made do with what I was given well enough to be proud of it. And to think I have something to share about the road I took.

I don't know if this book will be useful for you, but I hope it will be. I can tell you I had a great good time writing it, and sometimes—but not now—I wished I never had to stop.

—rpg
Redwood City
2002

Acknowledgments

I belong to two writers' communities: the software patterns writers' community, which is eagerly creating a new—and new type of—literature in the world of computing and software, and the Warren Wilson Master of Fine Arts (MFA) Program for Writers alumni, the Wallies. Each of these two communities is generous beyond anything xenia could predict and more than a modest writer like me deserves. If you are a writer, then you know what kind of communities these are, and if you aren't, you can't imagine the warmth, support, and generosity spawned by the work of trying to write what is impossible to write.

When I asked these two communities about their thoughts on the writers' workshop, I was flooded. Literally the size of my manuscript nearly doubled in length with the advice and stories I got, and the reminders of what I once knew but had forgotten. I would like to thank them first.

Beth Thomas, Bob Hanmer, Bobby Woolf, Brian Marick, Bridget Balthrop Morton, Browning Porter, Bruce Anderson, Carolyn West, Dave West, Dawn O'Dell, Dirk Riehle, Don Olson, Faith Holsaert, Gerard Meszaros, Ian Wilson, James O. Coplien, James Reed, John Gribble, John LeTourneau, John Vlissides, Jutta Eckstein, Kathy Collisson, Ken Auer, Kent Beck, Klaus Marquardt, Laure-Anne Bosselaar, Lauren Yaffe, Linda Rising, Mari Coates, Mark Solomon, Markus Völter, Martha Rhodes, Martha Carlson-Bradley, Margaret Kaufman, Neil Harrison, Norm Kerth, Priscilla Orr, Ralph Johnson, Rebecca Rikner, Richard Helms, Richard Schmitt, Steve Fay, and Ward Cunningham.

James O. Coplien and Bobby Woolf wrote down the writers' workshop process as we first practiced it in the software patterns community ("A Pattern Language for Writers' Workshops," in *Pattern Languages of Program Design 4*), and Neil Harrison wrote down how to shepherd ("The Language of the Shepherds: A Pattern Language for Shepherds and Sheep," unpublished but on the Web), each in fine pattern languages—without these I would have had to actually remember what we did and learned.

Linda Elkin provided detailed and provocative comments on the manuscript for this book, and without her help it would have been a feeble book indeed.

I particularly would like to thank the teachers who tried their darnedest to teach me to write: Heather McHugh, Stephen Dobyns, Michael Collier, and Thomas Lux. At Warren Wilson College, Ellen Bryant Voigt and Peter Turchi combined to create the most congenial and productive writers' workshops I have ever encountered. The following were some of my workshop leaders at writers' workshops around the United States: Brenda Hillman, Sandra McPherson, Jane Hirshfield, Walter Pavlich, Gary Snyder, Pattianne Rogers, Bob Hass, Ed Hirsch, Gerald Stern, Mark Strand, Timothy Liu, Mark Jarman, Carl Philips, Tom Andrews, Marianne Boruch, Eleanor Wilner, Tony Hoagland, Steve Orlen, Joan Aleshire, Agha Shahid Ali, Reginald Gibbons, Larry Levis, Campbell McGrath, Renate Wood, Brooks Haxton, Michael Ryan, and Alan Williamson.

And especially: My friend Guy L. Steele Jr. kept me alive; my partner, Jo A. Lawless, kept me loved; my daughter, Mika Toribara, and son, Joseph Tracy, kept me young; and my long-time colleague and close friend Ron Goldman kept me honest (sort of).

Introduction

Throughout my years of schooling, I received Ds and the occasional C in my English courses. My confidence in my ability to write was quite low as I entered my first writers' workshop. It's true I had spent years working on improving my writing on-the-job, but I still carried the scars from my teachers' assessments of my inability to express ideas as an adolescent.

During my virgin writers' workshop experience, I learned something about my particular paper, what worked well, what was confusing, etc. But beyond those interesting pieces of feedback, I learned something more important—I learned I could write something that others appreciated.

This workshop healed my scars, savagely inflicted upon my young mind by English teachers who knew harsh feedback was good for me. This experience gave me the confidence to write a book, which is now published and selling well.

—ANONYMOUS, BUT IT COULD BE YOU

Writing is one of the craziest things to do—it's hard, and often what gets written surprises the writer. After the hard job of getting a draft, the writer is elated and the result reads great—a masterpiece in the making and a life of fame and accolades; the writer can do anything. Then the writers' workshop.

For many people the expectation of their first writers' workshop is that it will be a glorious affirmation of their own talent and skill as a writer, but for many at the end of the writer's first workshop experience, there is emptiness—the experience has neither affirmed nor condemned. For some there are tears, doubts, shame. For a few there is only the question: How could I have ever felt I had talent?

The writer goes on, or the writer quits.

∽

The writers' workshop has been in use for decades by fiction writers, poets, and writers of creative nonfiction, and in the realm of creative writing it is praised as essential and criticized as vicious, loved and hated.* Like any long-lived institution, the writers' workshop has drifted from its origins, and some of the aspects that make workshops wonderful have been rubbed away or replaced by others having less effectiveness or good will—that is, like all magic bits, the magic has been worn off as the energy of its practice dissipates.

In 1994 the writers' workshop had a rebirth—in another field, with entirely new participants, and in a setting where the magic both reappeared and was understood. Since 1994 the writers' workshop format has been in use by the software patterns community, both as a way to improve patterns and pattern languages and as a way to share knowledge and experience, as a sort of alternative to presentations and standard scientific workshops.[2]

The patterns community experienced the writers' workshop mojo right away, but the important news is that this particular community, perhaps like few others, has the habit and practice of trying to understand and articulate why beautiful things are beautiful and why comfortable things give comfort. The workshop—something wildly new and unconventional to them—was studied and its nuances captured.

What makes the writers' workshop tick is roughly what makes large, open-source software projects tick, where sometimes hundreds or thousands of programmers are working with shared source code. We see it in creative brainstorming sessions where a diverse group is brought together in fast-communication situations. We can also see it in the swarming behavior of all sorts of groups in which order emerges where there once was chaos.

---

* I use the term *creative* to distinguish the *creative writing* community from other communities that write. These other communities are full of highly creative people. When you see phrases like *creative writing* and *creative workshops*, read them as jargon.

But knowing how and why a thing works when it works is different from being able to make it work any given time. The writers' workshop works through sociology and psychology; it is only as good as its participants; its direction depends on the work at hand and the order it is read; it can spin cruelly wrong; but it usually brings out the best in us.

~

The writers' workshop is bundled paradoxes: the private act of writing mixed with group criticism, the gift economy of shared works mixed with mercenary workshop moderators, and the generosity of supportive comments in a forum that seems better suited for cutting people down.

Writing is an intensely private, solitary act; the writers' workshop is one of the few parts of the process in which the public—the *other* in the guise of colleagues and strangers—is invited in. For the writer new to the writers' workshop, it appears to be a forum in which the writer, infallible and exhausted, faces the first check, the first test of the work itself, and given these expectations, the test can be harsh. Where moments before the feeling was total power, during and after, the feeling may be total incompetence.

On the flip side, writers experienced with the workshop bring work they are unsure of but feel contains a kernel perhaps without direction, and the workshop helps find that direction. Before the workshop they feel uncertain about the work, but after it they are brimming with new ideas and enthusiasm. Workshops are where writers gain invaluable advice and feedback, and in the best of circumstances, workshops are where writers learn to trust themselves and grow beyond the workshop.

The work goes on, the words improve, the ideas are sharpened, what was important is made bold, what is irrelevant is trimmed, the awkward matures to grace. And the transformation from pure thought to thought-in-words on the page goes on.

The arc from doubt to elation and omnipotence to doubt to completion is common to all creative activities. Its absence is the prime symptom of a mere job, rote engineering, repetition. That something like the writers' workshop is needed in this process needs explanation. In this book I hope to answer this question and more.

We will look at the writers' workshop process, and I will point out as best I can what conditions are required for it to work. I want to try to provide an understanding of how it works, and lay out a road map to its workings both as a ritual and as experience—how to run one, how to participate in one, how to survive one, and how to use it to further your own work.

˜

I come from a background of both the arts and the sciences: My principal education and activities are from the world of mathematics and computer science; my second education and avocation is creative writing—poetry, in fact. I have experienced the writers' workshop in both realms. In creative writing it is a more emotional experience because the stuff that's on the page perhaps means more to the writer as a person than does the more technical and "objective" stuff on the pages written by a software developer, computer researcher, or manager. In creative writing, the discussions tend to be about the narrative structure, what the piece is about, how it is constructed, craft elements and how to improve them, aesthetic concerns, and the positions and stances of the narrator and audience. In the technical world, the experience is more antiseptic—a little more about the stuff than about the person, but not overwhelmingly so—and objective; the discussions tend to be more about the facts presented, the accuracy of the claims, the technical and scientific basis for judging the correctness of the material, and less about presentation and aesthetics, even though the strength and intention of the writers' workshop is to the writing.

The writers' workshop is a dance, and without knowing the steps, a participant might trip, even fall. Feet could be sprained or even broken—one should never participate in a writers' workshop without an introduction to it of some sort and the ground rules being set. You need a moderator or workshop leader—someone with experience and, even better, expertise in the workshop and a master writer. The feet that are most badly hurt will not be those of the experienced, but those of a new writer, a young person, and it's not out of the realm of possibility that a career might be changed by the wrong kind of statement at the wrong time. The conversations in a writers' workshop are not a debate, not a chat, not an argument, not a forum to show off, not a flame war, not a love-fest, not a shouting match, not a lecture, not a demonstration, and certainly not a cakewalk.

But the young writer is not the only one at risk: I've seen seasoned writers—poets with hundreds of poems in their portfolio and dozens of writers' workshops behind them—break down, run from the room in tears, leave a conference that was devastatingly unaffordable after the wrong two or three comments. I have watched senior computer scientists with dozens of publications turn bright bright red in embarrassment and then anger. The workshop is a crucible in which every part of the human equation is tested: creation, destruction, leadership, control, privacy, exhibitionism, voyeurism, love, hatred, fear, collaboration, cooperation, order, chaos, victory, devastation, humility, pride, shyness, bravado, and spirituality. For technical people, the raw emotion is surprising; for the creative writer the clinical coldness is alarming.

When it works well, though, the writers' workshop works better than almost anything else at getting to the best work in the shortest time. If you're trying to get quickly to the release of a usable work, you will get there faster without the writers' workshop process, but if your goal is the best work, the writers' workshop will get you there faster.

Through this book, I hope to introduce or reintroduce the ideas of the writers' workshop to a wide audience: to writers new to the workshop, to writers who want to understand how the workshop works, to new writers who want to find out how to get good fast, to veteran workshoppers who have experienced too many bad parts of workshops, to technical people and scientists who have never thought of their work as including writing, to businesspeople looking for better ways to improve collateral material and presentations, and to software developers.

For creative writers for whom the writers' workshop has perhaps grown stale and drifted from its roots—by talking about how and why it works, I hope to rekindle your faith in it and help you find a renewed focus on the work and on the gifts the workshop represents. For scientists and technologists already using the writers' workshop, I hope to bring you some of the insights of the creative writing community on writing and their more pedagogical use of the workshop so that you can use the workshop more effectively and more thoroughly.

∼

The book is broken into two major parts, introduced by a two-chapter overview. To understand why the writers' workshop can work requires an idea or a model of writing and the writing process. I have no choice but to give you my view of writing and process, and I hope you'll recognize some aspects of it in the work you do. For both creative writers and scientists it is a creative act with risks involved. The first part of the book covers these topics and is called The Work of Making Things.

Part 2, Writers' Workshop, explains the steps in the writers' workshop and provides stories and examples of what goes on in the workshop. It refers to concepts and discussions in Part 1. Readers who wish just to find out what the workshop is and how to run one can simply read Chapter 1, Writers' Workshop Overview, and Part 2, Writers' Workshop.

I've mashed together examples from both the scientific and the literary writers' workshop. By doing this I hope to introduce the two communities to each other, because I believe there is more commonality between them than either would admit. But I've tried to make my discussions of topics particular to each community understandable to the other.

For clarity I'll use the term *creative workshop* for the workshop as practiced in the creative writing community and the term *technical workshop* for the workshop in the technical, scientific, and business communities. *Workshop* refers to both varieties. Similarly, I will distinguish between *creative writing* and *technical writing*, though by the latter, I'm not talking about documenting software or technology but writing in a technical or scientific vein.

I hope to present everything I know about the workshop and how to make it work for you. And if you are a creative maker of things working on your own, I hope to present enough for you to get the writers' workshop going and working for you so you can make things better and get good fast.

CHAPTER ONE

Writers' Workshop Overview

The writers' workshop begins when ten or so people decide to read, review, and critique each other's work under the guidance of a moderator. The workshop is a formal gathering, perhaps over a series of sessions, that lasts at least as long as it takes to go through everyone's work—and the group can stay together continuing to review later drafts and new work, much like a sewing circle or poker game. The longer the group stays together the better—up to a point where you need to bring in new people.

The seed for the writers' workshop as we now know it was planted at the end of the nineteenth century at the University of Iowa. The result was the Iowa Writers' Workshop, which is one of the best known and most prestigious of the creative writing programs in the United States.[3] The writers' workshop has been in use by the writing community ever since, and it is among the most effective ways for novice and intermediate writers to get good fast and to learn the critical skills to continue to improve.

The writers' workshop is one of several somewhat counterintuitive practices in which what seems like an individual art or craft is done or assisted by a group or crowd. Other practices, which I'll describe in Chapter 2, include brainstorming, open-source development, pair programming, and the design charrette.

The fundamental approach used by the writers' workshop is not limited to writing, drawings, and designs, but can be applied—and has been applied—to anything that people make: software, patterns, pattern languages, organizations, presentations, brochures, marketing campaigns, business plans, companies, plays, performances, music, conference plans, food, interior decoration, landscaping, hairstyles, perfume choices, and on and on. The writers' workshop brings together people who make things and the things they have made in a way that enables effective criticism and suggestions for improvement while maintaining an atmosphere in which the individual is not harmed by the experience of people criticizing the work.

The formality and stylized behavior of the writers' workshop is what makes it work. There are three roles one can play in a workshop: the author, the moderator, or a participant.

Already-organized writers' workshops exist for both the creative writing and the software patterns worlds. For the creative writing world, there are dozens of national workshops like the Bread Loaf Writers' Conference and the Sewanee Writers' Conference, and dozens of Master of Fine Arts programs based on the writers' workshop format. Dozens or hundreds of summer programs offer writers' workshops lasting from a few days to a couple of weeks—attending one is a good way to work your way into the workshop community. Many community colleges and universities, through their extension programs, organize writers' workshops, but these can vary in quality. The formats of these workshops are not all the same but hold a family resemblance. Later I'll look at some of the variations and what they're all about. If you wish to try one of the variations on the writers' workshop, it's a good idea to find out what variation it uses, the usual experience level, and, if possible, the culture that the workshop maintains. Workshops develop their own rituals, myths, ways of behaving, stances toward hierarchies, and so forth. The culture of a workshop can make the experience delightful or nightmarish.

For the software patterns world, there are international workshops like the Conference on Pattern Languages of Programs and the European Conference on Pattern Languages of Programs (PLoP and EuroPLoP, respectively). There are also a number of regional PLoPs—as they're called—and readers' and writers' groups for patterns.[4] Check the Web if you want to join an existing writers' workshop.

∼

The original idea behind the writers' workshop was to do a *close reading* of a work, to use the term F. R. Leavis coined for the practice of looking at the words on the page rather than at the intentions of the author or the historical and aesthetic context of the work. Under this philosophy, the workshop doesn't care much what the author feels about what he or she wrote, only what's on the page. This corresponds to the philosophy of the New Critics, which held that the work was its own "being," with its own internal consistency and coherence, which could be studied apart from the author. Moreover, this approach is nearly identical to that of the Russian formalists, who thought that the proper approach to literature was to study how literary texts actually worked, their structures and devices. These origins explain the reliance of the workshop on the text and the author as fly on the wall even in informal workshops in which the author is closer to the action than in the original conception.

There are a variety of workshop formats and practices, but to give an idea of what a workshop is like, let me present how a technical writers' workshop works in the software patterns community. Note that the following process is followed for each author in the workshop.

Before the group first gets together to review a particular piece, the piece is handed out so that the group can prepare. Each reader may write notes on the piece in preparation. When the group is ready to start, it forms into a circle. The group's ground rules are stated by the moderator, who may use a variation of the rules I talk about in this book. The author selects and reads aloud a short passage from the work or the entire work if it's short enough. He or she may ask the members of the group to focus on a particular concern. The author is allowed to introduce the piece exactly as it would be introduced when consumed or performed.

At this point until near the end of the session, the author does not speak; all conversation is directed, if to anyone, to the moderator. In fact, the moderator should keep people from looking at the author or speaking directly to him or her.

The moderator asks for the piece to be summarized. In this section the only thing discussed is what the piece seems to be about—if being about something is appropriate—or what the group members got from the piece. No criticism is allowed here: The idea is to get only a sense of how the piece was perceived. This is an area in which the creative writers' and technical writers' workshops differ most: The technical writers' workshop, because the texts are largely factual, focuses on the content of the work more than does the creative writers' workshop.

Once the moderator determines that little new information is coming out, the group moves on to discuss what "worked" in the piece, what people liked or found effective. This is the place where positive comments are made.

Once there is nothing new being said, the group turns to improving the piece. Sometimes a participant cannot say how to make an improvement, but the ideal situation is to present a fix along with the criticism—and some technical workshops require all comments for improvement to be in the form of a fix.

Finally, the author is allowed to ask questions of the group—perhaps clearing up points that were made or asking about specific parts of the piece. The author is not allowed to defend the work.

The group then thanks the author.

A workshop for one piece usually takes about forty-five minutes to an hour. Sometimes an author has two or more pieces reviewed, one after another. The duration of attention to a piece and how many of one author's pieces are reviewed in one session vary considerably from workshop to workshop.

There is a variation that allocates about fifteen minutes to each author. These workshops are usually intended for people in an ongoing workshop and who are writing new pieces all the time. The format of the workshop is usually the same as for the longer version, but scaled down to fifteen minutes.

In some workshops, an audience is allowed to observe the workshop in addition to the participant authors. In general, this is a risky thing to do because of the possible embarrassment for the authors.

Despite the apparent simplicity of the writers' workshop, it is remarkably effective. Since 1994, when I introduced the writers' workshop to the software patterns community, there has been a set of yearly technical conferences on the topic of patterns and pattern languages in which the main activity is writers' workshops instead of presentations or freeform discussions.

Besides using the writers' workshop format for creative writing, I have seen it used effectively as a replacement for paper presentations, for trying to improve an organization, and for preparing the collateral material for a product launch including presentations. Participants who are new to the format have commented that it seems to get more information out of the work in far less time and that a standard review process that might require weeks can take place in one or two days.

During the first technical conference based on a writers' workshop, a computer scientist colleague of mine took me aside and asked about the format and where it came from. After I explained it to her, she said that it was remarkable how it brought out twice the content in half the time.

The format of the workshop is designed to simulate the impossible situation of a group of very friendly, intelligent people discussing the piece, with the author's being an unobserved observer. The moderator and the form keep the focus, and the rules keep the discussion friendly and positive.

By just reading a description of the writers' workshop, you may not think that the approach is anything special or that it would work well at all. Even though the workshop format has been used for decades by the creative writing community, if you're not an artist, the workshop seems to be a vehicle for honing some work of self-expression, not the serious code review or marketing review you need to get done pronto. So here's the story of how the idea was introduced to the software patterns community.

In April 1994 the Hillside Group held a retreat at Sequoia Seminars, a small meeting center in Boulder Creek, California—in the Santa Cruz Mountains between San Jose, at the base of the San Francisco Bay, and Santa Cruz, coastal resort town and refuge to aging hippies. Boulder Creek is off the main roads, and the conference center is way up in the redwoods, rustic with a few small cabins with mostly working showers. We shared two or three to a cabin to save money and foster a sense of community. The Hillside Group was founded as a kind of "friends of Kent Beck" organization,* but officially we were aimed at the goal of promoting the ideas of the architect Christopher Alexander—especially the idea of patterns and pattern languages—to the realm of software development. The group was uniform only in sharing a "surfacey" sort of love of Alexander and his ideas, but otherwise we claimed a diversity that was refreshing at the time and unsettling: researchers from IBM and academia, Europeans, gamesters, an Australian, founders of companies, unknown consultants, and fundamentalist Christians. Typical, to an extent, for the times was the absence of women in the group.

The Hillside Group was named at its first meeting, when the members went up on a hillside and, using Alexander's book, *A Pattern Language*, designed in their heads a building nearby. The Boulder Creek meeting—about six months later—was called to review a draft of a book (later called *Design Patterns*) and to plan a conference—or at least talk about the idea. Software patterns were then largely unknown to the general software development community, as was the work of Alexander.

Alexander's work in *A Pattern Language* was to try to find what made some towns, cities, buildings, and rooms beautiful and livable, though he shied away from those words—he used "the quality without a name" and "habitable." Taken

---

* Kent Beck is an influential software developer and thinker.

as a group, the Hillside Group was not after the same thing, but focused more on what made certain software designs, especially object-oriented designs, special.

Patterns and pattern languages are a form in the literary sense of being somewhat stylized, written expositions explaining parts of design with these desirable qualities. A pattern talks about a context of building and the forces or considerations apparent to the designer's mind at that time and presents instructions on what to build to balance the forces as best as can be done. A pattern language is a set of patterns that can be used to build a whole thing—a room, a town, or a city. And a pattern language can be large enough that it includes other pattern languages within it.

Patterns and pattern languages are therefore about building a literature, and as with any literature, masterpieces are needed along with a way to move people along from readers to novice writers to accomplished writers to masters of the craft. At the time, and ever since, patterns and pattern languages have been a bit outside the mainstream of computer science—perhaps not by much—because software patterns are about describing what works and has worked well rather than finding new ideas. Most existing refereed journals and conferences won't accept submissions consisting of patterns and pattern languages, because those venues value novelty and puzzle solving, which patterns people scorn to a degree.

One way of understanding the situation is to think of patterns and pattern languages as a different paradigm from the one then in place for understanding how to build software. Within the old paradigm, which could be described as *formalist*, normal work was proceeding by looking at the formal properties of programs, systems, programming languages, architecture, and development practices. Patterns and pattern languages try to look at how to build software based on what has worked beautifully in the past. These practices are written down as a literature with a particular form or in a particular genre—the pattern and pattern language. Because patterns and pattern languages represent a different paradigm from the predominant one, the normal publishing outlets for the formalist paradigm don't recognize the validity—or even the rationality—of the patterns paradigm.

To address these publishing and paradigm problems, we needed a way to build a literature, which meant a publishing outlet, a conference, and a process for developing authors. We viewed as not effective the existing processes for developing scientific and technical writing. We gathered in Boulder Creek to work on this, and to work on the bonding exercises the group came to favor. In this case it was a ropes course—problem-solving exercises, trust-building exercises, and a climb to a platform on a tree where each person did a swan dive into nowhere to be caught by a belay rope held by friends and colleagues.

The conference had been decided on earlier, and a major topic for the retreat was to plan its details. Not many Hillside members at the retreat had much experience planning and running conferences, and of considerable concern was that the conference be unique, reflecting the nature of the patterns movement as we saw it shaping up. I had been involved with writers' workshops in my fledgling career as a poet, and I thought—suddenly, as I recall—that the workshop format might make for an interesting statement of uniqueness. Hillside was trying to build a literature, and the conference was hoped to be a funnel for patterns and pattern languages to be published, so why not use the process that seemed to serve the creative writing community well?

I described the idea and format, much in the way I did earlier in this chapter. Because Hillside is a group of people filled with respect for each other, I was able to describe it in great detail and without interruption. At the end, the group sat in stillness—we were in a large common meeting room with large picture windows looking out onto a redwood grove in mid-April, when the Santa Cruz mountains frequently enjoy a very heavy dew or light rain every night. After a few minutes, one of the members said, "That sucks." One by one, the group explained why they thought the idea was not good and was contrary to the philosophy of Hillside, and those reasons focused on the heavy degree of criticism that the workshop promoted—how this would be disruptive to the process of encouraging people to take risks writing a new literature, and how it was too academic an approach. Because I wasn't sure it was a great idea, I didn't defend it much.

Did I know it would work? In workshops I had attended, I had seen authors hurt and insulted by other authors and by the workshop leaders. I had heard great poets tell beginners that only their closest relatives might want to read their work. I had seen experienced writers who had drifted away from the workshop and ridiculed those who stuck with it. I had seen entire sessions focus on whether it was right to write a particular poem rather than about any of the craft of it.

No, I wasn't sure the writers' workshop would work, because if poets are highly critical of each other, just imagine how critical technical and scientific people could be. Ralph Johnson, though, was sympathetic to the irony of the situation: that my idea was being criticized while the rest of them were concerned about too much criticism in the workshop. He proposed we try it.

No one was eager to be the first victim, but Ward Cunningham had brought a nice pattern language and he volunteered. Mindful of the criticism, and having thought a little about the pitfalls of the workshop and having heard the poets describe it as intending to be a cushioned experience, I moderated that first workshop with tenderness and care—or with what of those things I could muster. We followed exactly the steps described above, and we went through Ward's pattern language, discovering new things, uncovering questions that perplexed us, finding unexplored corners of the work, talking about the writing and the form of the piece. We took about ninety minutes.

When it ended, the room was still again. Outside, the grove of redwoods began to darken and the drops that hadn't evaporated during the afternoon kept dripping down. Bruce Anderson, who was among the more vocal critics of the idea, spoke first, "Well, I must admit the damn thing seems to work quite well, wouldn't you all say?"

There's a concept with much currency in the writers' world that seems to have not made it to most of the technical professions: generosity. The generosity of the group in workshopping Ward certainly came into play, and it was by far the most civil and productive writers' workshop I had ever experienced. Because I had never moderated one before, I had my own fears to attend to. The generosity of that first experience seems to have carried over into the technical community's practice of the writers' workshop.

We spent the rest of the day designing rules so that an audience could watch a workshop, and trying to understand how the whole thing would work. Some of that understanding and later thinking about it is contained in this book.

At that retreat, we instituted a number of practices not typically used at traditional technical and scientific conferences and workshops: the use of the writers' workshop as the only or primary way to "present" papers, shepherding work before and after workshopping it, a book series for publication of the best work at the conference after a further period of shepherding, games as part of a conference in order to set the mood for new thinking, and crowded group accommodations (including sharing rooms) at the conference site so that latenight discussions would be possible. The concept of shepherding—used in technical journals to an extent in the form of editorship—was expanded and strengthened, so that an expert would routinely work with authors for a few weeks or months before the writers' workshop took place.

I've had experience introducing the workshop in two other settings. In 1998, the company I was working for decided to launch a major new product on short notice. It was the practice of that company to marshal lots of material for such launches, which typically took place in an on-stage setting with associated videos and major press coverage. This was an exceptional launch by being larger than normal, but the usual time for preparation was shortened by a factor of two.

We had to prepare a presentation, two white papers, a set of customer scenarios, a stage script, a video, a sales training guide, two brochures, and two press releases. We had marketing people from all over the company from a number of locations and several contract people and contract houses working on it. In a typical launch, all materials are reviewed by most of the core people in the launch team and the marketing people, and each review could take a week or two for proper grueling commentary and responses, with schedules arranged on an ad hoc basis.

Instead, I suggested the writers' workshop. We read papers, watched a presentation, looked at brochure mock-ups, and went through storyboards. Some of what was reviewed was spoken work, some written—along with visual materials. We took one long day to workshop all this. Though not everyone exited the room a confirmed fan of the workshop—marketing people sometimes can be good at criticism and not so good at generosity—all agreed we got more done in that one-day workshop and the one-day preparation for it than in the more typical multiweek process.

The third time I introduced the idea was to workshop the Hillside Group itself as an organization in the year 2000. After six years of good success in promoting patterns and pattern languages, the patterns community had matured faster than the Hillside Group had as an organization. We needed to revise the Hillside Group, and what better way than the writers' workshop? We had an off-site meeting after a conference, and we wanted to revitalize Hillside. After choosing an "author" from the group of founding members attending the meeting, we launched into a writers' workshop. The author began by stating what Hillside was. Next, we summarized what we thought Hillside was and had accomplished over the years. Then we discussed what worked well and what we liked about Hillside and its activities. After that we started to make suggestions on how to improve the organization. Finally, the "author" asked about specific suggestions. Perhaps you can imagine a discussion like this about an organization you are in that seems to be having its difficulties. What is its mission? What would you keep? What are you doing well that could be spread to the rest of the organization? How would you change it? These are the main topics to cover. And for people who are used to the ritual and with how to take advantage of the spontaneous bouncing of ideas off each other, it would seem this would work well. And it did.

In the three cases just discussed, the initial reaction was strong skepticism followed by jubilation at the results. These stories are meant to accomplish one thing only: to convince you that no matter how silly or inappropriate you may consider the idea of applying the writers' workshop to your situation, it might work a lot better than you think and be just the way to get moving.

CHAPTER TWO

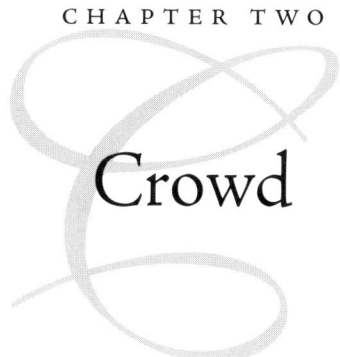

Crowd

There is a counterintuitive feel to the writers' workshop. It is one of several group activities aimed at assisting what is normally thought of as an individual act—of craft, of art, of invention, of creation. Brainstorms, critiques, charrettes, pair programming, open-source software projects, even master classes.

Brainstorming is gathering people, and through specific processes that either focus or liberate, the group uses association and dissociation to come up with more ideas than a single person can. The group can be in more frames of mind at the same time than a single person can, and different people's interests and knowledge can be triggered by what others say and do in the brainstorming session. Games and idea-generating exercises involving both the mental and physical can assist such groups. Ideas are captured on whiteboards, blackboards, pieces and sheets and rolls of paper, the wall—anywhere so that there is plenty of material to trigger new ideas. Relationships are marked down, missing relationships are sought. The result is usually more ideas than the sum the group could come up with as individuals and then lumped together.

In painting classes, students' work is reviewed regularly—say, every week—by the other students and the instructor in a process sometimes called a *critique*. In good critiques, as with the writers' workshop, a democratic ethos, in which each student is assumed to have something worthwhile to say, works well. In the critique, people can hear what's working and what's not and talk about craft and technique as way of reflecting while doing.

The *charrette* began as a teaching method in the École des Beaux-Arts in Paris. The students would be given a design problem. When they were finished, their drawings would be placed on a small pushcart—a charrette—to be critiqued by the faculty and students. Today a charrette is a team or several teams of designers from a variety of disciplines including sometimes the clients who work together in a public forum or on-site to put together a comprehensive solution taking into account all the disciplines represented. Their goal is to produce a design that addresses a wide range of considerations: design elements, green spaces, recreational needs, parking, traffic, landscaping, safety, and water management. At any given time, some are planning a street, some are sketching houses or buildings, and others are determining the effects of drainage. Constant invention and ongoing discussion and negotiation within a short time frame combine to produce a set of drawings that reveals a vision.

In *open source*, the source code to a piece of software is developed in the open by a process of public discussion about requirements, design, and implementation along with the implementation work. In this way, it's an ongoing writers' workshop applied to the development software by a group of developers. Or, you can look at a writers' workshop as a open-source project with just one main developer—the author—for each piece. Open-source development is in contrast to the more commonly used closed-source process, in which a small group of software developers work on the source code, which is hidden from public view. Where a closed-source project might have fifty people working with the source code and its design, the same project in an open-source setting might have hundreds or thousands of people looking at it, thinking about it, using it experimentally, and commenting on the system the source code represents.

Pair programming brings two programmers together to work on a single program in front of one computer or computer terminal. By discussing the program being written as it is written, the two programmers will likely produce a better, more correct, and more appropriate program than if either of them worked alone or if their interactions were only occasional.

I have also participated in paper-writing projects in this exact manner. For a number of important papers I wrote with a coauthor, the two of us would sit down in front of a computer with one of us controlling the keyboard. We would talk about what to write, and then one of us would type while the other watched. Some revision would take place when the nontyping partner would point something out. Sometimes when the typist was thinking about how to say the next bit, the other person would grab the keyboard and revise or add new material. In most cases, drafts written this way were of considerably higher quality than those written by one person alone.

A *master class* is when a virtuoso performer teaches a group of advanced or professional-level performers. Not only is ordinary teaching going on, but students perform small exercises and the teacher critiques and uses the examples to teach. It's like a group music lesson, but one in which the fine points of craft, technique, and musicality take the forefront and each student is assumed to be quite accomplished, which implies a degree of respect and a level playing field.

All of these collaborative practices share reasons for their success with each other and with the writers' workshop. In each, groups get together and the group achieves more than an individual would. Something about human interaction is involved. Something about having the work in front of the group is crucial.

The most reliably operating reason for such practices to work is that it brings to bear many eyes and minds to a piece to find mistakes or errors, such as factual errors, grammatical errors, structural errors, lack of clarity, bugs in software, cultural missteps, illogic, typos, and so on. A motto in the open-source world is that every bug is trivial given sufficiently many eyes. For artists, using writers' workshops to find errors doesn't compromise their aesthetic sensibilities—unless errors are part of the aesthetic intention of the work, most artists would appreciate being able to remove these mistakes. For small works or for repetitive works, checking for errors probably wouldn't require a dozen people dedicating a lot of effort to it, and so for this type of work the writers' workshop might not be appropriate.

The second—apparently related—reason that these collaborative practices work is that they bring to bear enough different points of view, expertise, and interests to deepen the work in places where its maker is not as facile. For example, suppose someone were to write a story about a Kansas farmer who in the year 2002 was paid by a company with a distinctive logo to plant his fields with plants and flowers so that when the flowers came into bloom, the field would display that logo when viewed from the air. As part of the story, the company was planning to make a TV commercial using the field as seen from different angles in the air. But the meat of the story is really about the fallout to the family in their community because the company is controversial in some way.

This storyline would make sense perhaps only in a pre-1995 time setting, because an ad made after that would likely use digital imaging to create the illusion that the field had been planted with the logo pattern rather than using real plants in a field. A writer unfamiliar with the use of computers in advertising and film would perhaps not realize that the premise of the story would be rejected by any technically savvy readers unless there were some other explanation for why the company wanted a real field, or unless the narrative was strong enough to cause such readers to suspend disbelief in this area.

To a workshopper with a computer background, this flaw in the story would seem like a serious bug or mistake, whereas to the writer and perhaps other writers, this flaw would seem like an esoteric detail. It would depend on the readership and other aspects of the work whether this "error" were acceptable, but it would be an error of a sort. Though it's up to the author to decide whether this flaw is significant enough to be addressed, the diversity of the workshop membership can provide information like this that is not otherwise readily available.

An author, though, cannot depend on workshop members having the expertise the author's work needs or on the willingness of a workshop member with the right expertise to spend additional time working with the author on the work. Different workshoppers have different interests, and some might be willing to invest work in specialized areas to help improve the work. Even though the volunteer work may last only a few hours or a few weeks, it may represent work that is invaluable to the success of the work.

Open source provides these benefits in different degrees. Because the work is ongoing and the instrumentality of interaction is the Internet, there are potentially more people looking for errors and the amount of volunteer work may be more extensive and longer term. In a sense, the members of the open-source community working on a project have an actual maker relationship to the work for the long term. Pair programming and design charrettes can be long-term efforts, and unlike open-source development, pair programming, design charrettes, and brainstorming sessions are face-to-face. Brainstorms, critiques, and master classes are usually short-term collaborations. Different durations means that the nature and depth of involvement and investment of the workshop members in a particular work will vary.

In the writers' workshop whatever degree of ownership the members have is more ephemeral than some other collaborations but it is just as real—workshop members can easily come to feel that the work is theirs and care about how it can be moved forward. This can be seen in the behavior of some workshop members in a poetry workshop. It is not uncommon for a participant, while preparing for the workshop, to revise another participant's poem extensively and then in the workshop to present that revision. To do this requires some degree of internalizing the work, more so than simply coming up with comments and criticisms.

A motto of the open-source community that seems to apply to these collaborative efforts is "scratch your own itch." This means that individuals will work on something when they get a direct benefit from their work. For example, someone who has a need for constraints in a calendaring program might work on adding that capability to the calendar. Later in the book, I will talk about other reasons for volunteering effort that aren't as selfish, but even this selfish reason can and does enter into writers' workshops.

For some works such as product launches, marketing collateral, and software, the members of the workshop have a large investment or interest in the work and it is their itch being scratched. But even in workshops in which artists or individual makers are reviewing their work, there is a selfish interest in trying to improve or hone one's own skills or understanding of craft by participating. One can learn how to talk about a work in workshops. For new creative writers, for example, literary and craft-related vocabulary and concepts can be mysterious. This vocabulary and related concepts can open up new ways for a writer to view his or her work, and the workshop will illustrate them with concrete examples from real work.

When I'm in a poetry workshop, I find I learn the most by listening and contributing to discussions about other work, particularly work that is unlike what I do. My itch is to improve how I work, and I can do that by working for a time on someone else's piece, where I can look at the work without too much personal investment in the outcome—I don't take personally any criticism of my suggestions or of the work itself. The work is on its own and is not enmeshed in my identity; my interest is to improve the work, whatever that might mean.

Another effect of listening to discussions about someone else's work is the extent to which the comments made about that other work can apply to one's own work. When the workshop examines the difficulties in a particular other piece, I can sometimes quite clearly see those difficulties in my own work. I don't have, for example, the distraction of my heart pounding in my ears to distract me when listening to comments about other work.

One of the things that happens in creative writing is that details are selected—in fact, Cezanne once said that all art is selected details. Such details can have a special meaning to the writer (or artist). It might be hard for the writer of the piece to alter those details or remove them if they seem too important to the writer or if he or she starts thinking about truthfulness or accuracy. I have heard writers object to changing a detail because "that's not what really happened," as if history or the truth had a personal stake in the art. Sometimes it does if that's part of the aesthetic, but the piece almost always has its own requirements that don't have as much to do with writer and the writer's life and history as one might think.

There is almost, at times, a sentimental attachment to the reality of the triggering situation—facts somehow demand to be part a story when the story has no need for them. This can happen in technical work as well as in creative work. Once I was working on the specification of a programming language. In this language there is a thing called a symbol, with which it is possible to associate other information. But its most important property is that a symbol can have a value associated with it, just as with a global variable. In all the existing implementations of this language, symbols are allocated storage, some of which is used to hold the value, if it has one. A colleague and I were working on a glossary for the specification, and he defined a symbol as an object, a part of whose storage includes the place to store its value. I argued that all we needed to do was to say that there was a value associated with the symbol but to not specify how the association was implemented; my point was that we could thus free implementers to try other implementations. My colleague argued that all the implementations did it with an included piece of storage and since that was the fact, we should say so. In this case, the facts of the situation would have led to a worse specification by limiting the freedom of the implementer.[5]

By working on other people's work, a workshop participant can practice this skill of stepping back, which is the skill required for revision. Stepping back is a way to see where irrelevant facts are intruding on the piece.

Regardless of whether your work or another's is being discussed, you hear many different points of view, ways of thinking about the work, concerns, approaches, techniques, processes, what is in the work, what parts fit together well, and other surprising and new things: This imagery is sexual or angry, the pace speeds up at the end, an alternative technical approach is conspicuous by its absence, or these two patterns fit especially well with each other. And these things are presented in the context of a work and not in the abstract. It is a sort of out-loud reflection of craft or technical issues similar to putting a microphone on the head coach during a professional football game—you hear the thought process while it is going on. This is a powerful itch to scratch: learning from the masters. Or at least from your experienced and interesting colleagues.

Such out-loud thinking is central to pair programming, design charrettes, and brainstorming, for which an important effect is for ideas to bounce off each other and generate new ones. This operates well in the writers' workshop when the discussion of a piece goes off in directions none of the reviewers had prepared for or even realized were possible.

The open-source community believes in "release early, release often," and the extreme programming community speaks of continuous integration. Like open source, extreme programming is a software development methodology; *releasing* means creating an executable version of the software for people to use, and an *integration* is making a new complete working version of some software as soon as new parts are complete and have been meshed in with existing software. In software, releasing often or doing continuous integrations means that the software can be tested in its entirety so that the code doesn't drift off into a corner where it either doesn't work or isn't useful to the people who will use it.

The writers' workshop itself is a release of the work. Without a writers' workshop or some other review mechanism, the maker of the work would work in isolation and do one grand release. By opening up the work to other workshop members, that work is being released earlier than it would have been, and the earlier something is released, the more—and more easily—it can be fixed. If the work is completely off base—let's say it's a new Web authoring system and its architecture or user-visible model is wrong—then it might be impossible to fix the work at all near its final release, whereas an early release might illuminate the problems and bring to the table possible approaches.

Releasing a draft early is hard because you may not think that the work is at its best. In the open-source world "release early, release often" makes sense only once the software is basically usable. Similarly, you should workshop work only when it is far enough along to be complete in some way. Determining when a work is ready for a workshop is usually subjective but one would generally not workshop a first draft—it would have to be quite a good first draft and generally not strike people as being one.

Some workshops, however, are designed for early work. Both the creative and the technical communities have workshops in which, for example, beginning writers write short pieces that are reviewed briefly that day or the next. For beginning writers, getting ideas about the direction a piece can take and what its heart is can make a difference to a writer's confidence and to his or her ability to see what's going to work. In the creative writing community, there are several national writers' workshops where each poet writes a poem overnight and it's reviewed the next day.

Releasing often occurs in the writers' workshop when the workshop group stays together for longer than one go-around or when the writer revises the work after one workshop and takes it to another. When some workshop groups keep going for months or years, the work can be "released" to the workshop several times before it is released to the public. There are advantages to staying with the same workshop because the members get to know each other. And there are advantages of changing workshops because you get more eyes and more points of view and areas of expertise.

In the software development world, the code review is related to the writers' workshop, sometimes having a different structure or a different amount of structure. In both cases, the maker of an artifact sits down with other people who look at and critique the artifact. People who have used the writers' workshop format for code reviews have found it pleasant and beneficial because it not only finds problems with the code and its design, but also helps add strength to existing strengths and boosts confidence in the making process.

∼

The writers' workshop also seems to work because there is something about writing that is special with respect to how its mechanisms operate within the brain. Two stories illustrate this.

The first is the story of Neil, a fourteen-year-old English boy who suffered an apparent inability to recall his daily experiences, along with other cognitive difficulties, after radiation treatment for a brain tumor. After he was released from the hospital, though, he did fairly well at school, which puzzled the psychologists working with him. They soon discovered that in many instances, though he was unable to speak about what had just happened to him or what he had just read, he could write down those things clearly. His parents then provided him with a notebook with which he could communicate about his daily experiences, which he was unable to do orally.[6]

This example provides a startling clue that the way our brains retrieve information for the purpose of speaking is quite different from how it is for writing. This could imply that writing indeed is magical in the sense that what we write may not be available to us through speaking and perhaps, therefore, not seemingly available to us at all.

It is a recurring comment in the writing community that fiction writers, in particular, write in order to "see how it comes out." This is as true for me doing technical and scientific writing as it is for writing poetry. I frequently sit down to write in order to find out what I really think about something or when I want to get deeper into a technical puzzle I am having. When I write poetry, there is usually some trigger that starts it off—I'll talk about triggers more later—but then the poem seems to take off on its own and I make observations that were never apparent in the conception or in the real world, for that matter. In fact, this book is the result of such an exercise—I had no idea how much I knew about the writers' workshop until I wrote this book.

Stephen King talks about this in *On Writing*:

> You may wonder where plot is in all this. The answer . . . is nowhere. . . . I believe plotting and the spontaneity of real creation aren't compatible. . . . I want you to understand that my basic belief about the making of stories is that they pretty much make themselves. The job of the writer is to give them a place to grow.

The second story comes from a writing colleague of mine who for seven years worked with emotionally disturbed children. As she describes them, they ranged from the abandoned, weird, and abused to psychotics and schizophrenics. Her job was to teach them high school English. These children had no real interest in academics, and generally they were scattered about the classroom acting out their defense mechanisms and illnesses.

She decided to try something like a writers' workshop. She asked each of them to write an episode from their life in full detail. They were told that nothing they wrote would leave the room unless she had a legal requirement to do so, such as if they wrote a suicide note. The stated purpose was to write vividly.

When a student was done with his or her first draft, only the teacher, my colleague, would look at it. She was careful never to talk about the content of the episode but only the writing and how to make it better. Most of the discussion had to do with adding detail. After the episode was revised, the student would show it to one other peer of his or her choice. The students were carefully coached on what kinds of comments were allowed: nothing judgmental. Then the student would revise. And so on, as long as he or she was interested in working on the episode.

My colleague reported this to me:

> The most important aspect of this was my edict not to respond to the content. Somehow doing this seemed to free them to write stories and communicate details that they had shared with no one else, not even their psychiatrists. They would bring the story to me and expect an emotional or therapy-like reaction, because this is what

> they usually got. What they received instead was a cold assessment of the writing and usually a request for more detail. "So, you write here that he didn't want to waste the bullet so he killed the deer with a nail." Show, don't tell.
>
> One boy wrote about how his uncle used to take him out to abuse pets. It was a fun and funny thing to do. They'd drive around until they saw a wandering cat or dog. While he was processing the story enough to write it, some great change came upon him. He came to me with the story in hand and very wound up. He had realized, he said, that this was wrong. He had never considered it wrong before. Everything in his ghettoized and violent past had taught him that it was cool. He very much looked up to his uncle, and his uncle had taught him that it was cool. It was a thrilling epiphany for him. It was like his vision of the world had been altered forever.

She also mentioned another story in which, possibly, memories no longer available to be spoken were available to be written:

> One student claimed to everyone that he did not remember the conditions of the orphanage in Rio where he was raised. He actually remembered everything. He became obsessed with writing his story. He wouldn't speak it, but he would write it. This boy who claimed that he was illiterate, claimed he couldn't read, declared himself stupid, wrote and revised hundreds of pages.

These stories point out that there is something deep and strange about writing, and further, that there is something about talking about the technique that can free the writer. Perhaps it brings the courage to write something, perhaps it enables an otherwise inaccessible memory to be written about, and perhaps it engages a kind of self-observation or observation within the self that enables us to see things in the world that we had been unable to see before. It's almost as if we consciously act as midwife to some of the work, and that by attending to the midwife's job we can make healthier babies. The writers' workshop is using collaboration to attend to the midwife's job with a variety of methods that aren't otherwise available.

∽

The writers' workshop is a social way to improve a work, be it artistic, technical, textual, visual, code, organizations, or performances. The work can be the product of an individual or a group, it could have a strong aesthetic component or not, or it can be the result of a creative act or of a purely factual or representational effort. The writers' workshop can operate effectively whenever there is the possibility of improving the work in more ways than correcting errors. When it is effective, it can be surprisingly effective, and it can help individuals when discussing others' work as much or more as when their own work is being discussed—the workshop can be a remarkable learning tool.

The writers' workshop has been in use by the creative and artistic communities for a very long time, and by part of the software community for a number of years. It shares principles with the open source and other collaborative communities, and it is not dissimilar to some code reviews. Occasionally, the writers' workshop has been used to review and improve communities, organizations, processes, and performances. Again, these are all things that can be improved by work, practice, and reflection.

PART ONE

The Work of Making Things

CHAPTER THREE

Triggers and Practice

Artists, writers, poets, software developers, software designers, software architects, pattern writers, presentation writers, marketing people, documentation and manual writers, people—such as managers and other leaders—who create and nurture communities, web designers, interface designers, and lots of other people have something essential in common: They make things under risk. At some point an individual works alone, if even for only a short period, and the work is then revealed and can be judged. How can we create a context in which taking risks like this isn't so scary?

I want to make a distinction between *risky making* and *repetitive making*.[7] In repetitive making, a mostly predetermined amount of work of a definite sort produces a mostly predictable result. In risky making, failure is a possibility. In both cases, the results might be disappointing, but only in risky making is there the real possibility of complete failure.

Artifacts are made by people, and therefore risky making shares many commonalities regardless of what is being made. Understanding the writers' workshop is easier if we expose some of these commonalities.

The work is difficult: Something is being made that has never been made before—making new things requires thinking about what to make and how to make it, and the making. Something must be pulled from nothing, even though the raw materials are all around. Because of this, the possibility of failure exists; in fact, failure is quite probable.

Risky making requires a kind of skill: People with more of the skill seem to produce better results—but the skill can be improved by practicing and paying attention while practicing. In most cases, the practice amounts to actually doing the work, and one way to notice improvement is to observe how many of the works produced are good.

Art, at first, seems different from making technological artifacts because art seems to require talent, and talent seems to be a gift that some have and others don't. For example, making software seems like repetitive making—an engineering task or a craft that can produce predictable results with a predictable amount and type of work, or perhaps a form of problem solving. Likewise, writing patterns seems to be analysis followed by summing up, almost a mechanical task. An entire industry and a host of software methodologies have sprung up based on the belief that writing software is a repetitive, noncreative activity. The Computer Science Department at Stanford University moved from the School of Arts and Sciences to the School of Engineering, signaling the establishment of this belief.

And if not talent, some form of creativity seems to be involved in making art that is not so important in engineering. Once we look closely into making art, it isn't so obvious that a magical, scarce thing called creativity is required for art. Rather, good artists have a willingness to look at more approaches and at different approaches. And perhaps good artists are particularly attuned to opportunities that appear in daily life to create work. Being prepared to seize what shows itself is more important than an abstract characteristic like creativity, which is hard to define. William Stafford, in *Writing the Australian Crawl*, put it this way: "Art is a reckless encounter with whatever comes along."

Art, we're told, has to do with self-expression, and we are tempted to imagine the artist as a wild-haired, wide-eyed seeker running through the desert in search of the self, but in fact art is simply making things in one's own way, guided by the skills and inclinations at hand, experiences, the materials at hand, and the triggers that present themselves. Triggers play the role that most see as creativity or self-expression. A trigger is any place, person, rhythm, or image that presents itself; any metaphor that comes to mind; or anything else that leads the maker to make a work. Often the trigger appears in the final work, and if the work contains a lot of private triggers, it is sometimes considered hermetic. For example, for many writers, places are triggers because a place can locate a mood and characters, and a place has details that can be described, with the descriptions being able to accrete narrative and emotional force and structure. Many writers have a partially imaginary, partially real landscape or townscape in mind when they begin work, and others use a real landscape that has witnessed partially real, partially imaginary events involving partially real, partially imaginary characters. Details that appear in a writer's work can seem odd because they seem arbitrary or play a role larger than their intrinsic importance indicates.

In *The Triggering Town*, Richard Hugo describes the role of triggers in poetry:

> *A poem can be said to have two subjects, the initiating or triggering subject, which starts the poem or "causes" the poem to be written, and the real or generated subject, which the poem comes to say or mean, and which is generated or discovered in the poem during the writing. That's not quite right because it suggests that the poet recognizes the real subject. The poet may not be aware of what the real subject is but only [has] some instinctive feeling that the poem is done.*

Triggers are part of our makeup, and creative writers take advantage of them. We can see this when we walk into a strange cafeteria with a full tray. You don't know anyone there, and maybe lots of seats are available. Looking and looking, you finally decide on a table to sit at, who to sit next to. How do you do that? By looking at a person's face, what he or she is wearing, what else that person has at the table—what books, what newspaper, what section the newspaper is open to—you make up a sort of story about the person, and you decide which story you want to be part of. The people in the cafeteria are triggers, and their fictional stories come out through you.

Triggers that occur while making technological things include existing mechanisms, algorithms, approaches, inspirations via solutions to similar problems, patterns, cultural forces, and anything else that might "remind" the maker how to approach the making. A trigger can appear in a final work as the "fingerprints" of the maker on the work. When we say that an engineer, for example, approaches many problems from the same or similar directions, we are talking about the way triggers work for that person.

Because triggers play an important role in both art and technology making, and because triggers in art seem to correspond to creativity and self-expression whereas in technology they correspond to training, experience, and habit in problem solving, the differences between making art and making technology fall away and we are left with a universal making phenomenon. Albert Einstein said this about creativity: "Imagination is more important than knowledge. Knowledge is limited. Imagination encircles the world.... The secret to creativity is knowing how to hide your sources."

And, importantly, triggers, along with the work itself, are outside the individual, although they may be vitally important to the individual and of a personal or private nature. This enables us to address the work without addressing the maker of the work directly, and this is how the writers' workshop works.

Art is made by ordinary people, and whatever amount of talent they have is part of what they bring to the work, and it is always exactly as much talent as they need. Perseverance, knowledge of craft, background experiences, triggers, circumstances, and materials, among others, are equal partners in producing art.

Let's look at software: Software is made by people with the widest possible degrees of problem-solving skill, engineering background, and knowledge of craft. Mostly, the results of trying to produce software are not predictable, and neither can the amount and type of work required to get something done be predicted unless the same software and the exact tasks needed to make it have been done many times in the past. Just like artists, some programmers seem to have more talent than others, but in both cases talent is a concept that slips from our grip the more we try to grab on to it. We find people who appear to have modest talent making masterpieces, and conversely, people apparently with great talent fail over and over. But in any individual, the effect of talent—if it even exists—falls from importance as more and more things are made and as what is learned takes on more of the heavy lifting.

~

Regardless of the different outward appearances of the processes for making art and technological things, there is always an aspect of a risky making process that is personal, something that seems to happen within the maker and that is expressed in the materials at hand. We often see this personal aspect of risky making in the period of anticipation or even fear between unveiling a work and the audience's reaction during which the maker is nervous. The nervousness implies that to the maker, judgment of the work is a judgment of the maker, which can happen only when doing the work is somehow personal.

For an expert carpenter making another cabinet of a particular, frequently made design, the real difference between one piece and another has mostly to do with the nature of the materials and mistakes. For this reason, the carpenter's opinion of the piece, though perhaps more harsh than others', is accurate—it matches the audience's pretty closely—whereas an artist, let's say, can be completely off in judging an audience's reaction. An artist can feel hurt when a piece is considered bad, just as a software engineer can feel pain when the system is considered a kludge.

Fear of audience reaction is fear of failing to get *acceptance* and *approval*. Acceptance and approval are related but different things. Acceptance is when what is produced is accepted as a valid artifact—for an artist, acceptance happens when a piece is considered art, the real thing. Approval is when the audience likes the piece. For risky makers, seeking acceptance and approval signals an attitude that might prove counterproductive to improving, even with the assistance of a writers' workshop. Here's why.

Fear is at the center of the concerns of risky makers, and the writers' workshop is a mechanism—an institution, a ritual, and a technique—for addressing fear, for finding a way to make the piece work for the maker, and for seeing what the process of making is really about.

Fear comes in two varieties: One is fear that focuses on the maker, and the other is fear that focuses on others. Fear inspired by the self has to do with the validity of the maker as a maker: Am I pretending I can do this, do I have enough talent, can I make things perfect, and am I merely my work?

Acceptance fear is a self-based fear: Am I capable of producing a legitimate work—can I write a real poem, can I make a commercial software application, am I really a writer, do I write enough to deserve to call myself a writer, is my work interesting enough, am I boring, trivial, too superficial, too intense? Other self-based fears come from comparisons: I'm not as good as I want to be, I'm not as good as I was last year, I'm not as good as another writer I know, I'm not as good as this particular famous writer.

Some fears inspired by the other have to do with the quality of the individual's work or the level of talent—that is, approval. Did people enjoy reading my work, did they find it inspiring or enriching, will it be considered a masterpiece? Other fears have to do with revealing too much about the self because writing—especially creative writing—opens the blinds on your mind, feelings, and spirit, and writing is more revealing than conversation, perhaps because it is a more slowly created and more slowly absorbed form of communication. Fears of exposure of vulnerability can lead to emotional backlash and self-doubt.

Fears based on acceptance and approval are related because, to the maker obsessed with such fears, legitimacy as an individual and approval by others is granted by others and not by oneself.

The problem with fear is that it can make us stop and finally quit. Fear can make us put the judgment of the work too far into the foreground of our making, so that rather than attending to the work, we are attending to the fear. Fear can make us try to make each work more than it can be—because we fear the failure of making a lesser work than we imagine is possible.

But the problem is that fear keeps us from attending to the work and getting better at it. Instead, we look to others or to the cosmos for help getting better, but the only way to get better at making things is to make things, to make lots of them, to think about how we are making them, and to realize that to produce something truly great—whether art or technology—we need to produce a lot of those things and, pretty much, select the best of them, even while the trend is ever upward, though not monotonically.

Fear is the source of strength for the internal censor, the internal editor and critic who seems to look over our shoulders and tell us we are frauds and fakes, that we need to be better people to be better writers. We need to find a way out of this.

The work teaches us. It's like practice: The number of times we do something is the best indicator of how good we will be. Craft will improve, and our ability to focus just on those things that make the work great will improve because some things become routine or we recognize them as unimportant. The best lesson for the work we are doing right now is the work we just finished. Because the work is at the center of making things, we encourage makers to focus on the work rather than on self- or other-centered fear. When they attend to the work and not to themselves as flawed writers, they are able to see more clearly what the work is teaching, and they are able to invite others into their process of making things.

But when a risky maker allows fear to take over, perhaps that person will stop working on a piece. If the fear is too great or if the hiatus lasts too long, then the making may stop forever. And in this case it is impossible for the maker to improve.

The arc toward maturity for the maker can be uncertain: When a person begins to make things whose making poses a risk to himself or herself, then skill level and experience are low or rough; the pieces made are likely to be inept. Some makers will approach these muddled beginnings with humor and humility, and most will press on. Encouragement will come from people close to the maker, those who care about what he or she makes because it is the person who matters, not the work. At some point, the possibility that the maker is good at it will pop up, and at that point fear can start to play a large role. There is the possibility of downward spiral here: The maker is eager to show off, but if the response is not supportive, the maker can stop making things or slow the pace of production. As a result, the maker cannot get better or can get better only slowly, and a gap arises between what a novice—who hopes to get good fast—wishes to accomplish and what he or she can do, because getting good is a function of the number of tries more than anything else.

On the other hand, one must look critically at the work to judge how to get better at it, and outside critics can bring more eyes and minds to bear on the problem. And so with such help, a person can get better faster. This is also a situation in which fear can take over and drive risky makers away from their task of focusing on the work.

Richard Hugo described the value of practice in *The Triggering Town*:

> Once a spectator said, after Jack Nicklaus had chipped a shot in from the sand trap, "That's pretty lucky." Nicklaus is [supposed] to have replied, "Right. But I notice the more I practice, the luckier I get." If you write often, perhaps every day, you will stay in shape and will be better able to receive those good poems, which are finally a matter of luck, and get them down. Lucky accidents seldom happen to writers who don't work. You will find that you may rewrite and rewrite a poem and it never seems quite right. Then a much better poem may come rather fast and you wonder why you bothered with all that work in the earlier poem. Actually, the hard work you do on one poem is put in on all poems. The hard work on the first poem is responsible for the sudden ease of the second. If you just sit around waiting for the easy ones, nothing will come. Get to work.

Getting better at risky making requires practice. Practice requires continuing, even in the face of apparent and real failures. At some point, some people need to hear from others that what the person is doing—practicing at risky making—is accepted and approved. This is where the risk becomes real, makes it into the experienced world.

If the others are friends or family members attuned to the feelings of the maker, things will likely go well. Naturally, the maker will suspect that his or her friends are merely being polite or acting as friends and family should, and will insist on taking the work to strangers. But sometimes one's family or friends won't understand the need to write or appreciate what has been written—approval will be blind approval. If the others are strangers, then the results are unpredictable.

This is the crucial point in the early arc of improvement. The wrong reaction can cause the fledgling maker to quit and then stop. The writers' workshop is possibly the least risky group of strangers one can find. Experienced moderators know this and take steps to ensure each author gets the best experience that can be reasonably expected.

∼

Risky making is the best and hardest kind of making, and the best way to reduce the fear that can stop us from taking enough risks to get better is to share that risk with others who know what these risks mean. Herds, flocks, and swarms know this. But it's a paradox—to learn how to do the most solitary creative task takes practice and a crowd. The crowd is what the writers' workshop provides, and this is why more experienced writers sometimes drift away—they don't need to share the risk with anyone else anymore.

CHAPTER FOUR

Work in Progress

In our high-aspiration world, the focus is frequently on end points: the start of a great new project, filled with anticipation and confidence; the end of the project, when it is revealed as a great performance. We (falsely) believe creativity is private, the product of the muse or an angel, perhaps spiked by a visit from Federico García Lorca's *duende*—a black soul tingling the centers of the work.[8] With this in mind we welcome news of the start of a new work of creation: a new pattern language, a new system or framework, a new book on methodology, a new novel under way. We drift into anticipation. When the work appears, there's great fanfare again. As members of the audience—for we have no other choice— we admire or we don't. Maybe we will judge the work and recommend it, or give it a bad review and warn against it.

As an author there could be nothing worse than this way of life: You are faced with a long slog alone followed by a verdict, and it's hard in such a situation to separate the judgment of the work from a judgment about you. The author contributes to this in two ways through one action: by claiming the work exclusively during its creation, you merge it with yourself—you are its sole progenitor, and all its successes are yours as are its failures. And by claiming the work exclusively during its creation, you push away the world, create a boundary, make an inside and an outside, placing all who might judge the work on the outside, placing you alone in the center.

This is the natural way of our times: Art is taken to be self-expression, and without the unique and clearly identifiable self at the center of the web of making, how could there be self-expression? Science and technology hold the possibility of fortune and fame—the possibility of owning the idea is intriguing to our selfish needs, and their selfishness is no criticism. The tradition of scientific publication mandates a clear creator, and originality is the benchmark of worth. Both these argue for the lonely way of making in private and unveiling in public.

The act of unveiling a work separates the work from the author, from any human presence behind the scenes; the reader is invited to judge based solely on the selfish needs of that reader. If the work is found lacking—for whatever incidental or crucial reason—the reader has no reason whatever to convey either the nature of the problems or their degrees. What can be taken away by the author is a mere vote recorded, and a purely anonymous one at that. And if the work is found useful or wonderful, little or nothing is recorded about that either—it is an anonymous transaction among mere donors rather than a human interaction in which learning could take place.

Making something is sweaty, hard work filled with false starts and foolishness, sometimes sentimentality, personal demons, and doubts, and even spelling mistakes. The writer sits at the desk and stares at the page, at the screen, and nothing happens, and when it does, what bubbles up is sometimes just what is most full of floatable gas. Think of software development: What might end up being a fine system in the end was built with poor planning, the code looks funny, there were hundreds or thousands or tens of thousands of bugs, the system acted goofy many times, its developers ate pizza while gaping at the screen and drooled Coke on the keyboard, some fell asleep fixing bad indentation, and in general, it was a mess.

Of course, few would want to pull the curtain aside to reveal this sort of reality, and the nature of the work while in the midst of such clamor is likely to reflect that clamor. In the software development world, corporate closed doors shield the development process from the outside lest the grime and bacteria of the real process be too graphically revealed.

But what would happen if the curtain were to be pulled aside in midstream? What would happen if instead of a grand performance on opening night, the work in progress were opened up by a humble author for the aid and assistance of colleagues both close and distant? What if the work presented were not the final work ready for judgment but a work in progress in need of help presented by a needy author? What if the audience were invited to be co-owners, coauthors?

There is still an inside and outside, but those invited by the author to help now sit on the inside, they can become coconspirators, coauthors of a sort—criticism someone makes on the inside can be as easily taken as a criticism of that critic as of the author, in a spiritual or moral sense. When the author invites you to help, you join the author at the center of the web of making, because the author has given you a gift or several: You have received the gift of the work itself, which is a work with a purpose and the worth of its doing, and you have received the gift of honor as a sort of coauthor even if you will never be listed on the cover. You have been honored by trust and an appreciation of your skills and talent, and of your trustworthiness, because the journey from the beginning of a project to its end is a personal one, it is just as messy as described earlier, and only the closest can be easily called into that scene.

Now you and the author are both in the same little boat cast away from the safety of finished things, and the way out is through the work itself. It belongs to each equally for that brief time, and as both of you focus on it sitting there in front of you, the *other* as critic—the judging stranger—is only in the periphery, comments about the piece are about the piece and not about either of you.

This is the magic of the gift.

⁓

The idea of the work in progress fuels the best aspect of the writers' workshop: A writers' workshop is a circle of authors who have decided to give the gift of their works in progress to the group in order to create a gift-based exchange aimed at improving the pieces in question.

The alternative is the grand performance, where the only two reactions are approval and rejection. A writers' workshop aims to be a writing family in the small, egoless—pursuing the life of the work, focused on the work and not on the individual, though sympathetic to the labor needed to complete the work. A good writers' workshop is where the author feels that any risks taken in the work will be seen and appreciated for what they are and not seen as evidence of personal flaws or weaknesses.

The creative writers' workshop can be one of the most intimate situations one could encounter outside the bedroom. A poet friend who has run writers' workshops for years tells this story of one of her students: "One of my students once told me that the reason she continues coming to my workshop year after year was that it was the one place where she was able to relate to others as her true/real self on a very deep level, that close attention to her writing improved both her writing and her life."

Even the technical writers' workshop can be more intimate than many technical people and scientists can handle. The quirks of writing style, hidden prejudices, private agendas, faulty reasoning based on hidden assumptions—all of these can come out, revealing the person beneath the writing. Pride exists everywhere, and the writers' workshop can uncover it.

∽

I have participated in hundreds of writers' workshops, in the creative writing, software, and business arenas. When the writers' workshop fails—as it sometimes does—the results can be explosive.

For creative writers, the work can be personal, and for some the risk of the workshop's not forming a gift-giving circle can be too high. Such writers may find the experience devastating, and others will avoid the workshop altogether or quickly leave it. I've been in poetry writers' workshops where individuals have fled in tears, left the particular workshop, abandoned all workshops, and have quit writing. In the creative writing community, apparently fewer people than in the technical and scientific writing community recognize that the writers' workshop is a gift-based community. Some in the creative writing community still hold on to remnants of the performance attitude and the idea that by cutting down another's work, one's reputation is enhanced—as if the one who can rip another writer the hardest is somehow the most artistic.

In the software world, I have observed individuals become embarrassed, turning beet red on hearing certain comments, but this is rare. The difference between the two communities is that the creative writing community is older, more personally invested in the work, and, in general, more jaded to the workshop. The software community is younger, more professionally invested in work, and more enamored of the workshop and how it seems to work through magic.

∽

The adoption of work in progress as an attitude has three consequences: It provides the gift that starts the community, it determines the culture of the community, and it provides a safety net for the individual contributor.

When writers individually decide to give the gift of their partially formed works to the others, each hopes for several things: to receive affirmation of the worth of the work and of the self behind the work (acceptance and approval); to receive ideas on how to complete and perfect the work; and to be exposed to the ideas and interactions of the group.

The writers' workshop is formed by the creation of a "work-in-progress" community with a shared purpose and shared culture. The shared purpose is to repair and celebrate the work, and the shared culture provides rituals and rules of behavior that work to keep the spirit of gift-giving healthy within the community.

The individual in the writers' workshop survives the experience by taking a stance separated from the work itself. By viewing his or her own piece as a work in progress, the author can form around the piece a moat that shields the self from the sting of criticism. After all, the work is not completed and therefore does not represent the self's best work.

Just as each work in the writers' workshop is a work in progress, the workshop itself is a work in progress. The group forms and might last only as long as it takes to review all the pieces, or it may go for many years and many reviews of single pieces and several pieces by each contributor. In either case, the workshop is a community and it evolves each minute, with each interaction, at each stage of review, with each new piece. The workshop accumulates stories and shared experiences, and the richness of the experiences includes the works themselves, just as books read in common form a ground field between two people.

∼

Making things requires the discipline of having made lots of them. Not only must a person master certain craft techniques, but he or she must have the confidence that what is important will be attended to and what's incidental can be ignored to some extent. When we look at what separates amateur from professional photographers, we see some superficial things: Professionals might have more cameras or more expensive cameras, they might have more sophisticated darkroom materials, and they might even have business cards announcing themselves as photographers. But the biggest difference is how much film they have shot and how much film they shoot for each subject.

A professional photographer has shot many thousands of rolls of film, and probably has thought carefully about why the results of each picture were as they were. Looking at the education of artists, a common thread is that they have thought about what they are doing while and after doing it.

And there is lots of doing. The reason to make a lot of whatever one makes is to become used to the degree to which it can pour out rather than being forced out. This way we come to see where conscious thought and design are required rather than subconscious craft and technique. When I decide almost unconsciously now how to indent code, it is the result of having observed good indentation, done a lot of indentation while thinking about it, and done a lot without thinking too much about it.

A professional photographer will shoot many, many shots of the same subject, bracketing exposure, trying different exposure durations, moving the camera around, trying different angles, different lighting, different filters, different props if that makes sense. The results will be in a distribution—a few not so good, most pretty good, and maybe a few that are really great. Now all the photographer has to do is select the best ones and work with them a bit in the darkroom or on the computer.

The number of photographs taken to get some good shots can be staggering. For one piece in *National Geographic Magazine* using twenty-two photographs, the photographer took about forty thousand photographs—this is over a thousand rolls of film to select just twenty-two photos. This might seem like a typographic error or a fluke. Here is an excerpt from a story about another photographer, Joel Sartore:

> *The standards are incredibly high. For a photo story on Nebraska that ran in the November 1998* Geographic, *Sartore had eight weeks total to shoot, which he broke up into several one and two-week intervals over two years of time. Of the 31,320 photos he shot for the Nebraska story, only 16 ran in the magazine.*

Between 60 percent and 75 percent of a photographer's time doing a shooting project like this is spent researching the subjects, planning how and when to take the pictures, getting in position, and other things peripheral to what we think of as the actual photographing.[9] Once the film is shot, the best photographs are selected and then the photographer works in the darkroom or with Adobe Photoshop to perfect them. We all believe the perfection part of the story, but we don't believe as deeply or appreciate the selection part.

Another example is filmmaking. The movie *Apocalypse Now* runs under 2½ hours. To get those 2½ hours, the filmmakers shot 250 hours of film. That means that for every hour of film on screen in the final version, over 100 hours of film were shot.[10] Once the film is shot and selected, the work of perfection goes on in the darkroom, perhaps on a computer workstation, and then in the editing room.

Great art is a process of making lots of things, knowing how to select the good ones, and knowing how to perfect them—making stuff, choosing critically, making some mistakes, being able to recognize them, and then being able to correct them.[11] Making art is not magic, and it can be done by ordinary folks.[12] But we also need to learn how to look critically at what we produce and to dissociate it from ourselves so that criticizing the work is not criticizing its maker. The writers' workshop is one of the best ways of doing that.

By cracking open the process and inviting people to participate in the work in progress, we can learn how to attend to the partially made work, how to select the good parts, and how to perfect them. We learn the critical skills to judge our own work by watching others apply their critical skills to our work and to others'— and by practicing it ourselves on work we are not personally invested in. That is, the work-in-progress method is one of the best ways to learn critical skills at all stages of risky making.[13]

What is a writers' workshop? It is a gift-based community whose gifts are works in progress and suggestions by a group of newly formed coauthors. It provides acceptance (yes, you can make such things) and approval (yes, what you make is good and we like it).

Like parents and close relatives, the workshop watches in appreciation while the new author tries to stand and walk, and almost any good effort toward this end will be rewarded. The workshop is where the results of taking a risk are rewarded, if in no other way than by providing enough of an affirmation that the maker is encouraged to go on and make more things, to try new things, to take more risks, to reflect on what works and what doesn't, to select what is best, and to perfect it.

For experienced writers, the rewards are the gift and community and the deepening of what already has begun to be learned—because there is no such thing as having mastered writing, one can continue to improve and understand the craft. And if not that, the craft can be changed and reinvented.

CHAPTER FIVE

The Gift

The writers' workshop begins with some people's decision to give each other the gift of their work in progress, and a more experienced individual's decision to give the gift of experience and expertise as a workshop leader. The magic of the gift.

The magic of the gift is not something new—it's always been part of human culture. The *gift economy* has been studied deeply. It's how our families are held together. It's how many ancient and contemporary cultures are held together. It forms the center of many religions. The writers' workshop works best when it is most firmly based on a gift economy.

In a gift economy, gifts are exchanged, forming a bond based on mutual obligation: In the simplest form of gift exchange, when one person gives a gift to another, the receiver becomes obligated to the giver, but not in a purely mercenary way—rather, the recipient becomes very much like a member of the giver's family, in which the mutual obligations are many, varied, and long lasting. More sophisticated forms involve more than two parties—in fact the cosmos may become involved. A person may give a gift with the realistic expectation that someday a gift of equal or greater use value will be received, or that the recipient will pass on a further gift. Sacrifices and many religious ceremonies are gift-economy-based. In an open-source project, the gift of source code is reciprocated by suggestions, bug reports, debugging, hard work, praise, and more source code.

In a writers' workshop, the gift of a manuscript—a work in progress—is reciprocated by revisions, suggestions, and commentary.

Gift economies are embedded within noneconomic institutions like kinship, marriage, hospitality, artistic patronage, and ritual friendship. The bond is so like flesh and blood that the Greek gift economy persisted alongside a vigorously growing commodity economy for several centuries.

In a commodity economy, the value of an item is abstracted into some other sort of object whose intrinsic value is unrelated to its "purchasing power." For gold coins this characterization makes less sense than it does for paper money, which is the ultimate abstraction: Paper money is completely real and yet unrelated to what it abstracts—so much so that it is possible through the medium of paper money to make a completely fair trade between otherwise incommensurate things, such as five hundred cotton candy cones for one handgun through the alienable intermediary of $500.[14]

Most importantly, the commodity economy depends on scarcity. Its most famous law is that of diminishing returns, whose working requires a limited supply.[15] Scarcity of material or scarcity of competitors makes high profit margins. It works through competition.

The gift economy is an economy of abundance—the gifts exchanged are inexhaustible, consisting of ritualized friendship and hospitality.

The gift and commodity economies have coexisted for millennia, generally with the most intimate relationships governed by gift, not money. Tribes based purely on gift economies will barter and exchange money for goods with outsiders. A healthy Western family operates on a gift economy.

Gifts are given without the expectation of direct gifts in return. By making your work a gift, you invite the reader into the circle of something akin to a family, and you can expect the spirit of *xenia*—"a bond of solidarity manifesting itself in an exchange of goods and services"—to take over interactions.[16] A gift has both economic and spiritual content. It is personal. In giving a gift, the giver's goal is to become as empty as possible.

What gift to bring to the workshop? It matters what you bring to the workshop and how open you are to being critiqued. Sometimes an author will bring a piece that he or she considers nearly done. Perhaps the author is looking to impress the moderator for some reason. Perhaps the work has been submitted already for publication or for assignment of an adviser in a degree program. For such an author, negative criticism could be harder to handle. Some writers recommend bringing work where about half of it seems like it's in real trouble. When that work is reviewed in a workshop, the author is more likely to be eager to receive any kind of help and suggestions.

It is very important to enter the workshop with the idea that the work you are bringing as a gift is a work in progress. It is not perfect; it is not finished; it is not you. You also need to know that this is true for all the other participants. Writing anything—patterns, conference papers, fiction, poetry—is hard and gets easier, if it ever does, only with time and repetition of the process of writing. This is true for every person in the workshop. The gifts, then, are given in a spirit of xenia.

There are other ways to get your work reviewed: Friends and colleagues are one avenue, and peer review is another.

Many writers ask their friends to look at what they have written. In some cases this works well because the friends are writers, perhaps, and provide thoughtful, encouraging, and critical comments. If a good working relationship has developed between a writer and his or her friends, then this can be a superb way to get the right sort of feedback. Developing such a relationship, though, can take years, and sometimes the early stages can be rough while each person experiments with things to say and how to say them.

Authors of scientific conference and journal papers are familiar with the process of *anonymous peer review*. In such a review an unidentified reviewer provides written comments to a review committee or an editor, and these comments are passed on to the author. This process, though common, can easily break down.

First the good aspects. Reviewers in such situations are generally senior experts in the domain the author is writing about. In many cases the author would rarely have the chance to have the paper reviewed by someone of such stature and experience. Comments from such a reviewer are quite often very useful. Sometimes such a reviewer will try to act as a mentor to the author and help his or her career along.

Now the bad. Rarely does something like this happen. The anonymity of the reviewer often acts as a cloak that covers jealousy or scientific rivalry; the lure of the unsigned review sometimes causes the reviewer to turn up the heat on the author; frequently, newly famous reviewers will turn up the heat even more as an unconscious way to preen. In the worst case, the reviewer might have a grudge against the author and uses the hidden position of power to snipe.

The purpose of anonymous review is to provide dignity to the review process: By hiding identities, the reviewer is able to be honest; and with an honest reviewer, the author gets the best feedback and the conference or journal gets the best advice and hence, the best papers. Science marches on.

Unfortunately, in anonymous peer review there is no way for the human dimension to be communicated between author and reviewer. The author has no opportunity to know for sure that the reviewer down deep cares about the paper, and the reviewer is doing little more than sending a message in a bottle, hoping it lands somewhere and that his or her honest concern will somehow come through clearly when coupled with any critical remarks the reviewer might need to express. Understanding each other's backgrounds, the context of the work and of the remarks, and the broad context in which the work lives cannot be explored except through dialogue, which is not possible in a single, one-way communication. Where the intention was that anonymity would guarantee dignity, the result was to separate two people in what would normally be a very human interaction.

For journals this can work because the review process can take several iterations in which a paper is reviewed, revised, reviewed, and revised. In such cases, the duration and ongoing nature of the relationship allows human nature to take its course, and the exchanges begin to resemble gift exchanges and dialogues rather than a contest.

For conferences, though, program committees rarely like to accept papers that require significant revision, because there is no time to ensure that the changes have been adequately made. Many program committees assume that the paper submitted is the one that will appear and so the best review is the one that says the paper is fine as is. In these cases, improvements are not made and no one learns anything from the exercise. Though the conference may get acceptable papers, even the conference attendees might notice the raw, unfinished character to the papers. In a single-shot relationship, gift exchange is chancy and dialogue is impossible—the safety that anonymity affords doesn't get to pay off.

Both friend and peer review processes have an ad hoc tint to them: There are no rules of engagement between the author and reviewer beyond the structure of the encounter. Once the reviewer knows he or she is a reviewer, the way the reviewer acts is up to that person, and the author can expect almost anything to happen—good or bad.

Further, rarely can an author get more than a couple of reviews for any particular work. It's unusual to have a staff of friend/reviewers, and most peer review situations provide one or two reviewers per paper only. The author then doesn't have the choice of a number of reviews to choose from, and sometimes the author will not find comments that are sensible to the author because there might not be a meeting of sensibilities.

A final problem happens in large organizations when things like marketing and other collateral material are produced, where a formal review process requires particular colleagues to review work. In some organizations there can be strong beliefs about ownership and sign-offs. Some individuals believe that they own a particular product or marketing area, and if someone outside that area produces the work, such individuals are apt to be unkind toward it. Others believe that they need to sign off on such work because they will be held accountable for any mistakes made in it.

Many corporate organizations do not foster an atmosphere of helping. Few companies reward people for accepting help from others (or for helping, for that matter). Instead, many value initiative and the ability to get things done alone. Though reviews under these circumstances are frequently adequate, they tend to have the critical, uncaring nature of anonymous peer review. Moreover, scheduling and following through with the schedule can be rough, and sometimes a simple review can take weeks.

In the patterns community especially—and in some others—there is a special sort of reviewer called a *shepherd*. The job of the shepherd is to help the author make the best work possible in a short time. A shepherd is usually not anonymous and spends enough time to oversee at least one revision cycle. The journal editorial process sometimes works as a shepherding process.

The gift nature of both sides of a shepherding relationship seems close to the surface, because the primary cause of its infrequent breakdown seems to be due to incidental problems like time constraints and schedule mismatches. When the process works—and it almost always does—it is perhaps the best process there is for rapidly improving a work through outside assistance. Improving a work is not necessarily the same as learning how to improve it. If the shepherd is a skilled teacher, such learning can take place, but this is a special relationship.[17] The shepherding process depends on two things: a pool of qualified and experienced shepherds, and the luck of the draw. Shepherds work with authors one on one—get the wrong ones working together and it may not work well at all. And perhaps the area an author is working in won't have a shepherding culture.

For example, such a culture seems not to exist in the writing arts, though some shepherding takes place. Creative writing does not have anonymous peer review, and most literary journals suggest only the most minor revisions for accepted work. Poets who like the idea of a shepherd will probably have to pay for one or try to find one in an educational setting. Once money is involved in the process—once you're in the outer circle where everyone is in it for the same reasons—the gift nature of the exchange is hampered, and the xenia effect will not get started. Or it will get started in fewer cases.[18]

∽

A chance meeting on Lexington Avenue in New York, deep in rush hour on a rained-on November afternoon with darkness infiltrating—though the clouds have cleared to the west, making a shaft of pink that lights the streets at the intersections—and Bill hands Michelle her birthday gift a day early. The gift's a surprise—early, a random location, nothing special about the setting except the atmospherics made by weather, time, and chance. Compare this to the birthday party where, once the candles are blown out, gifts appear and are opened. The setting is ready and the attendees all know what to expect, how to behave (mostly), and how to appreciate what is given. The gift is in its proper setting, a ritualistic one in which roles are known and outcomes predictable. Indeed, the meeting on Lex will be recalled for years, but not savored quite the same way—it will be adored for its unusualness, not for the gift, which in a birthday ritual might have been its centerpiece.

A ritualistic setting can establish rules that enable the important factors in the ritual to be fulfilled. At the birthday party, it's unlikely someone will pie the birthday girl, but on Lexington Avenue anything can happen.

This is the point of a writers' workshop as a formal setting or ritual. Once into the details of the ritual, once firmly seated in its setting, the ritual itself will enable the gifts of writing to be exchanged and critiques to be made. Rituals like this are a human activity and enable people's humanity to come forward if it's available.

The writers' workshop begins with the gift of a work in progress—already this is unlike the anonymous peer review, in which a polished, apparently ready-for-publication work is submitted for publication—and in exchange a community of authors discusses the work in a formal setting. Because the authors review papers by all the authors in the circle, the level of trust in the group can get quite high, and be higher still if they remain together for even more reviews of revisions and later work.

Software people seem to have little problem handling a ritualistic or formal setting and seem willing to follow rules; they see the value in ritual though they may not acknowledge it—it's a matter of degree. A software developer is always under the control of a programming language and computers whose rules are as black and white as they can be. Perhaps the mind-set of a software developer is similar to a game player's, who likes to maneuver according to rules. Certainly quite a few software developers are gamers.

Software developers are used to working within a development process or methodology in which rules dictate how and when to interact with others in a team of developers. In some software methodologies there is a ritualized but sometimes unrecognizable version of helping. The writers' workshop can seem like such a process or a methodology, and so those connections act as familiar anchors in the software writer's world. Many technical people and scientists are like software developers in appreciating some degree of rules and formalism—their mathematical training ensures this, and so they also may find the ritual of the writers' workshop familiar and comforting.

Creative writers, on the other hand, seem to like to be more informal and get to the heart of the matter, foregoing any preliminaries. In many cases they skip the preliminaries and get to the good part: criticizing.

Often, failures of the creative writers' workshop happen when the issue of "what the writer wants to do" arises, or when the other authors in the circle are interested in talking about how they would handle writing a piece like the one under consideration. The workshop members sometimes want to find out the author's motives for writing the piece and to approach the suggestions that way. For example, the workshop participants might try to figure out whether the author is the mother or daughter in an apparent mother/daughter conflict, and would try to proceed from that information. Other times, workshop participants will try to approach a work by talking about what they would do were they to write the poem. Sometimes this is a useful approach, but only if the discussion doesn't focus on the workshop participants' personal issues and quirks.

In many failure cases, writers want to find the narrative or the writer's issue or issues in the work and then respond to that rather than to craft and concerns of writing as writing. Other failures have to do with getting stuck in various ways. Sometimes the group will not be able to tell what a poem is about, and will go round and round on that point alone. The moderator needs to watch for this and react quickly.

Other times workshop failures have to do with the subject or theme. The following is from a recent graduate from an MFA program:

> *In one of my last MFA workshop experiences, I had submitted a poem that was dismissed because of its theme. For almost 45 minutes. I learned what? That I can't make such a poem? Or that I can't make one that way—that direction would've been really useful and craft-oriented yet the workshop carried on against the poem's theme and the writer's doltish neglect of said theme through our American literary history . . . good grief. I might as well have been told not to write about love, marriage, adolescence, childhood, etc., because those themes have been covered, too!*

Sometimes the writers around the workshop circle want to revise the work themselves, as if it were theirs all along. In some cases, a participant or moderator will actually revise the work and read it aloud as their suggestion for improvement. This can work, but this might not be an approach that teaches the author the most about his or her work.

These examples are failures of the ritual or formal nature of the workshop to take hold, which diminishes the gift nature of the exchange, turning it into a one-upmanship contest instead of something more like—but not exactly like—a support group. In other failed workshops, the conversations always circle back on each other, the moderator seems weak, the discussion is aimed at the writer, who cannot (usually) respond, because he or she is trying to follow the rules.

Furthermore, the creative writer is putting more of the personally vulnerable part of himself or herself into the work than the software guy who is writing about a technique or explaining a scientific breakthrough. In both cases the work is important to the author, but for the scientist, let's say, there is always the obstinate, unexplainable physical world that failure can be shared with.

But technical workshops can fail as well. A typical failure is to focus exclusively on the technical content of the piece to the exclusion of the writing. This is also a common problem in fiction workshops, where the focus can slip into just

CHAPTER FIVE *The Gift*   49

the narrative structure and the characters. Prose, whether technical writing, fiction, or nonfiction, is just as subject to good writing—words on the page, how they sound, images, rhythm, and so on—as poetry, and the workshop should attend to the writing as well as to the content.

For creative writers and other nontechnical people, it seems that trying to regain, even artificially, the air of naïveté of the ritual and its setting might help. Try to follow the rules blindly, even childishly; think of the rules as a form almost like a poetic form, and see whether you can say what you're itching to say while obeying those rules. Maybe the rules add more to the situation than you might think.

But the crux of the workshop is the gifts—they turn the group into a family, and as the group works together, family-type behavior is established. Conversations have a familiar feel, special rituals pop up, a private language based on shared experiences is created: the work in progress; the carefully considered but not overly prepared comments; the dialog that explores the space of each work in unpredictable ways. Bonds are formed. Friendships can be made.

In our long-term relationships, we observe the best and worst of our partners. When I mentioned that beginning writers can expect a good response from their families because those families care only about the joy that a beginning writer experiences in having accomplished something, I didn't mention explicitly that such acceptance—if it comes at all—comes even when the work is inept and not good at all.[19] The workshop, urged into existence and its good nature sponsored by its gifts and framed by its rituals, can provide—when it works at its best—this same kind of support, but from strangers whose comments might just reflect what they really think about the work: inept, but making progress, and with some darn good promise.

Gift-giving involves emptying oneself, and along with this emptiness comes risk-taking, creation, diversity. The Chilean poet Pablo Neruda speaks of gift-giving in this story from his childhood in the southern frontier of Chile:

> *I looked through the hole [in the fence] and saw a landscape like that behind our house, uncared for and wild. I moved back a few steps because I sensed vaguely that something was about to happen. All of a sudden a hand appeared—a tiny hand of*

a boy about my own age. By the time I came close again, the hand was gone, and in its place there was a marvellous white toy sheep.... I went into the house and brought out a treasure of my own: a pine cone, opened, full of odor and resin, which I adored. I set it down in the same spot and went off with the sheep.... Maybe this small and mysterious exchange of gifts remained inside me also, deep and indestructible, giving my poetry light.[20]

PART TWO

Writers' Workshop

CHAPTER SIX

The Players

The writers' workshop works best when the participants' roles are well laid out and understood by all, and the players are well matched. There are three roles in the writers' workshop: authors, a moderator or workshop leader (or two), and an audience. I use the term *workshop leader* when the person acts as a teacher as well as a moderator, and the term *workshop moderator* (or just *moderator*) when the person simply ensures that the workshop rules are followed. In a workshop, an audience is a group of people who are in attendance and perhaps are participating, but who are not authors of work that will be explored by this workshop. Creative workshops generally don't have audiences, though some, like Bread Loaf, do. The technical workshop, with its emphasis on summarizing the work, is more naturally suited for audiences.

The ideal size for a workshop is ten people. With ten, if each author takes about ninety minutes, it takes three to five days to go through all the work (one or two three-hour sessions per day, handling two writers per session). This is enough time for the people in the group to get to know each other well enough to know how to interpret and use the comments given. With fewer people, the total time together can be insufficient for each person to know what to do with the comments, whereas with more, the process can become tedious to some and comments can become tinged by the desire to get it over with.

If the workshop group continues beyond one round of work, or if the format calls for much shorter consideration of each work—say, fifteen minutes per person instead of ninety—then the ideal size is a bit smaller: about the size of a comfortable lunch group or afternoon get-together.

∼

The fundamental players are the authors whose works are being reviewed in the workshop. The authors have both the most to gain and the most to lose in the workshop: The comments they receive could make the work a masterpiece, or the experience could be so devastating that the work will be dropped altogether and the author could lose confidence in his or her ability to write. The format of the workshop is set up to maximize the likelihood of the good outcomes and minimize those of the bad ones.

Coauthors are handled just like individual authors: They participate as individuals when other work is being workshopped, and they act mostly like a single author when their work is being workshopped. That is, one of them reads the excerpt, they all sit quietly when the main part of the workshop is going on, and they can each ask questions later. Multiple authors of a single piece count as one person when a group is thinking about the ideal size for the workshop—the ideal size for one round of the workshop is thus ten pieces.

The moderator's job is to make sure that the ground rules are followed, that the author does not defend the work or inappropriately introduce it, that the author does not speak during the main part of the workshop, that the members of the group do not address the author, that the author is not embarrassed, and that the members remain courteous and focused only on the work and not the author or the author's intentions. The moderator should make sure that the comments and discussion are moving forward—and not in circles—and that points are made in a way the author can use for improvements to the work. In workshops where the moderator is also an author whose work will be or has been reviewed, the moderator should be careful in making comments since the moderator role can sometimes be viewed as a special one, perhaps slightly elevated or privileged. When it seems that by clarifying something about the work the group can more effectively move forward, the moderator may ask the author to clarify the point but never to defend. Some moderators are expert in the genre being workshopped, and can thus act as teachers.

Anyone who is not an author or a moderator is in the audience. There are two types of audiences: *participatory* and *nonparticipatory*.

The audience was a controversial addition to the traditional writers' workshop, introduced by the software patterns community as a way to share the experience of a writers' workshop with people who do not have work being critiqued by the workshop and who may or may not be authors themselves. In nonparticipatory manifestations, the audience sits in a circle around the writers' circle, and in participatory ones the audience sits among the authors. When the audience is separate and nonparticipatory, it acts as a true audience in that its members are expected not to speak, though sometimes an author whose work is under discussion will agree to allow them to participate. When the audience is part of the circle, its members act as authors with the only difference being that they do not have work under consideration. The ideal audience consists entirely of authors who have previously been in a writers' workshop.

In creative writing workshops, with some exceptions, there are no audiences, and in fact, the idea of one would be considered foreign and unnatural. The workshop in the technical world is formal and ritualistic, and therefore there are plenty of mechanisms for ensuring the safety and dignity of the author even with an audience present. The creative writing workshop, on the other hand, is considerably more informal and therefore has fewer checks within the authors' circle, let alone nonauthors.

Audience members—even those who have been authors in workshops before—should keep in mind that they don't have as much at stake in the workshop as the authors do. Nonparticipatory audience members should remain silent, and when invited to speak, they should take care with any critical comments, or not make them at all.

~

The first issue of roles is the relative experience levels of the participants. In the absence of other considerations, workshops would seem to work best when the overall experience levels of the authors are about the same, particularly if there are novice workshoppers in the group. For some, encountering dramatically more experienced people who have perhaps created more technically well-crafted work can be discouraging, especially for novices—though for many, seeing ordinary people who have attained a strong level of craft can be exhilarating. And to observe these experienced folks being critiqued can be difficult for novices because they can only imagine the comments they will get, and perhaps they will become fearful.

However, many considerations come into play. Most organized workshops insist on a minimum level of accomplishment as demonstrated by work submitted as part of an application to participate in the workshop, but any accomplishment level beyond that minimum is welcome. In technical workshops, there are also considerations surrounding the level of expertise in the domain area—someone who had never written or thought about banking software would likely have little to say about banking patterns. When you have a workshop full of novices, you need a very strong and experienced workshop leader or pair of them—the teaching needs to come from somewhere if the process is to work well.

Moreover, the makeup of the workshop depends on the pedagogical context of the workshop. Some workshops operate totally outside any such context, but many are part of a larger process of teaching writing. Some teachers use workshops as a kind of support group or scaffolding within which to establish a process of writing. Other workshops are part of a degree program that has other, supporting activities such as classroom teaching, essay writing, directed reading, and mentoring. The software patterns community has a series of organized workshops that are part of a cycle of teaching and preparation for publishing.

In my experience, the best workshop groups exhibit a bell-shaped distribution of experience levels: Most people are at about the same level, but there are several more experienced and a couple less experienced writers. The more experienced writers can act as teachers, and the less experienced ones can perhaps become inspired to try to excel.

There are four types of experience to consider when thinking about the composition of the group. First is the level of technical or content expertise. In software this is the technical training and experience of the person—advanced degrees, career success—which might mean that the person's work is at a deeper level or of concern more to experts in one domain. In the writing arts this can be the experience level of the writer: how many stories or poems the person has written. With more experience, there is a deeper knowledge of how to craft a story—not how to put words on the page, but how to make a story whose structure is effective. For poets this is the knowledge of how poems work. Technical expertise makes a difference in the level of the discussion, and novices can be frightened off by the experience of being part of a discussion too difficult to follow. Having a teacher as a workshop leader can make a big, positive difference—a teacher can quickly fill in some of the knowledge gaps novices might have and thus focus the discussion on the presentation. Moreover, someone who has written, let's say, five hundred poems will likely have different concerns from someone who has written fifty, despite talent or accomplishment.

Second is writing ability. This is the ability to craft lines, sentences, paragraphs, poems, stories, papers, essays, patterns, novels, and so forth. For writers, writing ability is highly correlated with the overall technical experience level, but even among writers there is a difference between how much the writing itself—the words in order on the page and how they sound and their meanings combine—is in the foreground of the story or poem and how much the story or images behind the words are. For technical people, writing may or may not be part of their normal activities, and so if the workshop is addressing patterns or a pattern language, or perhaps conference or journal papers, a difference in writing experience can be troubling for the more novice individuals, and the more experienced workshop members might become bored by so-called beginner comments.

Third is experience in the workshop. In software, because the writers' workshop is still relatively novel, the members of the workshop tend to follow the form and ethics of the ideal workshop very closely. As people become more experienced with workshops, they sometimes take shortcuts, are more critical, try to use the forum to establish themselves as top dogs, and in short, short-circuit the gift magic discussed previously. These problems haunt workshops in the writing arts, where the gift nature of the workshop and the fine points of its process are sometimes sidestepped and comments may be self-serving, sharp, and of little value to the authors. On the other hand, some workshop participants mature into good teachers who take a lot of time and care to provide useful critiques. To some extent, differences in workshop experience can be minimized by skillful leadership and an up-front set of guidelines for criticism. Such guidelines are discussed in Chapter 7, The Setting, and a sample set of guidelines is presented in Appendix B, Guidelines for Feedback.

Fourth is experience having one's work criticized. This experience can be gained through attending writers' workshops, but also through having it reviewed by colleagues and peers, supervisors, and writing teachers. Skins come in a variety of thicknesses, and it's sometimes hard to tell whether someone is going to fall apart or lash out when critiqued. Often, someone who is critical of other people does not react well to criticism. The writers' workshop is designed to minimize the risk to the author, but the risk is not zero. I have seen many people not handle it well.

If there are to be novices in the group, then it's best to set the overall group level as equal as possible in all four of these areas of experience—and get a good workshop leader. The same is true for genre: In the absence of other considerations, it is best to conduct a workshop as far as possible in the same genre by all members of the workshop. When the members of the group are all fairly experienced in the four dimensions, the genre can vary quite a bit, and for fiction writers, having poets in the workshop can make quite a positive difference and vice versa. But uniformity of genre can help deepen the experience for most people in most cases. Within the technical world, the works should be, as much as possible, the same writing genre—patterns, papers, code—and within the same or similar domain areas. One question not yet explored deeply in practice is how well a workshop works when there is a mixture of technical people and writers.

The moderator needs to be more experienced, in general, in all four areas than the other participants, but it is critical that the moderator be more experienced in workshops than the other members. If the group is very experienced, of course, a similar level of moderator experience is sufficient and is likely the only possible alternative.

When the experience levels match, then it is easier to engage the ethos of the gift. For more experienced people, the nature of the gift is understood—what is personally gained by giving the gift, how does it feel to give the gift of good commentary, what are the boundaries of behavior in this small gift exchange, how to behave at the different turns of the workshop, how the workshop evolves and matures in its meetings. For less experienced people, the workshop can seem foreign and intractable and can appear to be a sort of crucible in which the individual can be too easily hurt. Gifts are rarely given in many career and academic situations, especially those infected with an overly competitive nature, and thus, to some, the way this familylike behavior can appear out of nowhere can seem mysterious and unlikely. I find this mystery more in technical workshops that are mostly populated by men in competitive career situations, and very much less so in creative workshops.

When experience levels differ, either the technical comments (technical points in a technical workshop and genre-specific or literary points in a creative workshop) or the craft comments can be off balance. Some participants may make very specific and detailed comments, others may make more vague comments, and the overall effect can be a bit of confusion and people talking past each other. In such circumstances, an expert workshop leader can provide bridging comments and vocabulary as well as some teaching. If you are organizing a workshop and find that you have a group with very different experience levels, you can try partitioning the group into several, more closely matched subgroups.

It is important to think firmly of each author sitting in the circle having his or her work read and worked on as the final expert in the author's own subject area. The work each author presents is clearly his or her work, and even if the subject matter contains incorrect statements, the author is still the expert on the overall content, mistaken or not. This might sound odd, but there are benefits to this approach.

A writer I know who leads workshops said this about content:

> I usually operate on the theory that content can't be taught and that leaves us with technique.... If the conversation bogs into slow, boring, and/or irrelevant mud, I try to point out some obvious strengths and fixable weaknesses and keep it based as much as possible on technique or matters of logical follow-through. If somebody gets peckish in his or her commentary in class, I try to extract a teachable moment but otherwise head the mean-spiritedness off at the pass.

Let's look first at the writers' workshop for technical and scientific pieces, where the natural tendency of the workshop members is to look at the technical content, as they have been trained. When the author is thought of as authoritative, the tone of the workshop is elevated, and the circle members are more respectful and therefore kinder and more collegial. Even if the work contains blunders, the author will be able to receive this tough news more readily when he or she is treated with respect and as the expert in the area, and there is always the possibility that some other kind of piece can come out of the workshop experience than what was reviewed—perhaps an excellent report on a failed research project.

Three characteristics that a workshop member can bring to the workshop are brilliance, respect, and insight. Not all of us are brilliant, and no one is brilliant every day. Respect is a spiritual discipline that not everyone espouses. Insight depends on brilliance and respect—enough respect of the work and author that a person takes the time to search for insights to share—as well as knowledge, experience, and some luck. One writer I know says, "If a reader, in a workshop or in other circumstances, offers me respect and insight on the page, I feel blessed."

Insight and respect are deepened when a workshop group stays together over a long period. As you get to know the other authors, you appreciate more their expertise and talents, their points of view. As you become more familiar with their work and the way they write, your comments will reflect deeper insights. Wise workshop leaders insist that the participants treat each other with respect.

Keep in mind that this is a writers' workshop, not a technical review. Even in a technical workshop, you are focusing on the clear and appropriate presentation of material—often to other technical people, so that correctness is indeed an issue, particularly when claims are exaggerated or muddily made—and on the role of the author as writer, not on the role of the author as a possibly flawed researcher or developer, though that can come out.

In Chapter 2, I discussed how a workshop-like format was used with emotionally disturbed children and how its focus on the writing and not the content enabled the magic of the situation to emerge. As the teacher/moderator of this workshop explained, "The most important aspect of this was my edict not to respond to the content." This is a different way of saying that the author is the expert.

Similarly, in the creative writers' workshop, the author is to be taken as the expert in the work in front of the group, even though the participants may sometimes need to point out errors that creep into a work. A different presentation, different facts, a different structure, different craft elements, and different uses of writing techniques are all fair game along with errors and mistakes, but the writers in the circle must never claim the work of another author as their own. Nor should they diminish or even seem to diminish their respect for the author as the author of the work in front of them and its final version—and vision.

This may seem hard to do, but it isn't. You simply point out whatever factual errors appear in the piece, as politely as you can and with respect for the piece and the author, and then you resume thinking of the author as expert.

When a writer in the circle begins saying things like "You are wrong," that is the beginning of the work's hijacking. In fact, the tone of the workshop largely depends on the stance the participants take toward each other: helper or owner.

Some workshops turn into debates between members. Sometimes this signals a genuine dispute, which the author needs to think about, but sometimes it's just jockeying for position by the members. In such cases it pays to consider carefully who are the experts, and of what, in the context of the writers' workshop. The author is the expert about the piece—that is clear. People are experts about their own feelings and understanding. During a discussion it can never make sense for a reviewer to disagree with another reviewer making a statement about feelings ("I feel the work is too informal . . .") or a statement about lack of understanding ("I didn't understand the part about . . ."). Statements like "Of course you understand it" are merely showing off and claiming turf. The tone of the workshop deteriorates with such statements, and soon it is a display pit in which members are merely showing off rather than helping. The stance of "the author is the expert" doesn't prevent evidence to the contrary from being presented, but it does prevent two things: stealing the piece from the author and mowing down the author's dignity.

～

An important factor in the possible success of a workshop is the set of emotional needs and expectations its authors bring. If some authors are looking mostly for validation—approval and acceptance—then sometimes the mechanics of the workshop and the stances of the members toward each other can get in the way. Emotions are not out of bounds in a workshop. It is not uncommon for some ongoing workshops to engage in emotional discussions about commitment and the priorities of its members toward the workshop.

In workshops where most people are looking for validation, the expectation can be that the authors will read their work and what follows will be oohs and ahhs. Authors looking for real discussions will soon depart these workshops. Unfortunately, such authors are usually the ones needed to raise the level of the workshop. Workshops with generally similar expertise and expectation levels are found in universities and other organized workshops, such as the national workshops like Bread Loaf in the creative world and the various PLoPs in the patterns world.

～

Between the best, most experienced workshop leaders and the least experienced workshop moderators I have seen, there is a mighty gap. There is often a strong correlation between the skill of the leader and the quality of the workshop. The software and scientific worlds tend to have the least skilled workshop leaders, as do informal, self-organized creative writing workshops. Organized creative workshops are by far the most effective. Most organized workshops—from the large, national workshops to the small, local ones—select excellent facilitators who are also excellent writers and teachers, which is the best combination. Good workshop leaders focus the group on those things that can make the work the best it can be without the group's hijacking it from the author. Self-organized workshops, in which people who write happen to get together and the workshop moderator is casually selected, rely on the strength of the group for success.

A workshop leader, knowing what pieces are going to be reviewed on a particular day, can begin the workshop with a craft-oriented lecture or discussion, which can serve as a lesson on how to talk about the day's work. In this case the workshop leader is really a teacher and not a moderator. A similar effect of teaching a workshop how to respond can take place if the workshop is in the context of a course. A workshop leader described his method of preparing the participants in a poetry workshop: "The first hour is a seminar on some aspect of craft—say, line breaks, or prosody, or metaphor. We look at poems by published authors and discuss them as a group. Then we take a break and return to workshop student poems. The seminars inform the workshops, give students a vocabulary to talk about craft in poems."

For some technologists, the writing doesn't seem important or even interesting. Consequently, part of the work of the workshop is to instill a sense of importance to the writing in such technologists. A workshop leader can do this by teaching writing and clear presentation in the context of the technical material at hand.

At a technical workshop I once attended, an author brought an extensive pattern language for software development groups. The pattern language tried to show how to build a software development group that would not only be effective at producing code but also would be humane and fulfilling to the developers. Because the leader of that workshop was engaged at that time in revamping the development group he headed, he was conversant with different software development methodologies and was actively thinking about the very sorts of problems the author's pattern language was trying to solve. The workshop leader was able to ask the group numerous questions that explored the pattern language and that hinted at improvements and refinements to it. He would ask what-if questions and tied comments together in a way instructive both to the workshop participants and to the author.

Let's look first at the minimum requirements for a moderator. The moderator, besides moving the group through the stages of the workshop according to whatever time constraints have been agreed to, acts as a teacher of the workshop's steps to those who have not experienced it before and of the idiosyncrasies of that moderator's style. For example, some moderators are simply traffic directors who move the pieces and parts along, whereas others are more like commentators who summarize and synthesize comments, encourage the shy to participate, and contribute heavily themselves.

Being a moderator should never be a thought-free job. It takes some sensitivity to recognize that the positive phase of the comments is winding down even though there are new comments being made, and to be able to see that comments are going in circles and to collapse or coalesce them.

The moderator must ensure that the comments are as positively made as possible and that they do not take on the form or feel of an attack on the author. The other authors, mindful that their turns are next, should endeavor to help keep the workshop on an even keel, wording their comments as they would like such comments presented to them. They should feel that the moderator has an expert hand on the tiller.

A moderator can help maintain the dignity and safety of the author by engaging in *active listening*. In this situation, active listening means that the moderator and each reviewer are having a private dialog during each comment. The reviewer makes a remark and the moderator restates the remark in a neutral way, perhaps interpreting the remark into a suggestion for the author or softening an overly harsh statement. The moderator can also interpret and restate any emotions that the reviewer might have let slip in his or her remarks, again in a neutral or positive light. This way, the author is hearing the calm and dispassionate statements of the moderator last and so perhaps the setting is more safe for the author. In general, active listening is a last resort when a workshop group is not jelling properly.

Moderating can be learned. The novice moderator in training must be an experienced author and workshop participant. He or she ideally should be a good or natural teacher. It is easy to think of the moderator as nothing more than a timekeeper, when in fact it is the most important and difficult role in the workshop. The best way to train a moderator is to provide opportunities to observe good workshop leaders closely and to think about how and why they are successful or not. After that, the novice moderator can take the reins while an experienced moderator watches and is ready to correct and teach. For this to work, the group must agree to the training. Such training seems to have the effect of making the workshops more calm and productive, since there is a second activity obviously dedicated to learning going on at the same time whose tenor seems to rub off on the main business of the workshop.

As in any interesting system, there is a nontrivial interaction between the roles in the workshop—what sorts of people fill them determines how rich and varied the interactions in the workshop can be. The more expert the moderator or workshop leader, the more varied the workshop members can be in expertise and experience.

The dynamic in a workshop changes from piece to piece as the expertise of the moderator matches a piece more closely or less closely, and as the insights of the participants are more or less spot on. Where a workshop might click on one piece, it might fall flat on the next one. With enough variation in expertise and interests in the workshop group, each piece should receive useful feedback.

With a weaker moderator, the authors should be at about the same levels of technical, writing, and workshop experience, and that level should be high—as usual, a bit of variation in levels will work well. The moderator is ideally more experienced in all these areas, but sometimes a workshop will have a moderator who is nothing more than a director of the action. It is beneficial if the moderator is a teacher of the technical subject area of the pieces in the workshop, or of writing, but he or she should at least be familiar with the genre or technical areas of the pieces.

In many creative writing programs and national workshops, the workshop leaders are established writers—this is certainly true in major national workshops like Bread Loaf and Sewanee. In fact, each workshop group may have a hierarchy of workshop leaders: one or two established writers and perhaps a junior writer or a selected conference fellow who has published a book.[21] In this case, some degree of teaching is going on between the more senior and more junior writers along with the normal work of the workshop. In my experience, technical and scientific workshop moderators mostly deal with the mechanics of the workshop and making sure the tone is upheld. As a result, the moderator of these workshops is rarely a leader.

When there are two workshop leaders, they usually are essentially equals. The effect of having two leaders is that there is neither a single authoritative center of power nor a single point of view. This multidimensional perspective usually causes the workshop members to provide much more varied feedback—if for no other reason than that the territory of valid opinions either is or seems larger than when there is just one authoritative point of view.

One time I was in a workshop with two workshop leaders. One leader thought one of my poems was horrendous—actually an insult to her as a reader because she believed it was over-the-top intense, most of the line breaks were inept, and the narration was unbelievable. Further, it was one of my first unpunctuated poems, and many of the workshop members found that the lack of punctuation took the reader out of the poem. Her comments were expressed harshly. The other leader couldn't have had a more dramatically different point of view. He thought the intensity was part of the obsessive quality of the poem, the line breaks were good, and the narrative was all too believable. In short, she thought it sucked and he thought it was brilliant (more or less). My response was to mostly leave the poem alone because the confusion of lack of punctuation was one of the effects I was trying to get.[22]

In my first three creative writing workshop experiences—all within two months—my workshop leaders included Sandra McPherson, Brenda Hillman, Jane Hirshfield, Gary Snyder, Mark Strand, Timothy Liu, Ed Hirsch, Jack Gilbert, and Gerald Stern. One of the best workshop leaders I ever experienced is Ellen Bryant Voigt.

Ellen is able to work with very mismatched groups of writers, talking to the entire group in equally respectful and insightful ways. One thing she does is to find a theme or common thread to focus all discussions. Once I saw her focus on the free-verse line, which many of the workshop members were working with. Does the line reflect the way each author read his or her poems; was there a relationship between the look of the poem on the page and the sound of it in the ear?

When a group of peers comes together without an invited and acknowledged leader, a seriously mismatched group can have difficulties. The whole group dynamic can get seriously skewed when some people have a great deal more experience than others—or when some people assume they have more experience. There will be constant working out of the group's hierarchy rather than focusing on the work.

A strong workshop leader can help mismatched groups work well. A writer I know told me this story:

> *Maxine Kumin was a kind, generous, open workshop leader who seemed to believe that each person in the workshop was there to discover the best work he or she was up to that day, that year. She encouraged us to bring in revisions, but when we did, she wanted to see every draft that the group had seen—only one copy was necessary, although she encouraged us to bring everyone's work back each day, in case someone revised. She really listened to all, and seemed not to take sides or even interest in the varying levels or poetic bents of one or the other. Rather, she encouraged us to discover our own poetics.*
>
> *Maxine was very clear about some poems being as good as they would get, and not worth continuing with, even if they were unpublishable—although she believed*

only the poet could decide that. It was the idea that a poem would serve the poet, even if it ended up going nowhere. She focused on craft in a practical way, talking line by line sometimes, and other times discussing the assembly of a book-length work.

Another writer who leads workshops gave me her take on leading:

> I always tell the students that we are not a therapy group but a writing group, and that there will be occasions when they as individuals want to comment on the content, but that as a group, our task is to let the writer know when and where we "don't get it," assuming that our getting it is part of the writer's intention. We are also to point out (before getting to the I-don't-get-it stage) the poem's strengths. I try to step in quickly if someone starts to get personal—I turn the discussion back to craft. If a poem is really bad, I tend to speak first rather than last, so that I can model for the class how to address work that's "in a very early draft" or "an interesting early stage of development." I sometimes err on the side of tact, but my students are all adults, ranging in age from 25 to 85, and I know that tact allows them to hear better. There is almost no better hearing aid than that.
>
> After a session or two, they begin to develop trust in one another and know that a brave failure is more admirable than a safe blah line. I encourage that. I confess that sometimes I weary of being so supportive and at times, privately, may say to someone that the energy spent on overhauling something may be more than they need to expend. How about tossing this aside and starting fresh, a deliberate attempt to not use it as a basis for draft two? Something like that . . . I wouldn't say it in front of a group.

There is a difference between a personal discussion of content and no discussion of content. In a technical workshop and in creative workshops dealing with narrative, the content is fair game—though the author's expertise is not. A personal discussion is rarely appropriate when the topic is the author's personal relationship to the content.

~

Self-organized workshops can be full of danger. A self-organized workshop is when a group gets together and picks a workshop moderator. The success of the workshop, then, depends on the luck of the draw and how quickly the group forms into a supportive organization. If one experienced workshopper is also an author who needs his or her piece reviewed, then bad things can happen. The following story is highly unusual, but it illustrates that the workshop can go cruelly wrong unless enough of its parts are working well.

I once ran a writers' workshop as a way to review rapidly presentation and collateral material for a product launch that had too short a time allocated for ideal preparation. The workshop ran fine until it was time for my work to be reviewed. I made sure my work was among the last so that there would be experience enough with watching how I moderated that someone could assume that role effectively. Moreover, I figured that as an experienced workshopper and writer, I would be able to handle any comments that came up.

I underestimated the skill of people who were used to cutting each other down as part of their usual review process. The moderator sat by while not only my work but I was trashed by one particular person in the workshop. Not only was that part of the workshop a disaster, but it didn't reflect well on the form itself. These same people had tried to launch into other authors as well, but as moderator I had managed to quell them and to instruct at the same time. Unfortunately, the woman who trashed me was the director of the launch, and it would have been difficult for others to contradict her comments if, in fact, they disagreed with them.

This argues that you need to have something like a balanced field for the workshop, and that sometimes an outside moderator is best. When supervisors are part of the mix, it's hard to get, sometimes, a fair mixture of comments that are worded in a constructive way.

What might have worked in the aforementioned situation—but I have never tried it—would have been to have someone play the role of author of my piece while I moderated. The surrogate author would have been able, at least, to write down the comments accurately, and if they were familiar with the piece beforehand, they could have asked good questions in that part of the workshop.

In creative writers' workshops led by expert workshop leaders, the workshop leader is not another author in the circle, but is in a teaching role, and therefore, the workshop leader does not conduct a workshop on his or her own work, although it's not unheard of. In the situation just described, it would have been preferable for me not to have workshopped my pieces, but there was no choice.

When workshop leaders don't have their own work reviewed, the workshop can become unbalanced because the workshop leader is giving a different sort of gift. In fact, some workshops do become unbalanced in this case, but usually the gift of teaching and expertise works and balances well.

A lone writer can't get anywhere with a writers' workshop unless the other players are available. The best way to get into the workshop scene is to join one of the national or international workshops. You can find them in writing periodicals and catalogs (for creative writing workshops) and on-line. There you'll meet people whom you can ask about workshops local to your area. The organized workshops will have good workshop leaders or moderators, so you can see what it's like. Or you can try the local schools and bookstore bulletin boards to find like-minded people.

If you have a group of people of varying writing experience, you can try using this book and really, really following the rules to form your own workshop, but you should try to locate a workshop leader or moderator. A simple ground rule for workshops with lots of novices is that it should consist only of authors and an expert workshop leader or two.

∽

Writing is difficult, and it's easy to make mistakes or not do it as well as readers would like. Inept writing is not rare in early drafts, even from experienced or expert writers. The circle works best when its members are all in the same boat and no authors claim a privileged position above the others. The easiest and most effective way to achieve this is to populate the workshop with writers who are mostly at about the same level in writing and also at about the same level of expertise in their fields. The less experience the group has, the more important this ground rule is. When the least experienced workshop member is nonetheless an experienced writer with successes, this ground rule can be relaxed, and in fact the diversity of people and points of view of a divergent group can be wondrous and exhilarating.

Similarity of experience level brings commonality of experience, which can even out the responses in terms of their directness and potential venom: Hearing a criticism of one's work can be like taking a snake strike, and once a tough comment is made the author may not hear any subsequent comments through shame or rage. The responsibility of each member of the workshop is to prevent this. And it is the moderator's most important job.

CHAPTER SEVEN

The Setting

The primary purpose of most rules and rituals for the workshop is to create a safe setting for the authors. They are put in vulnerable positions by having their in-progress works put on display while not being able to speak or defend the work or themselves. For many authors, the trauma of letting people read unfinished, unpolished work can be significant—but this is the nature of the gift of that work. For the workshop to work, this situation must be comfortable, safe, and productive in helping authors with their works and with becoming better writers and designers. The ritual of the writers' workshop maximizes the effect of the gift-giving nature of the workshop: the gift of the unfinished work, of the time and expertise of the reviewers, of the teaching skills of the workshop leader, and of the emergent expertise of the group as a group mind.

Many workshops have an existing culture because they are part of an ongoing series, perhaps yearly (for example, Bread Loaf). Each workshop creates its own subculture by inheriting this existing culture and by following the rules of the workshop. This creates a setting that either is already or soon will be familiar to each participant—everyone knows how to behave and what the norms are for that behavior.

The culture of a workshop can range from a very informal, family-style interaction to a fairly competitive "let's see who is the best writer here" style. Some workshops foster open, mutual admiration of the participants, some are playful, others very serious. Some have rituals such as telling jokes between authors or holding dances. At residential workshops—where people gather for a week or more to hold the workshops—people sometimes share meals, gather in the evenings to chat or play, hang out at certain haunts in town.

There are two primary types of workshop distinguished by whether the work is written at the workshop for review, or whether prepared work is brought. In the first type, people typically write new material every day, which is reviewed the next; everyone is workshopped every day, and so the duration of an author's turn is usually quite short—about ten or fifteen minutes. In the second type, the work is submitted earlier, sometimes as part of an admissions process. Each author generally gets a longer session—up to sixty minutes—but there is usually only one session per author.

Authors and audience members should stay together for the duration of a workshop, which is the time it takes to review all the authors' work. By keeping the group together, a community of trust is built up through shared experiences and expressions that refer to the shared experiences—deepening the unique subculture of each workshop group. Each author's manuscript can also stay within this smaller community and thus increase the intimacy and trust of the workshop. It is a private place even though to each author it can seem dreadfully public.

The moderator is charged with maintaining the dignity of the silent author by not permitting the discussion to be directed at or about him or her—it is about the work and not the person. Creative and technical workshops deal with this a little differently from each other. For creative workshops, it's important for the moderator to note that everything reviewed is to be taken as fiction—this helps avoid the temptation some reviewers might feel to refer to a character as "you" and direct comments to the author, and sometimes it helps reviewers focus more on the writing and craft than on what the poem or story means to the author.

For technical workshops, the moderator should emphasize that the pieces are all works in progress. For technical writers, there is less opportunity that their works will be mistaken for autobiography, but because they write in fields where usually only polished, finished work is read, reviewers tend to approach every piece as polished.

The order of comments—summary, positive feedback, suggestions for improvement—is designed to maximize the comfort of the author in hearing the comments. The other participants thus act more like coauthors offering helpful suggestions rather than harsh criticisms.

All these things help create a safe setting for the author—there is a community of trust, a shared culture, and a common purpose. All successful collaborative efforts work exactly when all of these are lined up and in play at the same time.

∽

The physical setting of a workshop can be as simple as a plain, quiet room or a backyard or a library—but the way people are arranged can make a big difference to how well the workshop works. We want a level playing field, without barriers.

Many workshops take place in rooms normally set up as Western-style classrooms or as presentation rooms. Such rooms are designed around the idea that a speaker or teacher will stand in a special place so that hearing and seeing the presentation is easy. Tables are available for note taking. Additionally, tables act as a barrier between the listener or learner and the speaker or teacher, setting up a hierarchy in which the speaker or teacher—though in a more vulnerable position, exposed to the audience—is actually in a position of power. Because the speaker or teacher is exposed and can withstand it, he or she attains a position of power.

And in such a setting, the teacher or speaker gives while the audience mostly passively listens and receives. Though we are interested in the author as the default expert in the material presented, we also want to encourage a context in which gifts are exchanged, not merely given. We need a different formation than the classroom or auditorium.

The formation that favors no one in particular in Western culture is the circle, and if the circle comprises only authors with work to review, this is ideal. I will use the figure of a circle to indicate that configuration which places no one ahead or above anyone else.

When the workshop goes on for a long time, with lots of papers, notes, and beverages for the day, it is tempting to use a table or a couple of tables—a circular table or a group of rectangular ones arranged into a square. In creative writing workshops, such arrangements with tables are common, and given the more intense and personal nature of creative writing workshops, the tables work well because they form a small barrier behind which people can hide—hide at least in a symbolic way their innermost sensitivities.

The best situation is a circle of plain chairs with additional papers and drinks sitting on the floor. If the author whose work is being addressed sits outside the circle, which is a custom in some technical workshops, then a table for that author to make note-taking easier is acceptable. Otherwise a clipboard or a lap table works well enough.

This is an example of a cultural difference. In the European software patterns community, the author sitting outside the circle has come to symbolize the role of author as fly on the wall. Further, this makes it easier for the other participants to discuss the work without worrying about addressing him or her directly. Any facial expressions the author makes or his or her noises or motions while taking notes are out of sight and hearing. In a creative workshop, the role of fly on the wall is not as strong, and the expressions of the author are a way to calibrate how tough the comments are. What for the technical community seems a formality that reinforces the strengths of the workshop are elements of alienation to the creative community. An experienced creative workshop leader gave an example of how physical positioning can affect a participant's feeling of belonging to a group:

> *No one should sit in a way that makes them different or set apart from the others. For example, I once taught a workshop in which one woman wanted to sit on a pillow on the floor instead of the chairs all the others sat on. This set her apart from the group. When we looked around the circle, we didn't see her face. At the end of the workshop, she told me she was disappointed as she felt excluded from the group. You need to watch out for people who will do something to physically exclude themselves, and then complain that they felt emotionally excluded.*

The moderator—who is special by role—should not also be special by position. If there is a natural "head of the table" position, the moderator should avoid it. The moderator should face into the light from a large window rather than making the other authors do so. In fact, the moderator should assume the "weakest" geometric position. The moderator should be situated so as to seem like a mostly invisible friendly guide, a sort of Virgil guiding the traveler, as in Dante's *Inferno*.[23]

Authors should not sit in particularly extravagant ways. Some people like to take a second chair as a footstool or as a leaning post. Such postures reflect an overcasualness that belies the serious nature of the workshop, though in well-worn workshops with people who have been with each other for a long time, formality—or overformality—can be skipped.

Neither should the author sit right next to the moderator. Otherwise, comments directed by reviewers to the moderator will be unintentionally also directed physically toward the author. If the author sits opposite the moderator, the moderator can keep a close watch on the author for signs of problems or other signals.

Naturally, when a presentation or performance is being reviewed, the setting should be like its natural setting so that the workshop participants are exactly in the position the audience will be. After the presentation or performance, the workshop members should try to form a circle.

∼

The presence of an audience may make sense for a particular workshop. At some creative workshops (for example, Bread Loaf) there are people sometimes called *auditors* who are audience members. Several technical workshops (for example, EuroPLoP) always have some audience members.

Authors should be asked whether an audience is OK, or the workshop should have announced beforehand that audiences are welcome. The authors must be comfortable with the presence of an audience, and the members of a participatory audience should always be authors who have been workshopped before.

The question arises where the audience should sit. Outside the circle in a concentric circle is the logical place and shape for audiences who mostly listen. Sitting within the circle is the logical formation for audiences who participate as if authors.

When a nonparticipatory audience is large, there is the question of how they can all hear what is intended to be a casual but intimate conversation. Using microphones and an amplification system can be disruptive and unnatural. An interesting way to accommodate larger audiences is in a *natural amphitheater*.

The authors sit in their circle as usual. A third of the audience sits on the floor, right behind the circle of authors. Right behind each of those audience members, a second audience member sits in a chair. And right behind each of those audience members, a third audience member stands. So, in each spoke leading away from the inner circle, there are three people observing, each one's head being above the one in front. Each can hear and mostly see, and the arrangement is compact. The person sitting on the floor can lean back against the legs of the person in the chair to make things more comfortable, and the person standing can lean on the chair back of the person in front. Periodically (every five or ten minutes), the moderator will interrupt the workshop discussion and ask the audience members to switch. On this signal, the person on the floor moves to the chair, the person in the chair stands, and the standing person sits on the floor. This way each person gets an equal amount of time in the comfortable and less comfortable positions. The frequency of switching is based on concerns for physical comfort rather than the flow of the workshop.

Beyond the structure of the participants, the immediate workshop setting should be quiet enough that the author whose work is being reviewed can hear clearly. The more alive and whole the setting is, the better will be the quality of the workshop, though sometimes an overly attractive locale can be a distraction. Some prefer to hold workshops outdoors, but to some a bright sun or the sounds of birds or distant traffic can be too much. Try to be sensitive to the needs of those who seem most shy to express them rather than succumb to the whims of the vocal.

Writers' workshops are used to review and improve all sorts of artifacts and other things. For particular workshops, special settings might be appropriate. For business and marketing people looking at vision statements, marketing collateral, events, and organizations, working off-site can reduce company-related distractions and signal that the work is not strictly business as usual. This enables the workshop to develop a culture that is not a direct copy of the company culture, and in an unfamiliar setting, whatever hierarchical relationships might be inherited by the workshop can be shed or minimized.

Technical workshops benefit from a contemplative setting. Participants are working hard, sometimes reading papers and jotting down notes late into the night; the subject matter can be difficult; the works might be in the last stages of preparation for submission to a conference or publication. A quiet locale supports work like this. For example, two major software patterns workshops are held in relatively remote settings. The Conference on Pattern Languages of Programs (PLoP) takes place at the Allerton Conference Center, which is owned by the University of Illinois. Allerton Park is located outside Monticello, Illinois. The conference center is several miles through heavily wooded forests to the nearest neighbors, who are farmers. Monticello itself is a small town with only a few restaurants. Champaign-Urbana, where the university is located, is twenty-five miles away.

Many creative workshops are held in contemplative or cultural locations. The European Conference on Pattern Languages of Programs (EuroPLoP), for example, is held at Kloster Irsee—a former Benedictine monastery in the heart of Bavaria, Germany. The monastery's history can be traced back to the twelfth century. The conference center is in a very small town about forty minutes by train outside Munich.

∽

The setting for a workshop includes everything leading up to the first author's being introduced and the beginning of the work on that piece. If there are any special requirements for authors—such as overhead projectors—these should already have been taken care of.

The participants should introduce themselves to the whole group, perhaps with some comments about themselves that will make them more human to the workshop members. Some experienced moderators are good at proposing ingenious ways to do this. One particular approach I've seen that seems to work well in American workshops is for each participant to tell a little about his or her first car—how the person got it, why he or she liked it or didn't, and something the person did in or with that car.

The order of review should have already been set, or it can be set at the first meeting after introductions. If possible, the first piece reviewed should be by an author with workshop experience, and it should be a piece that will experience feedback typical of the bulk of pieces in the workshop—that is, not extreme either in expected praise or in suggestions for improvement, a piece that exemplifies a medium tone. For this to work, the workshop leader should receive the pieces enough beforehand to have prepared comments and set an order. In workshop gatherings where leaders rotate from workshop to workshop, the leader or leaders for a workshop session will have prepared for one or two specific authors, and so the schedule for the entire gathering will have been set. In this case, all the leaders will need to have their schedules globally determined. In my experience, in the absence of other considerations, workshops do best when the more novice writers in the workshop go near the beginning—first a few experienced authors to set the tone, then the more novice authors, followed by the most experienced ones.

If the moderator has any special rules or practices, those should be made clear before the review starts. It does not hurt for the moderator to go over the steps in the review process and to emphasize the reasons each person is there: to receive the gift of work in progress and to give the gift of useful comments for the betterment of each piece as if each participant shared ownership of it.

Some workshop leaders hand out a set of workshop guidelines that help ground participants.[24] Guidelines can be generic or can establish unique local rules and rituals. The following is from the last paragraph of workshop guidelines written by Warren Wilson College's *MFA Program for Writers Handbook*. Although this passage is not specifically about rules of behavior or etiquette, it presents a nice perspective on the writers' workshop:

> we are particularly proud of the tone of the workshops: supportive but rigorous, analytical but not judgmental, noncompetitive, vigilant against workshop jargon or preferred aesthetic. Participants should always feel free to question what seems weaknesses, poor choices, or inadvertent missteps, but should also recall that the piece has been snatched from the desktop, that some of its awkwardness may be the absence of authority that attends most work-in-progress, that it does not seek to represent the author's best or finished work. Workshop is not an occasion for merely congratulating the author nor "fixing" a flawed piece.... [T]he importance of workshop is the chance to enlarge one's capacity for strong work.

CHAPTER EIGHT

In Situ

The setting for the actual workshop is a matter of intimacy and the right accessories to facilitate the kind of exchanges needed for the workshop to work. The larger setting for a workshop is another matter. Some workshops take place in people's homes or in work settings during or after work. Here the settings are what they are. But for larger, national or international workshops, the setting for the whole workshop can make an interesting difference, and the larger venue allows for more variation and different activities than just a workshop.

Creating a good workshop setting is akin to creating a culture—or subculture, if you want to be pedantic about it. What makes up a culture? A culture is shared, socially learned knowledge and patterns of behavior. Knowledge includes symbols, norms concerning behavior in context, values, classifications of reality or a metaphysics, and worldviews. Patterns of behavior include rituals, manners, and defined individual roles.

Workshops create a gift-exchange culture based on shared experiences and common goals. The small workshops that people might join in an ad hoc manner follow the culture for workshops established and learned at larger, more global workshops. For creative writing these include the Bread Loaf Writers' Conference, the Squaw Valley Community of Writers Workshop in Poetry, and the various MFA workshops. For software patterns these include the Conference on Pattern Languages of Programs (PLoP), the European Conference on Pattern Languages of Programs (EuroPLoP), and the Southwestern Conference on

Pattern Languages of Programs (ChiliPLoP)—and to an extent the creative writing workshops that the founders of the patterns workshops attended.

Creative writing workshops have a distinctive vocabulary that comes from the technical vocabulary of literature (*postmodernism*, *sestina*, and *narrative structure*) and craft (*authority of voice* and *lineation*), and from special expressions based on the work of the workshop (such as *generosity* and *heart of the poem*). Veterans of particular workshops or schools have their own idioms and quirky sayings. For example, alumni of the MFA program at Warren Wilson College call themselves "Wallies" (after a lighthearted misremembering of the name of the school) and sometimes call their loved ones "sweatheart" (after a poem titled "I Love You Sweatheart," written by Tom Lux about a sign he saw spray-painted on an overpass near the school). Another favorite place for Warren Wilson alumni is Snake Lake, where students sometimes skinny dip—it too is the subject of another Tom Lux poem, called "Snake Lake."

Software patterns workshops share the vocabulary of computing, programming languages, object-oriented programming, and words and expressions referring to the concepts of the architect Christopher Alexander. The latter include words like *patterns*, *forces*, and *QWAN* (the quality without a name). An important book to the software patterns community, *Design Patterns*, is called "Gang of Four" because of its four authors, Erich Gamma, Richard Helm, Ralph Johnson, and John Vlissides.

Workshop members share experiences, which gives them a shared history and worldview. All are writers who struggle in their own ways, and all have been workshopped at one point or another (or are about to be). All are trying to build a literature through a series of conversations with other writers. The workshop itself is a ritual, and many members have shared experiences—"Remember that time Brian got so hot he jumped right into the pond, scum or no?" The national workshops that form a baseline of culture share common features and characteristics. Physically getting there is one of them.

Getting to Bread Loaf or PLoP is not a simple matter of flying to a major city and then taking a cab. When I go to Bread Loaf, I fly to Boston and rent a car. After grabbing a lobster roll at Legal's and a frappe at Bates Farm, I drive up through part of New Hampshire and over to Vermont. The two-lane follows a river shoveled out from a narrow valley for about five miles until just beyond the Vermont Castings woodstove outlet. Then I turn right and go past the sprawled farm where you can buy ferrets, then into the next town, where I gas up and turn left up the mountain past the ski area. Bread Loaf itself is a turn-of-the-nineteenth-century farm expanded with guest houses, a large barn for dances and adjoining classrooms, and a theater where readings are held in the evenings, all of it white with green trim and adirondack chairs spread about. Sometimes a lucky person gets to stay in the Frost house, which is nearby. All in a setting of rolling fields, oaks and maples, and the smell of fresh-cut hay.

PLoP is held at Allerton Park, Monticello, Illinois. To get there I fly to Willard Airport and rent a car. The quickest, most scenic way is due west through corn and soy fields, each one labeled with a seed sign from the seed supplier for that field—Viking, Steyer, Dekalb. Monticello is just thirty minutes away. From there I drive past the four giant silos by the railroad and then down a curving road past less flat fields until I get to where the road is lined with firs. I turn right into a fir-lined lane, across a small bridge that should be condemned, then left at the Fu Dog Garden to the main house, where the workshops are held. The grounds of Allerton Park are laced with hiking trails, one along the Sangamon River through a forest of red oak, silver maple, white oak, redbud, sycamore, and hickory. The trails and park are filled with occasional sculptures and apparent Greek and Roman ruins, including *The Death of the Last Centaur* and *The Sun Singer* (in dramatic isolation at the end of a road).

At both these workshops, participants share sleeping quarters and all meals; at night there is music and readings; both have a newspaper produced every day (*The Daily Crumb*, *The PLoP News*, and *Kloster Hearsay*).[25] At PLoP the workshop members often participate in the custom of exchanging small gifts—two I recall receiving were a thousand dollars of shredded, used money from a software developer who worked at the Federal Reserve Bank in New York and a stomach magnet for cows, which helps prevent a perforated stomach if a cow swallows a small piece of barbed wire. (This was from a guy whose wife is a veterinarian at the University of Illinois where some cows have stomach portholes for teaching and research purposes.)

The residencies at the MFA program at Warren Wilson College follow the same pattern: a location not easy to get to, a rural atmosphere, shared meals, non-resort accommodations, and various rituals like going into town once or twice over a ten-day period, dances, and the farm tour.

Being in a remote place has the added benefits of taking the workshop out of the ordinary flow of life and hence perhaps making something that has more significance than day-to-day existence. Writing is creating a literature, and a literature is art, even when it's a literature of science. It is important for a writer to know that what he or she is doing has a larger significance than just putting one word after another at night after the kids are in bed—though it is just as important to know that putting one word after another after the kids are in bed is exactly how you make art.

Being in a remote location heightens the senses, makes the group of writers feel more connected to each other than to the rest of the world, and helps build the culture. Shared experiences; shared goals.

Both the patterns and poetry workshops have a canon and revered writers. For patterns, it's *A Pattern Language, The Timeless Way of Building, Design Patterns,* Christopher Alexander, and the Gang of Four; for poets, it's Emily Dickinson, John Donne, Shakespeare (his sonnets), and perhaps Elizabeth Bishop and Walt Whitman. In both cases the canon goes on and on, but almost anyone in a workshop culture can point to its canon and "spiritual" leaders.

Snake Lake, "I Love You, Sweatheart," the creation of the Hillside Group, and the "Wally" moniker creation myth are all examples of shared stories and myths for their workshop communities. These shared stories are part of how newcomers learn the patterns of behavior and knowledge needed to move from novices to experienced members to leaders to elders.[26]

The code of ethics comes from the gift economy the workshop creates and the spirit of generosity based on the shared experience of the difficulty of writing and, in some cases, even knowing what writing really is, how to approach it, and how to come to grips with it. At workshops, one finds that the usually critical tone of review situations evaporates and people are less apt to carp at pieces than when in their natural work settings. This generosity sometimes extends to one's own writing.

Many creative writers experience strong insecurity about writing—and sometimes so do technical writers. The workshop is a forum created for writers to show generosity toward each other. Once this feeling of generosity is established, a good workshop leader will use it to teach the writers to treat themselves as respectfully and generously as they treat others.

The workshop is a ritual within a literature-building community, a pattern of behavior colored by generosity and gift giving. The custom of giving small tokens as gifts sprang up on its own, no one having made the connection to the gift-based nature of the workshop itself. This custom started at the first PLoP held in 1993. A poet attending a PLoP would recognize the culture, as would a patterns person visiting Bread Loaf.

Part of what makes a culture work in situations like writers' workshops is that the shared, learned behaviors set the workshop participants apart from business as usual. When I participated in a workshop led by Brenda Hillman, she advised me that when you are in doubt about how to revise, opt for making it strange. This seems to work also for creating a successful workshop setting and culture.

To this end we can also borrow some ideas from the brainstorming world. There, games and other creativity-loosening exercises are used to stimulate the group, to get its members out of its regular modes of working and thinking. In most of the software patterns workshops, there is a games master who between workshop sessions engages the entire population of the workshops in games and art projects. A common prop for games at patterns workshops is the parachute, which the participants can manipulate to form interesting shapes like a mushroom. Or they can move tennis balls around in a circle on the parachute as the participants stretch it out. For such kinetic games, the idea is to ask the group to achieve the goal without stating how, and without allowing for any planning, so that the group begins to practice self-organizing and creating structures where new thinking can evolve by small, local acts. This is what we expect to see in the workshops.

When there are several workshop groups at a conference, shared meals, shared housing, and games are ways of creating a common culture where otherwise a set of cultures might arise. At these larger workshops and conferences, authors often get significant benefit from interacting with other writers, and these conversations are cultivated by common activities and a common culture.

Games are an important part of the patterns culture—something not shared the same way by the creative writing community: You're more likely to see creative writers playing word games.

~

The larger national workshops or conferences made up of workshops have some opportunities not available in single-workshop settings. One is the opportunity to create a venue in which people can speak, live, and be immersed in writing. In addition to workshops, there can be readings, craft lectures, discussion groups, and one-on-one conferences in which a writer will meet with one of the workshop leaders in a focused discussion of the writer's work. The subject of writing can infiltrate the whole event.

Readings are a particularly effective way of building the workshop culture. With readings, you can introduce the workshop leaders and hear their sensibilities and what they pay attention to. You can also develop a canon. For example, at the Art of the Wild conference in Squaw Valley, California, Gary Snyder would give readings, even when he was not a workshop leader. He was on the same university faculty as the organizers of the conference, and he lived not too far away from Squaw Valley. His poetry exemplified the sort of nature-oriented writing the conference attended to.

In courses and classes at a workshop-based event, you can also build a canon and culture by what is taught and what isn't, and by how things are criticized. Care must be used to build such canons lest some writers feel left out—a canon that leaves out women writers in the creative world or people who program in Lisp in the software world can feel oppressive to women and Lisp programmers.

Just about any aspect of the workshop event can be used to build the culture, and the culture can last even when the conferences are a year apart. Even other workshops started by members of a conference workshop can bear the culture of that conference.

If an event consists of a number of workshops, then the organizers may consider rotating the workshop leaders among them. At the first workshop I attended, six or seven poets went from workshop to workshop. This way, workshop members can learn a variety of things from a variety of teachers by observing what each one homes in on and thereby how they think about work.

In such multiworkshop events, the workshops are partitioned into genres: poetry, fiction, nonfiction, and sometimes mixed fiction and poetry for creative writing workshops, and different domain or architectural areas for software and patterns—for example, telecom, middleware, user interface, or financial. This way the workshop members are more likely to be able to understand the discussions and participate well.

∽

Some workshops in both the creative writing and the software realms use a technique of writing at the workshop event. A couple of examples of this are the Squaw Valley Community of Writers Workshop in Poetry, the Napa Valley Writers' Conference, and EuroPLoP. At these week-long conferences, the writers are given writing assignments—usually every night. The next day, the students review what they wrote. In some cases, the workshop leaders participate, writing each night and having their pieces discussed in workshop each day.

Because the workshop is held in a writing-permeated atmosphere, this technique liberates writers who are possibly in need of expanding their palettes and trying new things. Sometimes the workshop leader will give a particular assignment. For example, one year when I was at Napa Valley, Jane Hirshfield gave the assignment to use the vocabulary of your job or profession to write a poem. That evening, Jack Gilbert gave a reading, and because I had done research in artificial intelligence, I wrote a poem called "Is Jack Gilbert's Mind a Computer?"

Because this workshop had the habit of also rotating workshop leaders, Ed Hirsch was going to lead the workshop. After a few other poems were looked at, it was my turn. Just then Jack Gilbert walked in. He asked Ed whether he could sit in. Ed looked around at us and said it was fine. At that point he turned to me and I mentioned in a quiet voice that maybe we wanted to look at someone else's poem first. Ed said, no, just go ahead. I added that maybe it wouldn't be a good idea to do mine. He said, no, it was fine, just go ahead. I insisted that perhaps there should be an exception made. Ed asked why and I said, well, here's the title: "Is Jack Gilbert's Mind a Computer?" Ed said, oh, I see, and he asked Jack did he mind? No. Did I, then, mind? No. We proceeded. The discussion first focused on the craft of writing applied to the poem and not its topic—reinforcing the idea that the author is the expert—and toward the end, Jack's interest in artificial intelligence came out and we had a brief discussion of the field. The culture of the workshop provided the good humor needed to get past what could have been an embarrassing session.

Later in the conference I had a one-on-one meeting with Ed. He pointed out a number of weaknesses in my writing. I mentioned that I was just trying to get better. During the workshop, he had talked about the concept of getting to the next level, each level a small step depending on what you paid attention to and how you applied it to your work. Just as I thanked him, he said, I think you've made it to the next level.

It was a small thing to say, but it helped me keep going and continue to practice and learn. It was a small thing, but it was something a workshop leader should be able to say and does say.

EuroPLoP and sometimes ChiliPLoP do the same sort of thing. A writing teacher will have a small group and teach them to write patterns. After a day or two of instruction, the students each choose a pattern that they think they know and then write it up overnight. A pattern can be as short as half a page and as long as ten pages. Often, some students have a tough time thinking of a pattern, usually because they believe they need to come up with an earth-shattering pattern in a technical area. But any pattern will do, even one that has been written up before. The teacher might spend about two or three hours helping students come up with their patterns and getting them unstuck while they write. Then off they go for the evening. The next day is spent reviewing the patterns. Some of these exercises go on to be shepherded, workshopped another time or two, and end up in books, so these impromptu writings can result in good work—the same for the poetry.

∼

One of the most significant contexts for a workshop is its educational setting, if it has any. Most of the workshops I've been talking about are outside an organized curriculum, but even these can be subject to a teaching style, practice, or theory espoused by the workshop leader. At Warren Wilson College, the workshop is an important but small part of a larger, practical theory of teaching writing. There the emphasis is on closely and individually supervised writing and revising while the student engages in critical writing on craft elements, along with extensive reading. Classroom work and workshops take place only during about three weeks of the year in a two-year program.

Other theorists talk about things like *role negotiation*, in which people try out different roles or personae while learning to write. The workshop, then, is a sort of theater in which the suitability of each role is tried out.

Though I have not experienced writers' workshops based on learning theories, I would be surprised if the kinds of effects described in this book were totally absent in any workshop. The simple theory of learning writing that I assume here is that you get better by practicing, that there are barriers to practicing, and that those barriers are similar among most people—and that the ways past them are similar too and can be applied in the context of the writers' workshop. I would be very surprised to hear of an effective way of learning or teaching writing that did not involve the student's doing a lot of writing.[27]

∼

Workshops are not held in a vacuum. Establishing the right culture can foster the exchange of gifts and set the tone of the workshop. It can create a setting in which the creation of literature is at the forefront. Seeing that there are other writers engaged in the same struggle as you and apparently making progress is a way to gain the strength to continue writing, which is the only way to get better. The only way.

CHAPTER NINE

Preparing for the Workshop

The workshop is a high-energy affair, potentially with emotional upheavals as well as lots of opinions and suggestions. Authors and reviewers need to prepare for the workshop to make it work for everyone. Fortunately, basic preparation for both authors and reviewers is easy—for authors because the preparation is just what one would do while carefully writing, and for reviewers because the workshop can rely on the differing interests and expertise of the reviewers to gather a wide diversity of comments without requiring each reviewer to scour the work for all possible comments.

Much of how to prepare depends on the culture and practices of the workshop you are attending. Workshops that work with well-worked drafts will not be suitable for early drafts; workshops that work on material written at the workshop will not be comfortable with polished drafts. Although many workshops either occasionally or always work with new work or work written on the spot, most are intended for work that has gone through several drafts and some polishing, and in the absence of evidence to the contrary, you should assume a workshop is of this variety.

First and foremost, the author should never submit a raw first draft to a workshop that is expecting well-worked drafts unless that is what the author intends to publish. The reviewers will, as a group, be doing a lot of work, and that work should not be wasted on a draft that will be heavily revised anyway. Unless you are one of those rare people whose first drafts are nearly publishable, do the workshop and yourself a favor by presenting a good attempt at a polished draft—something you think is on its way to being publishable, though still a work in progress. Over time, as your experience with writing increases, you will know better what a good work looks and feels like.

Writers find it useful, however, to have their early drafts reviewed in a workshop. The purpose of the workshop is to help the writer with whatever the writer needs help with. Sometimes, amazing writing comes right off the notebook page. The level of critique will change depending on the level of draft: For a newer piece, larger comments will dominate—such as a comment that an entire section is confusing—while for a well-worked piece, details will dominate. An ongoing workshop is an appropriate place to bring fresh work, including first drafts. This is true of both creative and technical workshops.

Some workshops are designed for new or even raw work—but make sure that's really the kind of workshop it is. Typically such workshops devote only about fifteen minutes to each piece.

Writers experienced with the workshop sometimes use the workshop for specific purposes. For example, some bring work in which about half of it seems like it's in real trouble—this helps them get in a mood to accept suggestions. Others bring work that they think is finished—perhaps to get a final polish or the final, small changes that will make the piece "done." And some bring a work to test it out on an audience—what they care about is the reaction of the audience to hearing the work read. Here is how one poet described her purpose in taking a poem to a workshop: "I often won't feel like a poem is really finished until I've read it to someone. It's a way for me to distance myself and actually hear it as I'm reading it to others. It takes on its own life." Most bring in work that has had at least one revision, but they know from their experience that the piece will be useful to the group somehow.

An issue that can be overlooked is how polished a look the piece should have, that is, how well typeset the piece is and the quality of paper it is printed on. Silly as this sounds, it can be a major contributor to the sense of gift giving and the work-in-progress nature of that gift. Too shabby, and the gift is more like a throwaway, a goodwill gesture of sorts but perhaps nothing more than a slightly more caring form of trash day. Too polished, and the work is maybe not so in-progress—it presents itself as intended as a finished work with the author looking for praise rather than for a form of coauthorship. Remember, the gift is the work in progress with an invitation to own it in a spiritual sense.

Perhaps the members of creative writing workshops don't think about this explicitly, but I rarely see wonderfully typeset manuscripts reviewed at poetry and fiction workshops. Almost all are simply typed double-spaced or have been prepared using a computer but with fonts and spacing chosen to give it the look of a typed manuscript of the old style. Is this just a tip of the hat to tradition, or is there something important about being neat but modest, something clearly taken from the midst of the author's studio, brought out to the workshop for some critical work, and then back in it goes before the final, final polish is put on?

I've noticed a significant difference between how the work I give my colleagues is treated if I typeset it carefully and print it on nice paper and if I do the same but put "Work in Progress" at the top of every page. In one case, the readers applaud or criticize; in the other, a discussion arises. Whether a piece is labeled a work in progress or advertises itself as such by clearly looking as if it is being worked on, the approach of reviewers seems to change from critic to coauthor.

Work in progress—the essence of a shared gift.

A second way to prepare for a workshop is to think about the kind of comments you are looking for. For a beginning writer, simply hearing whether something is basically good or bad will be enough, and perhaps some of the more detailed comments will not be important to the writer or not even noted by the author during the workshop. For an advanced writer, there may be only a couple of technical or smaller points that the writer wants opinions on. Other comments may not even be considered seriously or even listened to. Writers in between will have a general idea of their strengths and weaknesses and will be able to listen for comments validating the strengths and suggesting fixes for the weaknesses.

The nature of the feedback that a writer seeks can be as unique as each piece of work. For a creative workshop, a writer might want to hear about whether the narrative is clear and believable, whether the images and metaphors are clear and work with each other, whether a particular character is believable and her motivations clear, whether there is too much description in a specific spot, whether it's clear who's speaking when, whether the line breaks in a particular section work, whether the stanza about the white chickens is too much, whether there are too many spondees in the first two lines, and so on. For a technical workshop, a writer might want to hear whether it is clear what the piece is about, whether the introduction is appropriate for the audience, whether the names of the patterns are clear, whether there are other forces to account for in the pattern, whether there are enough examples and the motivating example is convincing, whether using the first person makes sense in this type of article, whether the references are complete, whether the pattern really should be two patterns, and so on.

The creative workshop focuses a little more on the craft and the writing, whereas a technical workshop focuses a little more on the content and how it's presented. In both types of workshops, the goal is to make the piece at hand the best it can be without taking it over. For creative writing, the effect of the writing is perhaps the largest part of what the work is; for technical writing, the presentation of content is perhaps the largest part. Therefore, we expect to see more focus on craft in the creative workshop than in the technical, but the difference is in degree and not an absolute.

The comments from a workshop—considering that there could be ten or more people commenting in rapid succession—can be overwhelming. The author will be able to capture only some of the comments. Sometimes authors pair up and both people take notes when one of their pieces is under consideration. Sometimes an author will ask someone else to take all the notes while the author simply listens for the large points and tone of the discussion. A writer explained it this way:

> *For those who tend not to hear when their own work is being discussed—it is a good thing to have someone whose judgment you trust and whose writing is legible take minutes of the comments made about your work. These include positive remarks as well as suggestions for revision or other avenues to realize what some regard as "the intention" of the writer. All but the most mature have experienced that deer-in-the-headlights feeling. It does seem a help to have a page of notes you haven't taken yourself.*

Another obvious solution is to tape record the workshop. However, the nature of the culture and interactions of the workshop don't lend themselves to such accurate and unambiguous records. Reviewers are much more comfortable and make more honest comments knowing they are ephemeral, recalled only by memory or incomplete notes. Some workshops may allow it if asked, but I would not recommend it for either a creative or a technical workshop.

There is sometimes a temptation for the author to not write down comments he or she disagrees with. The author should write these down too, because how he or she feels during the workshop may change upon reflection and the passing of time.

~

In a workshop sponsored by an organization, that sponsoring organization may provide ways to prepare. For example, in the software patterns community, some writers' workshops are held yearly in various locations around the world. The overall community supports a group of guides or *shepherds* who are experienced pattern writers and who are interested in helping the community by providing a couple of rounds of comments on papers before they are accepted by a workshop. Shepherds are, unfortunately, a rare resource in most situations in which a writers' workshop is appropriate, but an author sometimes can find some friends or colleagues who will act as informal shepherds. The author's preparation, then, consists of preparing for the experience of the workshop as well as doing what most writers do to prepare their pieces for publication.

Reviewers in patterns workshops usually prepare by reading the work and preparing comments right before the workshop that considers it—the night before or even during the preceding hour. There is usually no need to dig into the references, since they are likely—and ideally—only supporting material to the essence of the work under consideration. The comments should be written onto the manuscript itself for easy reference, and the marked-up manuscript can be given to the author.

There are advantages to preparing more thoroughly, however. If a reviewer is new to the workshop, he or she should be deeply familiar with the work in order to understand where the discussion is going and to contribute to it. The main point, though, of a more thorough preparation is to reflect—preferably in writing—on the craft of someone else's work as a way of understanding how the work's construction helps it achieve its ends. There are two approaches to learning writing: practice and paying attention to writing. You practice by writing lots and lots. Every word out of your head and onto a page is practice. You pay attention to writing by examining the craft elements of writers—including yourself—and writing about them. How do Dean Young's line breaks work? What makes Steele's prose so precise and transparent? What does the evolving form of Shakespeare's sonnets do? How does off-rhyme work in Yeats? How does Knuth make the mathematics behind his algorithms so clear and intuitive? Andre Dubus uses language in ways that few other writers do—the story is controlled entirely by the language, which carries it to the reader with the stealth and force of a tidal wave. How does he do that? By looking at one of his stories critically and focusing on the language and how it is working, you might figure it out. You can learn from workshop pieces in the same way, as one poet told me: "I kept thinking that having my own poems discussed would help more, but now I realize that I learned much more from both the preparation I'd do in reading the worksheets—the care in examining how the poet was crafting the poem—and in the actual workshop discussion that ensued with other poets."

Technical and scientific circles do not value good writing much. In fact, many academic settings don't. In computer science, there is a canon, but it is made up of books and papers whose content is considered important or seminal. Sometimes a book will become part of the canon by becoming part of the curriculum at many universities. Some have tried to raise the attention paid to good writing in the sciences, but the major thrust of technical writers' workshops remains the content and whether it is adequately presented.

If a reviewer decides to do a thorough review—as if he or she were the only reviewer of the piece—then the number of comments is likely to be high and the importance of some comments is likely to be low. With too many comments, the reviewer will dominate the discussion while trying to get them all out, and certainly a detailed review will contain small points and perhaps ones that are opinion or style rather than substantive. If you prepare thoroughly, try to partition your comments into two buckets: major comments and nits. Leave the nits out of the discussion but give the author the gift of them in written form as notes on the manuscript.

Some reviewers, being aware that the preparation can be relatively light, will try to review the paper while the workshop is in progress, perhaps by reading while others are commenting or by focusing only on the parts others have brought up. Certainly if this is the first reading by the reviewer, this is wasted effort as far as the author and workshop are concerned. This is pure laziness and typically results in a distraction to the more serious business of the workshop.

If the material has been read beforehand, then experienced reviewers might be able to contribute constructively to the workshop by coming up with comments on the fly, but it is a rare reviewer who can do this. On the other hand, all reviewers should be prepared to think on their feet because the comments often turn into discussions about the fine points of a suggestion or even the general direction of the suggestion. Frequently, a reviewer's comments reveal a lack of clarity in the presentation and what might have started as a discussion of the correctness, let's say, of part of the piece will turn into a discussion of how to make clear the already correct material.

The workshop often operates in a kind of brainstorming mode in which comments and ideas bounce off each other in unexpected ways. The results may thus be nothing that any reviewer thought of. The author is the direct beneficiary, but the other participants are learning from such unexpected comments.

The natural diversity of interests and experiences of the reviewers typically ensures a fairly broad—if not extensively broad—range of comments on the work. Normally the comments will not be as deep as a thorough analysis would be for any given part of the work, but that is not the goal of the workshop. The goal is to refine the experience and perhaps the utility of the work to the expected readership.

The workshop is by its nature a relatively shallow review—very few individual reviewers, aside from the leader, spend a lot of time poring over the manuscript, tracking down references, doing comparisons to other work, and so on. Any depth comes from the expertise or interest that the particular reviewers happen to bring and from the collaborative direction the discussion takes, which might be deep in some direction but often is a bit meandering.

If the author wishes in-depth analysis for a particular aspect of the piece, this should be conveyed considerably before the workshop as a special request to the reviewers, and whether this can be done is up to each workshop and moderator.

Saying that the workshop represents a shallow review could cause some to think the workshop is not very useful. Given a choice between a deep analysis and a shallow one, which seems more valuable? This is a cultural bias we have. There is a lot to be said for shallow review if it is also broad. In computing terms it's the difference between depth-first and breadth-first search. The philosopher Paul Feyerabend has an interesting take on shallow review: "Confusionists and superficial intellectuals *move ahead* while the 'deep' thinkers *descend* into the darker regions of the status quo or, to express it in a different way, they remain stuck in the mud."

If a workshop digs deeply into just a few areas, such discussion serves as a validation of the overall piece and encourages emphasis of those narrow areas, while perhaps the best thing for the piece would be for the author to see that those areas are unnecessary or undesirable. When the analysis focuses too sharply and deeply on those narrow areas, the workshop participants miss the big picture and the global relationships between these areas.

In creative writing workshops, for example, the author may discover a new or fresher approach to the piece or a way of looking at it that frees up its possibilities. Or the original trigger or scaffolding for a piece has remained in a distracting manner and needs to be removed, which would fix a problem of lack of artistic focus. A deep analysis might reveal apparently good reasons for the limited vision or for the trigger or scaffolding to remain—a result of overthinking the piece.

In technical workshops, finding a better set of forces might come from a shallow look at the domain and all the patterns in the piece rather than by focusing on the wording of the problem statement.

Note that the reviewers cannot prepare for some works: presentations, for example. For a presentation, the experience of receiving the presentation is the work being reviewed. The reviewers then prepare only by thinking about the workshop mechanics rather than by looking at material beforehand outside of whatever synopses or advertisements would be normally available to the intended audience.

For all types of workshops—software patterns, creative writing, marketing collateral—good preparation as a participant is to reflect on how you would like to be treated by the workshop. If you want to embarrass someone in a review or show off your critical skills, you should think about whether the workshop is for you. Perhaps you'll be able to get in your digs, but perhaps when it's your turn, your experience will not be good either.

Reflect, also, on what you know. If you will be reviewing someone's sonnet and you don't know too much about them, think about how many of your comments are simple reflections of your lack of knowledge. It is valid to comment on whether the chosen form or genre is the most appropriate, but don't do it out of ignorance.

Remember that different people have different aesthetics, and that a discussion about whether the aesthetics is appropriate is a rat hole. If you don't like language poetry, perhaps say it once, but try to help the author make the work the best it can be, not the something else you would like to make it.

In the creative writing workshop, you often hear comments like these: "What is this piece trying to be?" and "What is the center of this work?" These comments aim at an attitude in which the piece exists on its own in the world and the reviewers are trying to get at its essence and make the best of whatever it is. Though perhaps a little sappy, this attitude is good because it is work focused, not author focused.

One particular sort of preparation can be a little dangerous: the proposed rewrite. This sort of comment is fairly common in poetry workshops. When a revision consists mostly of deletions, this can be a good response to the piece. But in general, a proposed rewrite should be presented only after asking whether the author wishes to see it. In most cases, the proposed rewrite reflects what the reviewer would have written rather than what is best for the work as produced by the author. There is substantial likelihood the rewrite will seem insulting to the author. I have seen numerous situations in which a proposed rewrite of a poem by a poet of admired skill will be met with great excitement by the other reviewers—"that's wonderful," "ah, that gets to it well." Such secondary comments—a sort of miniworkshop of the newly presented piece—have the effect of telling the author that this other reviewer is a better poet than the author, and better at the author's own material. Dangerous ground.

∽

Moderators need to prepare differently. They must direct the workshop through each review, calling for the different parts of the review and ensuring that the formalities are maintained. The moderator should order the pieces so that the best learning experience is possible. Often it's best to start with a piece that is good and fairly far along though not finished, so that the workshop participants experience a thorough discussion of a piece that is neither too flawed—which would elicit perhaps a too-tough set of comments—nor too close to finished, which would spark a too-congratulatory discussion. After the first piece or two are settled on—based on both where they are in their arc of maturity and how well a discussion of them can teach the participants how to workshop—the remainder of the pieces should go in the order that makes the most pedagogical sense. Let's say, for example, that in a software patterns workshop, the pieces as a whole contain patterns and pattern languages that could form an arc from code patterns to design patterns to architecture patterns to user-interface patterns and finally to application or user-visible patterns. A good ordering might then be from the inside, code patterns out to the user-visible patterns—because user-visible patterns are less common among software patterns writers (though such patterns are more in line with the original philosophy of Christopher Alexander, the architect who developed the concept of patterns). Moreover, user-visible patterns engage a different sort of aesthetic concern—and perhaps a deeper one—than what most software developers are comfortable with.

The best workshops I've been in had strong moderators who were, in essence, teachers. This is how writers' workshops operate at the Warren Wilson MFA Program for Writers. Each workshop has two moderators who are each faculty members. Not only do they operate the workshop mechanics, but they provide a great deal of input on each piece.

Each moderator reads each work in detail beforehand and prepares comments. When the comments by the regular workshop members slow down or don't cover all the important points, the moderators step in. At times they will use a more Socratic method and ask leading questions. When the group is not sure about links to other works, genres, and historical precedents, the moderators jump in to fill the gaps. In short, the moderators have enough material of their own to fill the entire time for a piece, and they ration it out according to how the workshop is proceeding.

It is rare for a workshop outside the creative arts to operate like this—though this may change. Frequently the moderator of technical workshops simply sits at the controls of the workshop.

The best preparation for a moderator would be to read the work more carefully than a regular reviewer would and to be prepared to step in with comments for all the phases if no one else does. Being more deeply familiar with the work, such a moderator would be able to better synthesize and integrate the comments into something the author can use. By being able to ask probing questions, the level of discussion could be considerably raised.

Some authors find that it is helpful to talk to people who have attended an established workshop in order to get an idea of what the culture of the workshop is like. Is the workshop craft-focused; how deeply into a particular aesthetic is it; is it highly competitive or is it relaxed; is it mostly a celebration of writers and writing; does it have special events or themes such as game playing, beer drinking, or nature writing; is it safe for newcomers; is the workshop known for helping writers? And so on.

A writer should at least make sure of the style of workshop: Does it focus on existing work or does it rely on work written at the workshop? Perhaps a hesitant writer will not be comfortable producing new work under unfamiliar conditions, or would not like an audience for such work. A writer expecting to have deep interactions about craft issues in participant pieces will find unsatisfying a workshop that is light on the workshops and heavy on evening readings by successful writers.

If you are looking at a workshop that features workshop leaders who are established writers, you should find out how well those leaders teach and, to an extent, whether you like their writing. Find out whether those leaders enjoy helping. I've found that there is not usually a connection between how a leader teaches and the aesthetic his or her own work displays. Formalists teach language poets well, and patterns writers who focus on end-user-visible patterns can teach design pattern writers well.

Part of the preparation for the workshop is examining yourself to see whether the workshop will be useful for you. Sometimes you are at a place in your writing maturation where the workshop won't help or even could hurt you as a writer. Too much of a beginner and you could be overwhelmed; too experienced a writer and the workshop might simply annoy you or cause you to doubt yourself as a writer. An experienced poet I know told me the following:

> I wanted to work more independently—and I discovered that if I workshop a poem too early, I tend to get more lost and confused about the piece: all the comments about what it "could" do and "could" become make me feel as though I'm losing an intuitive sense of what the poem would have been on its own without too much deliberation and intellectualizing. Later on in the process, when I was surer that the poem had taken shape and reached its real ending, the workshop was helpful in showing me if the poem was actually as clear as I thought it was, that there weren't distractions or misleading elements in it. (As Joan Aleshire once said, if the poem is about your mother, you want to make sure your readers don't think it's about a hippopotamus.)

The workshop might not be for you if your expectations are wrong or perhaps too inwardly focused or not aimed at the work. Another poet described a particular workshop experience:

> I think I often lost ground with drafts that were workshopped there, and I don't even know why. I think now I was too edgy, too eager to be great, or perceived as great. I don't know. I do know that I thought at times that some critics wanted the

poem to take on a life as if they had written it, so that [my] poem would, with a few strokes of the pen, become [one of theirs]. I hated that, and struggled against it. On the other hand, I remember specific poems by others that were workshopped to my tremendous growth. I remember loving to read the assembled work, to see how and where we were all going, and often feeling proud to know such an amazing group of living, breathing writers.

This poet clearly got something profound from the workshop, but it was not the workshopping of her work. You should examine yourself before and after each workshop, and adjust your expectations and do what's best for you as a writer and your work.

～

Good preparation for both authors and reviewers for their first technical workshop is to attend one as an audience member, if possible, or to observe a demonstration of one, which is routinely provided, for example, at the software patterns conferences. For people trying out the workshop concept on their own, it would be best to enlist the assistance of an experienced moderator and to review just one paper, which is judged to be a strong piece to begin with, and to discuss the process before, during, and after the workshop with the experienced moderator.

Preparing for a workshop serves two purposes. First, it shows respect for the authors, who have worked hard on their pieces and who are exposing themselves to criticism. To cavalierly come to the workshop and think of comments on the fly is a rude statement. Second, the process of looking critically at work and writing down comments is a way to learn how to write. It is an attending-to that a writer needs to get better. It is a form of practicing. Articulating why something works or doesn't is a step toward viewing your own work with a trained eye.

CHAPTER TEN

Shepherds

A shepherd is an experienced author who is helping another author prepare for a writers' workshop. Shepherds are an important part of the software patterns community and culture, but they are not as significant a part of the creative writing workshop culture.[28] A shepherd typically reads a piece about a month before it is workshopped and provides advice on how to get it in shape. Often, the shepherd is part of an acceptance process for the workshop: The shepherd works with the author and makes a recommendation to the group responsible for inviting authors, so there is often a deadline associated with shepherding.

The shepherd is part of the overall workshop culture—the shepherd and author are exchanging gifts in the same spirit that drives the writers' workshop. He or she is perhaps one of the first outside readers for a work destined for the workshop. The relationship, though, is more clearly and narrowly defined. The shepherd is an acknowledged, experienced writer in the genre who also has significant experience in the writers' workshop, perhaps as a moderator or leader. The interaction will be brief but sharply directed. Although some publications use shepherds to help the author revise the work until it's done, the shepherd as described here is helping the author prepare the work for the workshop.

Let's look at how to be a good shepherd—and as a side-effect, a good reviewer.

Because most interaction is by email, there is the issue of how to establish a good working relationship that is not just another anonymous peer review. The interaction is short, so there is not a lot of time to go back and forth. A shepherd is a volunteer, and shepherding is usually done on the spur of the moment, which means it is most likely interrupting the shepherd's day job.

The first thing is to plan to do three iterations. A common mistake is for the shepherd to wait too long to get in the first batch of comments, and the author ends up with a long email message a couple of days before the shepherding period is over with.

Normally, to get in three iterations requires starting the work right away. For many people, putting a task aside temporarily is a good way to put it aside permanently. So planning three takes ensures something will happen quickly. Because experienced writers rarely need three iterations, you might finish the work earlier than expected. Planning three iterations over about a month establishes a schedule, which you should make as explicit as you can. If you come under new constraints, you should tell the author right away. The ideal relationship between author and shepherd is intense and immediate.

The shepherd is a critic and hence there can be a natural barrier between the shepherd and the author. You don't want to end up like an anonymous peer reviewer except with a name. You should contact the author right away, talk about yourself and your experience, and explain that you are hoping to get three iterations in. Tell the author that the work is his or her own and that you won't mind your comments being ignored. If you send email quickly to the author, this gets the personal relationship going while establishing a professional tone. When the shepherd immediately contacts the author, the author feels that the shepherd is eager to see the work and there is a buzz about the work that can only help. Early contact reinforces the idea that there will be three iterations, and the author will be prepared to work.

As a shepherd, you should try to keep whatever commitments you make to the author. This bolsters the author's confidence—if you fall down on sending comments when promised, it's easy for the author to read that as waning enthusiasm for the work. And as a shepherd, you should try to bring in the attitude and practices of the workshop itself: Summarize what you thought you read, say what is good about it, and make suggestions for improvement.

If you have trips or other known gaps in your schedule, you should mention them as soon as you can. This will help the author plan, and if you tell an author about a trip right before it happens, the author may think you planned the trip after agreeing to be a shepherd, which can only diminish the relationship and outcome. And it can convey to the author that the work and perhaps the author are not important to the shepherd.

Sometimes a shepherd will believe that the most respectful way to react to a piece is with the most thorough possible review—from the grandest statements about it down to the smallest typo. To the shepherd a big response seems to say that the work is big and deserves a lot of reaction. To the author it looks overwhelming, as if the piece needs a lot of work.

As a shepherd, you should start with a summary of what you believe you read and the largest issues. If you have planned a date by which you will have sent such comments, send what you have on that day even if you're not done. The author should receive something manageable at first, and it should be the most important things to think about. Don't worry that the comments are not well written—the author can likely figure out what you meant or can ask you. Treat this as a casual discussion over email, not a formal relationship. Showing your own vulnerabilities and weaknesses helps with communication—the fact you were chosen as a shepherd has already shown that you are expert. You don't need to prove this to the author.

But don't be so sloppy that it seems like you don't care about the author or the piece. Just be casual.

It is more important to keep to the schedule than to be thorough. We are never as thorough as we could be, and that's part of the charm of being human. Art is not thorough—it selects, it elides. Be kind—not complete.

Start by looking at the piece as a whole. Try to get a sense of it and tell the author what you read. If you are reading a pattern, read the problem and solution statements first; if a pattern language, read its sequences of patterns and the problems and solutions. Not only will you get a lay of the land that will help with later reading and study, but your reaction to these high-level issues can be the best feedback for the author to get right away. These comments will frame your later remarks and provide a clue to the lens you will use for further reading. Unlike in the writers' workshop, the shepherd and author can go back and forth on what the piece is trying to be and how the author is approaching bringing that out.

The author may be inclined to incorporate the shepherd's suggestions verbatim. There is time pressure from the deadlines, and the shepherd may seem to control whether the author gets into the workshop. If the author does this— thinking the shepherd will appreciate the flattery—the author is learning next to nothing. And the benefits of acting as if a coauthor can vanish when the shepherd is an actual coauthor—resentment, rivalry, and bad writing can take over.

To avoid this as a shepherd, you should frame your comments as questions. Why is this statement here? What are you trying to accomplish with this gesture? What does this passage really mean? Resist the temptation to rewrite, even in an elemental way by suggesting what you think the piece is saying.

This not only keeps the author thinking, but also reinforces that the author is the expert on the piece and you are simply an interested, inquiring reader. A shepherd should never appear to take over the piece and elevate himself or herself to author. Make your questions answerable, and if you think there is a clear answer, it's OK for your question to hint at it. Don't ask open-ended questions like, how does this compare to Feyerabend's take on conceptual relativism?

The shepherd should not care whether the author takes the shepherd's advice. There is no need to repeat advice as if the author didn't read it the first time. The author is the expert, and how the piece evolves is up to the author and no one else. This may mean that the shepherd needs to recommend against acceptance at a workshop or for publication, but that's the nature of writing. The shepherd, of course, needs to be honest about his or her role regarding the piece, and to keep the author informed of the shepherd's view on the progress of the piece, but never should the shepherd state or even hint that the author needs to do exactly what the shepherd thinks or else the piece won't be accepted. The shepherd should assist the author in making the piece the best it can be given that the author has the final say.

∽

Shepherding is not common. The editors of some journals act like shepherds. Shepherding is not a teaching role, but more of a guiding or coaching role. Experienced authors can be shepherds—being one is a gift back to the community.[29]

CHAPTER ELEVEN

The Author Reads

The workshop as ritual requires an initial gesture as opening: The author reads aloud a selection of the work. The reading should take only a few minutes—five at most. The author sometimes stands to read, though in most creative writing workshops, the author remains seated.

How the reading works depends on whether the workshop has a forty-five- or sixty-minute slot per author or just fifteen minutes. With longer time the author has the opportunity to read a longer piece or portion of a long piece, and in some cases, several people can read the same piece.

To begin, the moderator introduces the author, and the author or the moderator states the name of the piece. If the workshop leader's practice is to say something about how experienced the author is, this is the place for that. The author then effectively introduces himself or herself by reading—a paragraph, a section, usually something that is central to the piece. In poetry workshops, the entire poem is usually read, whereas in fiction workshops only a sample is read, similar in length to a one-page poem. For a software pattern or pattern language, a pattern or part of one would be read; for a paper, a page or paragraph would be read; and for code, some comments would be read. If there are several authors, usually only one of them reads.

The workshop is thus initiated. The workshop members can see and hear the author, can attach a person to the work. If the magic of xenia will ever take over, it will at this moment. The author's gift is made apparent and palpable; the author's own voice is attached to the gift. For poems, the author's own voice indicates the rhythm and pacing, and sometimes the reviewers can then better judge how the poem is working. For technical authors, the act of reading out loud is usually alien, and it thereby reinforces that the work at hand is an act of communication between people. For the rule- and ritual-conscious, this formal start of the workshop should frame the mind properly and get things rolling.

The inflection and other reading patterns the author exhibits can sometimes give hints about how to improve the work. For example, if the stresses the author puts in or the gestures he or she makes turn out to be central to the experience and those things are somehow absent from or contrary to the words on the page, the author needs to know it.

For the author, reading is the first engagement with the workshop and with the workshop leader and his or her rules. Simple as the reading seems, there are some delicate points about it. One is how much to say other than to read the material. In my first writers' workshop at a conference in Squaw Valley, Sandra McPherson, a warm and generous woman, listened quietly as the first author described the occasion of her poem's writing and the factual background needed to understand it. Two things are still clear in my memory: the look on Sandy's face as this poet went on about the poem, and the final comment by the poet: "and everyone knows, of course, that in the plaza of the Taos Pueblo, there are always two skinny dogs."

Sandy, who is an extraordinary teacher of poetry, asked the poet whether she intended to take her work door to door and explain to each person what it was about before the person read the work. Her point was that a work must stand on its own at some point; if it needs additional explanation, that explanation should be part of the work itself. As it turns out, for a reader to understand this poet's work, there needed to be a gloss or a set of notes at the end of the book of poems explaining the things that she had explained to us. This was one of the major outcomes of the workshop for her.

But there is a second lesson in this story. The way that Sandy made this point is crucial—she could have made her remark about going door to door sarcastically, or in a way that emphasized her cleverness. Had she done that, the poet might not have survived the workshop process—maybe even would have quit writing. As I said, Sandy is warm and generous, and that's how her remark came across. She had already engaged the group with her self-deprecating humor and sensitivity. When she talked about going door to door, the workshop members, including the poet whose work was being discussed, were smiling and taking it all in the lighthearted way it was intended.

Not all workshop leaders are as warm and generous as Sandy. Some have an agenda for the workshop. At my third poetry workshop that same summer—part of a larger conference—the workshop leader told me he had two jobs at workshops. One was to encourage the talented poets he found there with specific criticism and advice, and the other was to eliminate those would-be poets who had no talent so that the population of poetry writers would not be diluted by them. He had a hard, judgmental edge—not good enough and he would actively and insultingly turn you away, good enough and he would lavish you with praise while clearly saying how much work lay ahead. And he had the standing to put a sharp punch behind his harsh words. Luckily—and to me, inexplicably—I fell on the good side of his divide, along with only one or two others from the group of twenty.

On the first workshop day, he turned to each person in the room and asked what poets the person liked and why. He had already read everyone's submitted work. He was not kind. He told most people that not even their closest relatives would want to read their work. He told one woman that she should take up knitting if she needed a hobby that involved her hands, but she should stay away from the pen. When my turn came, he didn't ask me anything but talked about how it seemed I used a computer to write with and that he used a typewriter but was thinking about a computer. He mentioned right at the end that he thought I had some interesting pieces.

So strong a reputation did he have as a discourager of poets that when my turn to be workshopped came around on the last day, fifty audience members showed up to see who this guy was whom the big poet liked. His taking me under his wing that week had a complex effect on me. I was so thrilled with his encouragement that I went on to try seriously to write poetry, but I was despondent about how he treated the others, and I tried in my inept way to provide my own indirect encouragement for them. Others at the conference felt resentment toward this poet and toward me—and justifiably so. The spirit of xenia did not become established at that conference, and the poet's encouragement proved a hindrance to my progress as a poet because it led me to too-high expectations, which I was certain, underneath, that I couldn't achieve. It made me wary of writing a lot, because it seemed like everything I wrote had to live up to this poet's expectations.

Notice how strong an affect a workshop leader can have.

About five years later I happened to be on vacation in the Taos area. I decided one day to visit the Taos Pueblo. I sat in the central plaza of the pueblo, which is a major feature of all pueblos. After about fifteen minutes, I spotted two skinny dogs running along the sides of the buildings that formed the northern side of the plaza, then over to the stream in the center of the square, just as the poet mentioned would happen. Hmm . . .

The question of how much to say in explanation of a piece is a difficult one. When a novel is being reviewed, for example, it is not reasonable—and usually simply not possible—for the reviewers to read all of it beforehand. Therefore, the author needs to explain something about the context in order for the action and characters to make any sense. Similarly, for a larger work such as a book or for a work intended for the few researchers or practitioners who can understand it, the author needs to talk about the piece a little bit, setting it in context and telling what the intended reader will know about the subject, and perhaps a little about the subject itself.

If the prevalent view is to explain as little as possible, there is an alternative. The poet Browning Porter explained the alternative:

> *In my education in the 80s and 90s, poetry workshops usually insisted that the author say little or nothing to preface the work before the discussion. I never questioned this practice until I participated in a workshop with Alan Shapiro at the Bread Loaf Writers' Conference in 1996. He told us that the pre-workshop gag rule on the author was a vestige of the philosophy of the New Critics, a school of literary criticism by then over fifty years old. The New Critics believed in something called the "intentional fallacy," that the author and her agenda for the poem were irrelevant, even distracting, from the reader's experience. The poem should speak for itself.*
>
> *And perhaps it should, for the general reader. But a workshop participant is playing a specialized role. She has (we hope) read the poem in advance, as a general reader, but when the discussion opens, her role has changed. Now she is supposed to look under the hood of the poem.*
>
> *Before the workshop discussion began, Shapiro would have the author tell the group in concrete, specific terms what is happening in the poem. The gloss was strictly denotative. Not, "I was trying to say something about Man vs Nature," but "There's this guy who is obsessed with this whale who bit his leg off, and . . ."*

Some authors, faithful to the New Critical philosophy, will be resistant to this technique. In these cases, they may opt out by saying: "I have no intentions for this poem. Read in it what you like."

This practice can save the workshop valuable time that is often lost in trying to figure out what is actually going on in the piece. Often in poetry workshops, one hears exchanges like this:

"I thought the 'she' in the second stanza was the grandmother!"

"Oh, I thought it was the goldfish!"

"Maybe it's both!"

The pre-workshop gloss gets this business out of the way quickly. The author still gets the full benefit of hearing the alternate readings, because when she says, "In the second stanza the grandmother . . . ," a chorus of gasps will go up, and those who were confused will be eager to tell her that they thought she was a goldfish, and why, specifically.

For technical workshops—and probably for most creative workshops—I think the most effective feedback for the author includes how the work is perceived before it's explained. Perhaps a gloss after hearing summaries by workshop participants would work well, but because people are sometimes hesitant to admit they grossly misread a piece, the gloss probably should not come before the summaries.

Other genres, like presentations, require their own reading or presentation rules. For a presentation, for example, there is no preparation except for whatever abstracts or biographies would normally be available to the intended audience beforehand. And the work that is reviewed is the presentation itself.

When an organization or another far-out work is reviewed in a workshop, the person who acts as the author should explain the organization or work, its purpose or occasion, and anything else that can act as an introduction to the organization or work in this part of the workshop. When we workshopped the Hillside Group, the acting author explained why Hillside was created and what it did with the conferences every year.

Some poetry workshops have both the author and another person read the piece, and some even have the piece read only by someone else. There are a couple of points to having someone else read a work. One is for the group and the author in particular to hear what the piece sounds like in another voice. Frequently the group asks the best reader to read the work aloud, which sometimes represents the best reading for the work—this might help people get a better feel than if the author is a lousy reader of his or her own work, which is fairly common.

The other is for the group and the author to hear where a reader unfamiliar with the work stumbles, what any awkwardness in the writing sounds like, where people might naturally emphasize phrases and put in stresses, where the reader is impelled to read faster, where slower.

When both the author and another reader read the piece, the important question is who should read first. There are points in favor of each order.

Some believe the author should go last because the idea is for the author to hear how his or her work demands to be read without teaching the group how to read the work by going first. Others believe the author should go first so that people can understand how the author thinks about writing as revealed by the reading. This is particularly true for poets whose reading of their own work reflects how they read all work. An experienced poetry workshop leader found this to be true of most people: "I think it's important to hear how the author thinks the work should sound. In my experience, most people have a way of reading that they impose on everything they read. If you hear me read your poem, it will sound very similar to the way I read my own poems."

She went on to explain that the most information for the participants comes from how the author reads and that this information turns into better comments to the author. And when other people read the piece, they usually read it the way they would have had they not heard the author anyway.

One goal of the workshop for an author is to get as accurate a picture of the complete reaction to the work in progress as possible. Some of that picture emerges when the workshop reacts to hearing the work read aloud, and more emerges if the author hears the work read aloud by someone else.

The overall goal of the workshop is to observe readers brought into contact with the piece: What did the readers encounter, how did they react to it, what emotional responses did the readers have, how did the style and other writing choices affect them and their reception of the work, did the facts the author wanted to convey come across, and what happened to the reader during and after the reading experience?

Reading can't help but be an emotional experience, even for the most technical works. If a reader is so turned off by the words on the page, then the message, the facts, the lessons—the very meat of the work—will have been for nothing, as if the thoughts and work of the author had never existed at all.

∽

Not only are some authors more advanced than others in general, but some pieces are more polished or closer to being finished than others. You wouldn't expect every piece to be at the same stage of development and thus to be treated the same way by the workshop.

Any special instructions for the group regarding a piece are given at the beginning of the workshop session for that piece. Someone who has workshopped a piece several times and thinks it is complete will usually say so and will ask the workshop participants to look at specific things: For a design pattern, it might be the wording of the forces section; for a poem, it might be the flow of images or the sentimentality of the ending; and for any kind of work, it can be a specific section or passage. For someone who has just worked on revising a particular part of the piece, having the workshop focus on just that part might be the thing. Such requests should come after the piece is read aloud, because they thus won't affect how the piece is heard. The author should be aware that this is the time to make specific requests for attention and inattention, but the moderator should be sure to ask the author.

For workshops in which each author has a number of pieces, the moderator should also ask which piece the author wishes to do next rather than assuming an order. In such workshops each author is allocated a fair amount of time—on the order of ninety minutes—to do three short pieces. In workshops in which each author has one long piece, such as a short story, a technical paper, a presentation, or a pattern language, each author is allocated forty-five minutes to an hour. For a novel or another long piece, such as a large pattern language, the author needs to select a short-story-size piece of it for the workshop and perhaps provide the rest and definitely be prepared to summarize the rest, which is done during this part of the workshop.

For workshops that spend about fifteen minutes per piece, there is no time for multiple readers. The feedback is quick, and six to ten people workshop their work per session. The author simply reads the piece.

∽

The beginning, therefore, of workshopping a piece is highly ritualized in order to signal the start of a special sort of activity. For symmetry, the ending is also ritualized. It is as if the workshop experience for each reviewed piece takes place in an enclosure, and both entering and exiting the enclosure are signaled by rituals that essentially switch on and off, respectively, the special behavior within the review itself.

CHAPTER TWELVE

Fly on the Wall

The question we're exploring is how to get the best review of work while helping the author mature as a writer. There are two extremes: face-to-face, interactive discussions of a work between the author and reviewers, and anonymous review. Neither of these is a workshop setting, and both are routinely used by writers, creative or technical. The results are often good, but bad things can easily happen.

Many face-to-face reviews turn into discussions between the author and the reviewer when, for example, a comment by a reviewer spurs an explanation by the author, and sometimes these discussions turn into debates or arguments, with the author defending the work and the reviewers responding with justifications of their position, and so on. Debates and arguments can easily drift from the page to personalities, and whether the author can "prevail" in such exchanges is not important to the work at hand—what's important is whether the work by itself does its intended job, be that to convey information as in a technical article or to convey poetic truth.

At the other extreme, a group discussing a work by an absent author can display an honesty that might be hard to come by when the author is there, but sometimes the comments turn harsh and become nonconstructive as reviewers turn their attention to showing off their cleverness to each other. So, at one extreme we have the generosity created by the presence of the author potentially undermined by arguments about the comments, while at the other, the honesty created by the author's absence potentially undermined by the destructiveness of the comments.

In light of the possibility of the failures of these extremes, the ideal for the author would be to be a fly on the wall in a room where truthful but polite people were frankly discussing the work. Take away the defensiveness of the author when he or she speaks up for the work, and add the face and presence of the author to remind the reviewers that a real person is behind the work, who wants to make the work better and improve as a writer. Achieving this is the goal of the writers' workshop. Achieving it takes three ingredients.

First, the gift-giving nature of the workshop needs to kick in at some point. The reviewers and authors need to believe that they are giving the gifts of early access to work and of constructive feedback. Next, the authors must be and must feel that they are being protected by the moderator and by the other authors and audience members. Finally, the author must seem to be not present while in fact he or she actually is.

When conditions are right, the results are impressive. Indeed, the comments are honest but probing, and the dignity of the author is respected. Gift-giving is engaged, and plenty of good comments come out. Rarely is there a failure of the writers' workshop—failures need to be avoided because the stakes are high.

Being a fly on the wall is a fiction: The author may not be speaking, but the author is there, and his or her emotions are on display though not through speech. One creative workshop leader told me this: "The fact that the author is quiet and doesn't speak does not mean that he or she is not noticeably present in the room. One of the ways the participants remain mindful of the writer's feelings is that they are aware that the writer is present and is listening to everything that is said."

And being a fly on the wall can be hard on the author. Sometimes the author wants to defend the work or further explain it, or feels that the workshop members don't like him or her when critical things are being said. An author in the software patterns community described the discomfort and then the ultimate value of the fly-on-the-wall approach:

> It was very difficult to be a "fly on the wall" and not get excited about and respond (even just visually) to things being said. Being "gagged," I was forced to listen without mitigating or rationalizing. What was powerful about this was the realization that something I wrote communicated itself completely enough without my verbal explanations—or didn't. That's a major focus for writers' workshops outside of the

pattern world—discovering whether what you wrote communicated the concept/idea/feeling you intended to the reader. Sometimes the interpretation is vastly different than what you intended.

An author may not be able to listen to what is being said when he or she is arguing or defending the work. Only the gist can be heard when you're trying to think of how to word your rebuttal. And when you are arguing a position, it is nearly impossible to be open to changing your mind, which is trying to find all the ways to support the truth of what is on the page. Defending your work turns easily into a defense of yourself, particularly in heated exchanges in which each response—as a matter of the biology of speaking—is directed at you and not at the work.

∼

How can we create this fantasy? Some workshops—I have seen this only in technical workshops—ask the author, immediately upon completing the reading, to move outside the workshop circle. Some technical workshops provide table space just outside the circle for the author to use to take notes. In other technical workshops, the author merely moves his or her chair back a few inches as a symbolic gesture of leaving the circle. One technical workshop I know of actually speaks of the author's "now becoming a fly on the wall." In experienced technical workshops and most creative writing workshops, the author does not assume any special position or stance with respect to the reviewers.

From this point until the author is asked whether he or she has questions for the reviewers, the author is completely silent. The only exception to this is clarification. The moderator may ask the author to clarify or explain a point if he or she believes the discussion is bogged down and would proceed more effectively by knowing some fact or exactly what the author meant by a certain passage. Also, if the author notices that the discussion is actually going nowhere, he or she might ask the moderator to allow a point of clarification or some unwedging of the discussion. However, I've found that such occurrences are rare.

A variation of the fly-on-the-wall idea is to treat everything as fiction. In creative workshops there is a strong tendency to treat each piece as autobiographical or at least as the direct utterance of the author. Though there may be autobiographical triggers in the work, it is almost certainly intended to be taken as art, and discussions that assume it's autobiographical tend to pull the author and the author's life into the discussion, where it doesn't belong. In some creative workshops, the workshop leader will set guidelines that require each piece to be treated as fiction.

Both the fly-on-the-wall and the piece-as-fiction approaches require keeping the reviewers from addressing the author directly, referring to the author by name, or using the word "you." Most workshops settle on references like "the author" or "the writer." Moreover, the reviewers should not make eye contact with the author. Both these approaches also encourage people to focus on the content, the narrative, and the writing.

The moderator must be willing to step in and instruct the workshop on these points and insist on their being followed. For this reason, the moderator must feel that he or she has enough authority to do that. Sometimes it is better not to have someone be the moderator when his or her boss is a workshop participant. This is also why sometimes it is a good idea to have an outside moderator come in for a workshop.

Similarly, the moderator must try to keep the comments positive and not antagonistic or insulting. This requires a fair degree of sensitivity since a comment can become personal very quickly. Sometimes simply reminding people at every transition in the workshop can be enough.

∽

Every now and then an author being reviewed speaks up and defends the piece, especially during suggestions for improvement. The moderator should remind the author to remain silent, but if the author persists in speaking, the moderator should change tactics. The moderator should address the workshop participants and not the author, telling them that their comments are being worded too negatively, that only clear suggestions for improvement should be given until the workshop dynamic stabilizes, and that if a reviewer has a criticism to bring up without suggestions for how to improve it, the reviewer should hold off. That is, the moderator should turn down the temperature of the comments until the author becomes and remains silent and then see whether the workshop dynamic can evolve from there.

If the author persists, the moderator should address the author, telling him or her that the purpose of the workshop is for the author to get advice and suggestions from the group, and that the best way to do that is for the author to remain silent. The moderator should ask whether the author wants to get the feedback or terminate the session right then. That is, the moderator should ask the author for positive affirmation of the workshop rules. If the author does not ask for feedback or continues to speak up, the moderator should terminate the session.

Some people simply are not comfortable with the writers' workshop format for reviewing work. These are prime candidates for not being able to keep quiet, to be a fly on the wall. At one PLoP conference a well-known writer came and simply could not live without defending his paper. He never came to another conference.

∽

I've seen some creative writing workshops that are quite bad at maintaining this fly-on-the-wall illusion. I've heard comments like this in a poets' workshop: "Susan, I know you've had a lot of trouble with your mother, and so you need to address your daughter more warmly in this poem." In long-established workshops in which the members have become good friends, maybe this sort of direct and intimate discussion is appropriate, but even there I think it makes sense to look at the more formal incarnation of the workshop and decide whether it would serve the workshop members better than an overly informal creative writers' workshop.

In long-running workshops, there is also the danger of overfamiliarity: "You don't write like that—what are you doing?" Writers need a lot of room and unconditional acceptance to be allowed to explore and expand. Both by the workshop group's being too personal and direct, and by a group's being too comfortable and familiar with each other, the workshop can become limiting on its members.

Being a fly on the wall doesn't mean the author is ignored by the moderator. An alert moderator should be watching and judging the state of mind of the author at all times—the workshop exists for the authors. If the author seems bored—signaled by halted note-taking—the moderator can notice this and move on. If the author is clearly in distress, the moderator can try to alter the course or tone of the workshop. In some workshops, the author is allowed to signal the moderator when to move on to another comment or phase of the workshop.

Out of sight, but not out of mind.

∽

Another way for a workshop to create a fly-on-the-wall simulacrum is by reviewing the work anonymously. This, of course, works less well as the workshop stays together, but it is easier to avoid talking to and looking at the author when you're not sure who the author is.

Such a tactic works best in a school setting instead of with peers, mostly because a school setting is filled with all sorts of irrational rules to begin with, and it's likely a course will attract people who don't know each other anyway. With peers who have some familiarity with each other's work, it is sometimes easy to recognize writerly fingerprints on a work.

As a writer trying to be a fly on the wall, you should try before and during the workshop to remember that you are not your work—it is something you are trying to write, it's a work in progress, every writer has his or her minor works, it is not you they are talking about. Try to dissociate yourself from the work. Disown it. Think of it as a lost waif that you and the other workshoppers want to help get on in the world.

An author can sometimes remain calm by remembering that a lot of the real work of the workshop takes place for an author when the group is discussing someone else's piece. A writer told me the following:

> My experience in workshops—and my advice to others in them—is to expect nothing *when it is your work that is being discussed. The discussion is for the benefit of everyone else. People learn how to talk about writing, and learn how to listen to what other people say. But you can't really do either of those things too well when it's your work on the table.*
>
> *I always learned the most—about my own work—when I was listening to someone talking about the work of a third person. I really heard how her comments applied to my work, my needs, my interests. My ears weren't clogged with the pounding of my pulse.*

When an author remains silent, the discussion is cleaner, safer, and more dispassionate. This is the best way to learn. Moreover, when the workshop setting is safe there is no reason to expect nothing, and expecting nothing can be a way of distancing yourself when you are uncertain of your safety.

Of all the formal aspects of the workshop, two of them—maintaining the fiction of the author's not being present, and politeness—are the most important. Most workshop failures I've seen would have been avoided had these been heeded.

CHAPTER THIRTEEN

Summarize the Work

Review starts with the most basic feedback: What did people actually get from the work? Perhaps the comments start with a statement of the genre down to some level of detail: Was the work a design pattern aimed at C++ programmers, was it a piece of marketing collateral aimed at ISVs, was it a Shakespearean sonnet, was it a golden pitch aimed at analysts for a product launch? The more details about what type of piece the reader saw will help the author understand what has ended up on the page.

In all technical and some creative workshops, this is followed by a summary of the work, in as much detail as the moderator thinks makes sense for the piece and the time allowed. If the piece is a research paper, the questions might include: What was the methodology, what were the results, what evidence was produced and described, how did the author say it fit in with related work, and what conclusions were found? If the piece is a story, the reviewers might address the question: Who were the main characters and what happened, if anything? If the piece is a poem, the questions are: What was its narrative structure (if any), what was its lyric moment (if any), what imagery and figures were used, and what is the heart of the poem? Details.*

---

* See Creative Workshop: Summary, on page 190 in Appendix A, Examples, for an example of a summary of a difficult poem in nontechnical terms.

The comments should be stated in neutral, observational language. There should be no value judgments made at this point. For some who are sensitive to specific bits of content, it can be hard to resist summarizing the work using judging words. Stating a content or theme judgment mostly has the effect of declaring one's own political or philosophical stance, and it can be taken only as a recommendation to avoid that topic or theme. If you find the content or theme of a work too hard on your beliefs, it may be best to recuse yourself from the discussion.

The summary is extremely important for technical workshops.[†] Summaries are usually not part of some creative workshops. Two specific issues with summaries, especially for poetry, are that perhaps the group will go round and round trying to figure out "the meaning" or what they are seeing, and that the group might not have enough craft or literary vocabulary to express what they see, or perhaps because of this lack of vocabulary, they can't see certain things. The moderator needs to keep the conversation from going in circles. And even a novice group of poets and writers can point out things they noticed in the piece: Was there a story, and if so, what happened; were there words, descriptions, phrases, or sounds that stood out; were there repetitions; did images in the piece remind the reviewer of something they've read or heard somewhere else? These observations are something that a reader can respond to intellectually, emotionally, or narratively, not in an analytic breakdown. That is, a good summary of a creative piece is not simply a description of the text, such as "this poem has fourteen lines comprising eight sentences. . . ." Even though it's not as common in creative workshops, I think something like a summary to start with is important, and the workshop leader or moderator should try to keep things moving ahead.

~

At some level, every writer expects his or her writing to have some effect on the reader, which depends to some extent on the amount of information transfer—even in creative writing. In scientific writing, information transfer is paramount, even when the work is aimed at convincing or at establishing philosophical underpinnings. The author expects a somewhat common starting point for the reactions to the work. After a while, each author gets to know the other members

---

[†] See Technical Workshop: Summary, on page 197 in Appendix A, Examples, for a summary of a software pattern.

of the workshop and is able to identify some members who should understand the work well. By seeing what those members got out of the work, the author can get a good idea of how well the information was conveyed.

This can be especially important for technical work. Some papers are intended to be quite broad in their appeal and so their authors should not assume deep reader knowledge of a particular area; other pieces are aimed at researchers narrowly focused on one small question. A workshop with just the right membership can give extremely good feedback on whether the author has aimed right.

Even with extremely hermetic poetry, the poet would likely appreciate learning of potential misreadings based on different backgrounds, experiences, and cultures of readership. In one workshop I was in, an atheist from birth was surprised that one of her poems had a Christian reading—she had unknowingly used images from the gospel-story topos.[‡] She revised the piece to steer clear of this reading by changing only a few words.

In many creative writing workshops I've been in, writers have been surprised at the sexual connotations of some of their phrases and images. The problem is that the writer has a fairly clear picture of what's being written about—or about the trigger for the work—and the words on the page serve to remind the writer about that picture or trigger. As an example of a trigger that could confuse, I often write about a particular bridge near where I grew up. It has some odd facets: It is a turntable drawbridge, so that boats can pass through the bridge when the turntable section of the bridge is rotated to orient that part of the bridge's roadbed parallel to the river. The bridge is painted a shade of green that resembles pond scum. When I write a poem with that bridge in it, I see it, and sometimes I'll write about the color but leave out the turntable. In an early draft, some other part of my poem might depend on knowing it has a turntable, but the readers won't know it. In a case like this, the response of the writer to his or her own writing is both to what's on the page and additionally to something that is not, whereas the members of the workshop and general readers don't have the privileged information of the writer's trigger. This can cause the sort of blindness

---

[‡] Alex Preminger and T. V. F. Brogan, eds., in *The New Princeton Encyclopedia of Poetry and Poetics* (Princeton, N.J.: Princeton University Press, 1993), define a *topos* as "a conventionalized expression or passage in a text which comes to be used as a resource for the composition of subsequent texts." I generalize this notion to that of a story-generating story. Conventional use of the term would, for example, describe the use of phrases from or references to the Garden of Eden, whereas my generalization would call the Garden of Eden a topos because it can supply a narrative framework and elements for creating other stories—for example, a cartoon about Donald Duck in the Garden of Eden. We would, in this example, recognize the Garden of Eden story in the Donald Duck story.

to one's own work that can make it hermetic or inaccessible when such inaccessibility is not part of the intended aesthetic. A summary can point out problems like this one.

At least, the summary gives the author a good idea of what the remaining comments are about—each member's later comments will be on the work as the member has perceived it and not what the author believed the work to be. It may be hard during the workshop for an author to correlate what each person thought the work was about with the reviewer's later comments, so the author should take notes highlighting differences from the intended reading.

For patterns, a good place to start with a summary is the overall context and scope of the pattern or pattern language, and then to go into problem/solution descriptions, perhaps with some major forces noted. It may not make sense to go to this depth on all the patterns, but it is a good place to start thinking about the shape of the summary.

Many times, this is the most important part of the workshop experience for an author. If the author is way off in thinking that something is on the page when it actually isn't or if the work on the page is confusing, then hearing a sympathetic group of people struggling to talk about what's there or stating summaries that seem as if they are about a different piece can have quite an impact, especially because this part of the process is the least likely to set off strong critical remarks.

∽

The moderator has two major problems to contend with in this part of the process: how to know when to cut off summaries, and what to do if it is clear no one really knows what the piece is about.

Knowing when to cut off summaries is a matter of recognizing diminishing returns. When the same point is being made over and over, that is a clear sign. But sometimes the summaries seem like they are not getting to some points, or the moderator feels that there are more things to summarize but doesn't know clearly what they are. If the moderator thinks there may be other points, he or she should ask questions to try to get people to explore other areas. If it seems like the summaries are going in a circle, asking the group about it will usually get to the point quickly. The vastly more experienced moderator typical of organized creative writing workshops can supply missing summaries or direct attention where it has not sufficiently been given.

Creative and technical workshops face very different issues regarding clarity and understanding. Language use and understanding are the subject of thorough and varied scientific, linguistic, and philosophical discourse, but it might be possible to make headway in grasping the practical issues of the workshop by using a simple model. We start with the words on the page. Reading those words we get a story, a description, an argument, a picture, or a statement that is the result of a relatively cursory or literal apprehension of those words. If a story contains the sentence, "Adam ate an apple offered to him by Eve," the cursory or literal apprehension is likely something that people would describe as a picture or mental movie of a man being handed an apple and then eating it.

In addition to cursory or literal apprehension is the meaning, import, or interpretation of the words, which in many cases can be derived from the literal apprehension, sometimes directly and sometimes with the addition of cultural and personal views and tenets. This other level of understanding relates pieces of a work to each other, to the surrounding culture, to the reader, and to history. Some speak of this other level as their *response*. Given the sentence about Adam, the meaning or import could involve a reference to the biblical Garden of Eden story, a loss of innocence, or the introduction of temptation and evil into the world.

Given this model, *transparency* is when different people get the same or similar cursory or literal apprehensions, and *understandability* is when people have the same or similar meanings or imports. The sentence about Adam and Eve is transparent, but its meaning depends on the rest of the story as well as cultural and personal beliefs and knowledge of the Judeo-Christian creation story. Consider this sentence, "Eve interacted with Adam, and—God damn it—the apple was finished." Although the Bible story rings through, we cannot be sure what is actually happening. The picture or movie in one person's head could be the Bible story, and in another it could be the destruction of the apple after a violent encounter between Adam and Eve. The sentence is not transparent—it is confusing—and if we change the names of the players, it is likely not understandable to anyone.

Good technical writing is always transparent and understandable. Readers are never confused by what's on the page, and the meaning of the piece is quickly grasped, assuming the reader has the proper technical background.

Good creative writing *can* be neither transparent nor understandable if the aesthetic requires it—language poetry and some postmodern writing have this aesthetic. The following five lines are from the language poem "Sentences My Father Used," by Charles Bernstein:[§]

> Casts across otherwise unavailable fields.
> Makes plain. Ruffled. Is trying to
> alleviate his false: invalidate. Yet all is
> "to live out," by shut belief, the
> various, simply succeeds which.

This fragment can't be apprehended beyond the words on the page, and any meaning is gathered from the connotations and impression of the words. Within its aesthetic, this fragment is satisfying and there are many things a workshop could say about it.

Outside of aesthetics that reject it, creative writing should be, probably, transparent, though meaning can be obscure or absent. If there's a narrative, we should all know what is going on; if there's a description, we should all know what it describes; if there's an image in a poem, we should all see similar things. After that—our response to the piece—things can be up in the air. Technical writing has to go beyond this.

Summaries aim at unearthing confusions and misunderstandings. For technical workshops, it is proper to talk about both transparency and meaning; for creative workshops, it is usually fine to talk about transparency, but meaning is often off-limits.

If some part of a piece is confusing the workshop, the moderator should decide quickly how to handle it. In most cases, the right approach is simply to point out that this part of the piece is confusing and move on. Confusion during summary can become a teaching opportunity and perhaps good feedback for the author when reviewers state why they thought what they did about the piece. A creative workshop leader told me two stories about this.

> *I once ran a workshop in which a woman read a story about a nine-year-old girl. She did not mention her age anywhere in the story. Afterwards, she asked us how old we thought the girl was. Most guessed correctly eight or nine, but several thought she was about fourteen. I asked those reviewers why, and they all referred to one*

[§] Bernstein, Charles. *Controlling Interests*. New York: Roof Books, 1986.

small section in which the girl had noticed a slightly sexual interaction between two adults they thought a nine-year-old would not have noticed or interpreted that way. The writer had to revise only one paragraph of the story to straighten this out.

Another time, a woman read a poem and was surprised that the speaker was interpreted as being angry at someone when that wasn't what the author intended. When I asked the group why, they pointed out only two strong words. Changing those words gave the piece a different tone.

In these examples, what perhaps seemed to the author like major misunderstandings were traced to very small places in the pieces, and repairing those places was easy. This is why writing can be hard but workshops can help.

For a creative workshop, moving on is an easier option than for a technical workshop because confusion might not hamper understanding the creative piece on other levels. A piece may be intellectually confusing or have no logical meaning, but it might affect readers similarly on an emotional level. The first stanza of "Of Mere Being," by Wallace Stevens, has that quality:

The palm at the end of the mind,
Beyond the last thought, rises
In the bronze decor.

A gold-feathered bird
Sings in the palm, without human meaning,
Without human feeling, a foreign song.

You know then that it is not the reason
That makes us happy or unhappy.
The bird sings. Its feathers shine.

The palm stands on the edge of space.
The wind moves slowly in the branches.
The bird's fire-fangled feathers dangle down.

We can't be sure where (or when) "at the end of the mind" is, nor what is "the bronze decor." We can guess, and perhaps most people will guess the same thing. But emotionally we likely all feel the same thing, and the picture of a palm tree rising up is transparent—our doubts of transparency have to do with the context: *at the end of the mind, in the bronze decor.*

A piece might be transparent but have no obvious meaning. We would all paraphrase it similarly. The last stanza illustrates this well. We see the tree's fronds moving in the wind and an extravagant bird sitting up there. We wonder about the edge of space, but it doesn't seem to trip us up. As we wonder about this poem, we don't feel that it is a maze of ambiguity—we feel deeply puzzled but attracted. We wonder whether it is a metaphor or an allegory or a death poem or an *ars poetica*, but we're not troubled by not getting it.

A narrative might be transparent though in the end it might be impossible to talk about a lesson or moral or deeper meaning. The novel *Moby Dick*, by Herman Melville, has a crystal clear, transparent narrative but readers and critics have puzzled over it indefinitely because it seems to hold more than its measure.

In other cases of reviewer confusion, the moderator has a tough choice to make. Should the workshop proceed as usual, with people commenting and making suggestions about something they don't really get, or should the author be asked to explain—a sort of revision on the fly? If the confusion is not too deep, then perhaps it's best to let the workshop proceed and put the author in the position of seeing what the alternatives are for different readings. That is, later comments in the other phases of the review will be to a piece that the author likely didn't intend, but those comments might convince the author to turn it into that other piece. For a technical piece, in which confusion and misunderstanding are not tolerated, exploring where the problems come from is important. The moderator should be sure to come back to the points of confusion and misunderstanding during suggestions for improvement.

In some cases dwelling on the confusion and misunderstandings is the best teaching tool available at the moment—and the workshop is a teaching/learning laboratory. Again, an experienced moderator with teaching talent is best equipped to make the judgment here. Less experienced moderators can do something like take a time-out from the workshop and "go meta," which means stating that confusion seems to be in the cards and asking the participants whether it would be the right thing for the author to clarify.

A final, rare problem could face the moderator. Suppose that the summaries are way off the mark, and the moderator thinks that the piece is just not ready for a full workshop. This is much more likely when there was no filtering on the pieces beforehand, either through a submission or shepherding process—though if the workshop leader is careful about what kind of feedback to elicit, work fresh from the notebook can be workshopped successfully. If the moderator thinks the piece is not quite ready, that the time of the other participants is being wasted in going further, and that clarification will not help the situation, then the moderator can and should cut things off with the summaries. However, cutting things off here can be a problem if done ineptly.

∽

A problem with creative workshops occurs when someone says that he or she doesn't get something that is clear to most others. The danger is that the writer will be taught to oversimplify the work so that everyone will get it. The writer can end up with safe but dull writing in which everything is overexplained and there is no room for the imagination.

A similar, opposite problem occurs when the work is confusing and incomprehensible on all levels (intellectual, narrative, and emotional), yet the participants are afraid to say so because they don't want to seem dumb. If the workshop does summaries, there is no real danger of this, but most creative workshops are light on summaries or discuss only genre or form instead.

Language poetry and other work for which no value is supposed to be attached to meaning and literal apprehension can be difficult to summarize. It's important for the author or workshop leader to point out that for pieces like this, apprehension and meaning are not issues to consider.

For technical pieces, lack of understanding depends on the intended audience. A deep, narrow paper might not be accessible to a person not steeped in the domain. It's up to the author to decide who is in the audience and, as best as possible, to make this clear early in the piece.

∽

Some workshops, especially those in the design patterns community, rely on a single person providing the summary, asking others to pitch in only if the summary seems incomplete or a little off. Sometimes the off-by-a-little summaries provide some of the most important information to the author.

I don't recommend this approach—it's too important for the author to know what the workshop members thought they read so that he or she can gauge their further reactions. Almost everyone should contribute to the summary. If a workshop member agrees with someone else's summary, he or she should say so quickly.

Earlier I talked about acceptance and approval. Acceptance is when the author is told that he or she is indeed making what the author set out to make—a poem, a pattern, an essay, and so on. Approval is when the author is told he or she is doing a good job of it. The summary can provide acceptance to the author, by letting him or her hear that what the readers read is what the author wanted them to read, and that it was a piece in the genre the author intended.

So effective can be this stage of the workshop that some workshop leaders stay entirely within it, requiring that all comments be phrased as observations of what's on the page. The advantage of a summary-only workshop is that there are no statements like "I liked this" or "I hated that." When people start talking about their subjective feelings, it is tempting for the author to set up a scale of degrees of liking, loving, adoration, infatuation, and so forth. Sometimes when reviewers are talking about what they like, a member not making any comments can be taken as conveying disapproval or even as withholding acceptance. A workshop leader can try to head this off by noting at the start of a workshop that not everyone will speak up every time, that this is acceptable, and that an author shouldn't infer anything from it.

One writer with some experience with a summary-only form of workshop found some advantages to this form: "[It] gives the writer a good sense of what they've got and what they're missing without condemning anything or insisting on engraving anything in stone. It also delivers the workshop from being a forum for praising or trying to change the writer. It's truly liberating."

One of the ways a workshop can go wrong is if the summary period is too short and if later comments about the work in the other phases are actually about a misunderstood part of the work. The result can be a comical who's-on-first exchange.

The critical sections of a workshop review—summarize the work, positive feedback, suggestions for improvement—can be applied iteratively, which means the workshop can return to an earlier stage but not skip forward. For example, during the suggestions for improvement, more summary or positive feedback can be given if a new comment comes up or a forgotten one is remembered.

Some workshops err on the side of brief summaries, but I prefer to have the workshop spend a little too much time on this, trying to get everyone to speak up about the piece. Even for poetry, for which there usually is no such thing as "getting it," the poet can gain a lot by hearing all the ways the poem has been read rather than just a few.

I find the summaries to be one of the most important phases of the workshop for my own work, whether it's poetry or technical pieces. Hearing what reviewers understood from reading my piece helps me understand the origins of its strengths and weaknesses, and prepares me to understand where the upcoming comments come from. The language of summaries is neutral and helps keep emotions down while preparing authors to hear the rest of the reviews.

CHAPTER FOURTEEN

Positive Feedback

After the author has sweated through getting a piece together, revising and polishing it enough to workshop it; possibly after shepherds have done a couple of rounds of review and help; after the workshop participants have read and marked up their copies of the piece; after the ritual of the opening of the workshop, the reading, the special instructions; and after the summaries of what the workshop members read, what most people think of as the real work of the workshop gets going: finding and fixing problems.

Western culture and certainly engineering and science have taught us that an appropriate response to almost any critical situation is to find a problem and fix it. This attitude seems to have permeated the arts. So, imagine that each author goes home with some areas of his or her paper painted red and accompanied by suggestions for improvement. What is that author to make of the places not painted red? Were they OK? Are they available for alteration to help improve the red areas? Are some of them not OK but the workshop just didn't get to them?

Imagine—well, we don't have to, do we?—recall what it's like to have submitted a piece of yours for criticism and then to have only problems pointed out and possible solutions discussed, perhaps accompanied by the statement that everything else was OK. A feeling of uncertainty, a slight lack of enthusiasm, a bit of self-doubt?

The criticism part of the writers' workshop begins with giving the author positive feedback: What did the reviewers really like, what worked particularly well, what would the reviewers keep no matter what else changes about the piece, what parts are remembered best, what parts stayed with the reviewer?*

Since it's pretty hard to find a piece that has no pluses, this guarantees that the author will hear that there is something worthwhile about the work and that he or she should keep going with it. The author will hear that the people who will later be making comments about how to improve the work are doing so from a frame of mind that includes liking parts of it. This part of the process feels most like a gift-in-return to the author, and though most people will wish to return to the workshop to get constructive criticism, the good feeling of hearing what's good about one's work will be another strong reason.

Most importantly, the work will now end up effectively painted three colors: blue (let's say) for the good parts, white for those not mentioned, and red for those that need improvement. When looking at the piece later while revising, the author will see more easily what to leave alone, what to revise, and what is still in question.

~

The gift effect can sometimes dramatically kick in during this part of the workshop. A few positive comments and pretty soon there is lots to cheer the author, as one seasoned technical workshopper explained:

> Many times I've reviewed a workshop paper where I really could not think of anything positive to say. I didn't like the name. The solution didn't work for me, etc. What always happens, however, is that when someone begins with a positive comment, I suddenly see lots of things I can add. This never fails and now I look forward to seeing this miracle happen. It says something about the power of good or the ability we all have to pull each other up.

By looking at the positives of a piece, the members of the workshop can begin to work on a deepened sense of what makes pieces good. Western tradition tends to teach us that something is good if there is nothing bad about it—that all the broken parts have been fixed. By looking for good parts as well as not-so-good parts, and as a result of eventually noticing the places in between, the workshop

---

* For examples of positive feedback see page 187 for a creative workshop and page 197 for a technical workshop, both in Appendix A Examples.

members can teach each other the traits of "good stuff," both in writing and within the genre being workshopped.

It is then not simply a matter of finding and fixing "misfits." It's real work. I am reminded of the words of the architect Christopher Alexander, in his essay "The Perfection of Imperfection":

> *In our time, many of us have been taught to strive for an insane perfection that means nothing. To get wholeness, you must try instead to strive for this kind of perfection, where things that don't matter are left rough and unimportant, and the things that really matter are given deep attention. This is a perfection that seems imperfect. But it is a far deeper thing.*

Where can we find quality? It's the stuff on the page. The content can be compelling and its presentation can be well structured; its narrative structure—whether as part of a story, a poem, a technical or scientific paper, a presentation, collateral material, or any sort of performance—works toward carrying the work into the deepest parts of the reader. The paragraph and sentence structure can be conducive to reading and can carry their own interest through strength and fostering the ability to read right along without stumbling or rereading.

For technical and some creative pieces—and especially for presentations—graphics and artwork help determine how effective and beautiful they are. The use of figures and illustrations to illuminate a piece; how well the illustrations are done; the quality of the graphics; the appropriateness of colors; the use of dimensional and multivariate data, shading, resolution, and integrating words, images, and numbers can be done well or poorly.

The writing style overall can be good and serve the intention of the piece. Word choices, stylistic choices, images, use of metaphor and other figures, humor, informality, formality, storytelling even in technical pieces, and use of writing craft elements in whatever genre can add to and serve the piece well. Line breaks, meter, rhyme and near rhyme, rhythm, musicality, good noise, good lines, and strangeness too. All of these can be commented on. Even the typography can be done particularly well. For presentations and other performances, improvisational skill, energy, thoroughness, animation, informality, the speaking voice and its control, and any other factors serving the piece (or constituting the piece) can be praised. By the workshop's looking at each piece as an opportunity to learn, its members can begin to see how the elements of good writing combine to make an exceptional piece, something that is more than simply its information content.

Technical workshop members tend to ignore the actual writing—some fiction workshops fall into this as well, focusing almost entirely on the characters and what they do. This narrow approach may have two drawbacks. First, the author may not look at his or her own work along only technical and scientific—or character and plot—dimensions, but consider the writing part of the entire work. Second, we shouldn't really let the author get away with looking at the work so narrowly. Each piece needs to be read or heard (or performed), and—let's look at written pieces only—let's face it, the reader has to look at the words. In this sense, any work that an author produces is being placed among all written works; people who sit down to read the most technical work are doing something indistinguishable from reading literature, which often leads to great pleasure from the artistry of the words on the page. In a sense, then, every work can be considered a candidate for comparison to the great works of literature. And, let's keep facing it, we notice when a technical paper is well written. Why not work on that?

An author who particularly wants to hear about the writing should say so right after he or she reads aloud the poem, piece, or passage.

Part of the reason the writers' workshop works is that it contains within it the seeds of a technique called *positive deviance*. Positive deviance, as a group improvement process, is based on the observation that in every group of people engaged in some activity, most are doing the activity at the same, middle level, some are worse than that, and some excel. The idea is to spread the techniques of those who excel to the others. Groups this works for generally have a great deal of shared culture, practices, and beliefs, and therefore the likelihood of adopting the successful techniques is better than if those techniques originated outside the group.

Each piece in the writers' workshop very likely demonstrates this sort of bell-shaped distribution of writing levels: Most are at about the same, middle level, some are not as good, and some excel—like the red, white, and blue paint. When workshop reviewers point out sections they like or find well done or effective—the sections that excel—this encourages the author to raise the level of writing by doing more of the good stuff. Presumably, if a writer wrote the passages that excel, that person is capable, in theory, of writing that way consistently. By pointing to the author himself or herself as the model to follow, the workshop is not asking the author to do something he or she feels incapable of doing.

On the other hand, it might be a mystery to a writer what makes the good passages good, and the writer may not have any idea what to do to achieve that level uniformly. The author's ability to write at least short bursts of good writing, however, implies that uniformly good writing is not a priori beyond his or her grasp.

~

Even though the positive-feedback section is where only positive comments are allowed, it might not work out precisely that way, and some forms of praise can sound like faint praise. The moderator should keep a mental tab of the balance of positive and negative response an author is getting, and this requires getting started in this phase of the workshop. The moderator should also check on the author, seeing whether there are any signs of distress, even in this positive stage: Sometimes an author will expect particular responses here and will be upset not to hear them.

The moderator should remind the workshop members that a positive comment must be positive throughout the whole statement, not just at the beginning. A statement like the following is not positive: "The description of the character waking up is very effective, but . . ."

Keep in mind that this is the first critical response the author is hearing—and though it's intended to be positive, the tone of voice, equivocation, qualification, and gaps can sound like criticism to the sensitive ear. Some positive comments can create problems for the author. If the author is at a particular stage of revision and has decided that a passage, a sentence, or a word or two need to go, a positive comment about that part can make the author rethink the decision, possibly with the wrong results, but certainly it creates stress and doubt about the author's sense of expertise over the work.

Established writers who have not previously had their material reviewed in a workshop commonly believe the people in the workshop simply will do nothing but praise what they've written. Although good writers in whatever genre tend to get fewer suggestions for improvement than less adept writers, the differences are subtle. Not hearing everything praised may be a warning sign to the author, which begins a disastrous downward spiral.

Some writers—especially women—have difficulty hearing positive feedback, either believing it is given as a result of politeness and kindness rather than being accurate and deserved, or feeling that somehow they are taking too much of the workshop's time. In such cases, the writer effectively does not hear the positive feedback, might not write it down, and later might dismiss or deny it.[30] A workshop leader needs to ensure that the workshop members make statements voluntarily and that it is clear that each statement is honestly intended. This might mean that some participants won't speak during some sections of the workshop.

Even when an inexperienced author has observed the workshop for a few days before his or her turn, the response can be overwhelming to an author in the hot seat. The moderator's job is to notice this and do something about it—even cutting short the workshop or taking it over and monopolizing the comments for a while.

Under no circumstances should the moderator allow any negative or equivocating statements to be made during this part of the process. Not only is this not the time for it, but allowing such comments to leak into this part of the workshop weakens its effect in creating a safe setting for the author. The moderator should stop reviewers making "but" statements here—these are not positive comments.

Some moderators go so far as to ask members of the workshop who have not done so yet to state something they liked about the piece. I think this is generally not a good idea. Doing this invariably means that some people will have to say they liked something when they didn't. An insecure writer then has no reason to trust any of the positive feedback. The workshop moderator should emphasize that not everyone has to speak, so that the writer can trust that any positive feedback is intended and not said simply to be nice.

I have also seen workshops with beginners who are obviously waiting for these early steps to get done so that "the real stuff" can come out. Watch out for this.

∼

Some workshops, particularly in the software patterns community, have adopted certain shorthands for some situations. The most common one has to do with positive comments that are repeated. Conscientious workshop members recognize that if some aspect of a work is very good, the author deserves to hear that everyone thinks so. Without any shorthands, this can lead to lengthy repetitions of the same comment in different words.

The shorthand I have heard to cover this case is to say, "gush!" In many cases I have heard a comment followed by a virtual chorus of gushes. What this accomplishes is that it shortens the commentary while amplifying it at the same time.

∼

For the author, hearing a broad range of comments, from good to bad, is humanizing. The piece is not just a lightning rod for negativity, but an opportunity to see that one's work evokes a variety of responses. The good has been seen along with the not so good. The work is clearly the work of a human read by humans who can express more reactions than just hunt for bugs and repair them. For authors looking for approval—hearing that they are doing a good job of writing—this is where they will get that if anywhere.

The gift nature of the workshop is thus reinforced and the setting is rendered safe for not just this author but all others.

CHAPTER FIFTEEN

Suggestions for Improvement

The heart of the writers' workshop occurs when the group is asked to supply suggestions for improvement. Implied, of course, by "improvement" is the idea that the work has some relatively weak places. Because of this, the danger is that the reviewers will gravitate toward simply pointing out the problems, reasoning that because they are not the experts, the author will be in a better position to figure out how to repair the work. But the purpose of the workshop is to find avenues for improvement, not mere criticism.

Reviewers should remember that the author is the ultimate expert on the piece. For technical pieces and for creative ones, glaring factual and literature-review errors should be pointed out, but politely and perhaps as questions: "Didn't Peter Deutsch and Danny Bobrow work on reference counting garbage collectors back in 1976?" or "Didn't they use computers to generate crowd scenes for Roman gladiator movies starting in the late 1990s?" The purpose of the workshop is to make the piece the best it can be, to make it more of what it is, not to change it into something else, especially not what you as a reviewer want it to be.

Each comment in this phase of the process should be either a direct suggestion for improvement or a statement of a problem along with a suggestion for how to address it. Each suggestion needs to be concrete and something that the author can use, not a general suggestion like "fix it somehow."[31]

Here are two examples of good approaches for suggestions for improvement. In each of these, you'll see that the suggestion is concrete but leaves a lot for the author to do.

The first example comes from the software patterns community. Here the literary vehicle is the pattern or pattern language. A common problem in early drafts of a pattern is that the problem statement is too close to the solution statement. That is, the problem statement is sometimes of the form "How does one do X?" and the solution is "Do X using these steps." The issue is that even knowing that one needs to do X is already an embodiment of the solution—that is, knowing to do X is 90 percent of the insight. A good problem statement will begin with easily observable symptoms or other indications of an issue needing resolution, and those should be closer to what would be a good problem statement than the direct question of how to do a particular thing.

A good reviewer in a workshop will point out that a problem statement "anticipates" the solution, and he or she will then proceed to start backing up from the existing problem statement toward symptoms that should be readily observable in the existing context. The reviewer may not take the problem statement all the way back, but will instead start in one or two example directions, whereupon the author can see how to approach this deeper sort of seeing required to write excellent patterns.

The second example comes from the poetry community. A frequently used strategy by a poet is to use some trigger or initiating image or situation to start drafting the poem. Sometimes the trigger is a narrative, such as a sentimental visit to a graveyard. As the drafting and early revisions proceed, the real observation that will eventually form the heart of the poem will begin to emerge, and even in the first draft the seeds of this observation will likely make their appearances. That is, the real observation is not likely to be something actually seen in the graveyard, but it will be some observation about humanity or vision itself, and this real observation will be made by the poet while drafting the poem that began with the actual trigger—the visit to the graveyard.

In the workshop version of the poem, some of the original trigger or narrative may remain, acting as a distraction to the meat of the poem. A good reviewer will point out that some particular lines, phrases, words, and images seem to form the "scaffolding" of the poem. That is, the scaffolding is what the poet needed to get the poem—likened to a building to be built—framed, sheathed, and standing. But now that the poem is almost a freestanding building, the scaffolding should come down, unless that is part of the aesthetic of the work.

The author's first reaction might be "but, that's the way it happened," to which one could reply that faithfulness to the original facts is not required of poetry as it is of nonfiction and memoir (maybe). The author, seeing the scaffolding as such, is then in the best position to see how to remove it if that would be the best thing.

∽

Questions to ask about a piece of fiction include: Is the point of view consistent? Who is speaking and to whom? Does the point of view shift? Is there an effective conflict-crisis-resolution arc? How are plot (events deliberately laid out and ordered to reveal their significance) and story (events told in chronological order) related? Are the characters believable, introduced well? Is the dialogue consistent with the characters and the situations? Do we understand their thoughts well enough? Is the length reasonable for a story, a novella, a novel? Is the action clear and believable? Are there enough or too few details to render the dream vivid and continuous? Is there harmony between the conflict and characters? Is time used effectively? Are there unreliable narrators? Are they handled well? Are figures such as metaphors and similes handled well? Is there too much symbolism? Is it too much of an allegory? Is the language in the background, is it window dressing, or is it almost another character? Is it a good read?

In technical and scientific writing, you should ask the following, at least: Does the title reflect the content well enough? Does it attract the intended readers and repel those who cannot understand it? Do the abstract, introduction, literature review, and conclusions do their jobs? Do these parts help funnel and filter readers? Are all the relevant previous results noted? Are the arguments and evidence laid out logically and in proper order? Are the arguments and explanations clear and believable? Is there enough detail in the evidence and experiments to convince? Is the mathematics clear, and are theorems proved correctly and with the level of detail customary for papers like this? Is it clear that there is sufficient novelty or new results? Are they clearly pointed out? Are the figures, illustrations, graphs, diagrams, schematics, and other nontextual information designed and executed properly? Is the writing clear, vivid, and appropriate to the audience? Is the narrative structure clear and effective? Is the writing too ambiguous? Is the piece overall too shallow, or too deeply embedded in details? If the piece is a specification for implementors, does it underspecify or overspecify? Are historical precedents and lessons appropriately and clearly presented? Is the use of statistics correct and appropriate? Are any statistics, graphs, numbers, or images misleading? Is it fun to read?*

Technical, scientific, essay, and fiction writing all have excellent how-to books and courses. Reading these books and taking these courses should provide some background on how to respond to a piece in these genres.

∽

In the best workshops, this phase of commentary turns into an upward spiral of reinforcing comments with better and better approaches to the weaknesses. This not only provides ideas for the author but demonstrates that there are lots of ways to approach revision and not simply a particular right answer that the author stupidly missed. It will be obvious to the author from such reinforcing positive discussions that the workshop members want to help and that there isn't some deep flaw in the author's personality that prevents him or her from doing good writing—that good writing is simply hard to do.

Such behavior also demonstrates a feeling of temporary co-ownership that is a hallmark of the best workshops. A colleague in the computing world compared the results of standard reviews with those of the workshop:

> *After a "standard" review of a document I've written, I often feel the document is no longer mine but has morphed into a working document owned by the entire group, which is a good thing in many cases. But the workshop format allows for input from others while actually increasing the feeling of ownership of that document—at least it did for me. I realized that my goal was not to resolve every issue everyone raised or follow through on every suggestion, but to take what I believed would improve my document, and leave the rest.*

In some workshops that I thought were successful, some reviewers would argue that some of the supposed weaknesses were either fine as is or actually strengths. In fact, sometimes passages that were praised during the positive feedback phase would be brought up again here. The lesson is that there is a subjective or aesthetic component to all writing, and that the author has a lot of

---

* A more detailed example of suggestions for improving a technical workshop can be found on page 198 in Appendix A, Examples.

latitude in how and whether to revise the work. One poet described her experience in the Warren Wilson MFA program:

> In my first semester, I included a poem in the worksheets that I had already gotten lots of comments on by my adviser. He thought that one line in particular was great, and eventually used this line in my final evaluation as an example of me at my best. There was another line in the same poem that he thought I should delete—it was obscure, confusing. Then, in the workshop, the workshop leader suggested I cut the "great" line as it didn't work at all, was a distraction, included "Jesus," who really shouldn't be there, et cetera, et cetera. But, he loved the part that my adviser didn't get and thought it was such an interesting, intriguing idea that it practically made the poem.

As a writer in a workshop, you should be careful to accept only those suggestions that really ring true *to you*. You should never change your writing to suit the workshop or anyone in it when it doesn't feel right, unless you are doing so in order to practice writing in different ways. But for writing you really care about, it's important to try to rely on your own instincts and approach to writing whenever you can.

⁓

A puzzling tension in both the technical and the creative writing manifestations of the writers' workshop is the degree to which content—including subject and theme—should be directly discussed. Undoubtedly, the workshop works just fine when the discussion is limited to presentation and craft elements, the logical flow of information, and the poetic flow of images, figures, repetitions, and echoes.

In pattern workshops, the parts of the pattern, its explanation, its generality and specificity, whether the problem and solution are too intertwined—these are all valid discussions of the craft of the piece.

In creative writing, subject is not irrelevant to craft. The possibilities for theme are like a palette of materials from which the artist may select. Once a subject is chosen, its elements have a large say in how the work can unfold, as much as the decision whether to use watercolors or oils does for a painter. Subject matter that is too familiar or too strange may make it hard for a reader to appreciate the piece. When the discussion of subject touches on how it guides the unfolding of the piece, the workshop can do some valuable learning.

Whether a subject is worth taking up is perhaps best left out of the discussion, lest it turn into a debate on political correctness or sentimentality. Sometimes a reviewer's criticism will gravitate toward how worn-out a subject is. In this case, the best approach, probably, is for the workshop leader to point out that maybe the subject has been already well explored, and to urge the author to be aware of the burden the tradition of that subject imposes. Then it's time to look at how the piece at hand fails or succeeds in interesting us in spite of that burden. In other words, no subject is automatically off-limits, though it might seem so to some folks.

~

Some people in creative workshops find it difficult to talk about craft, for a variety of reasons. Every writer is making work with the same materials—syntax, units of speech, music, noise, repetition, echo, and symmetries. Yet the choices are distinctive to each writer, along with what is used and how it is used. By not speaking of craft, there would seem to be lost opportunities for deep learning about the how of making things.

A problem with talking about writing is that since everyone uses language all the time, most people are fluent in at least their own neck of a language or dialect. How large then is the gap between fluency and artistry in writing? Compare this to playing a guitar, painting, or sculpting where fluency with the medium is learned consciously and at an older age. What is intuitive about writing, then, is likely to be buried deeper in the memory or essentially hardwired into the brain. To some this means there is nothing to learn about writing, even when a person is confronted with the clear and explicit use of craft in poetry, for example.

Some aesthetic stances and philosophies can help members of a workshop discount craft and the actual writing. For some technical and scientific writers, what matters is what's being said, not how it is said. I've heard computer scientists tell me that if an idea is good enough, it doesn't matter how hard the reader has to work to get at it. For some creative writers, a sort of postmodern relativism pops up that says that everything that anyone does even in the name of art is good because all people are created equal.

For other writers there is the Romantic preference for nature over artifice— Allen Ginsberg's first word, best word. And as John Keats wrote in a letter to Joshua H. Reynolds in 1818, "If poetry comes not as naturally as leaves to a tree it had better not come at all."[32]

This can be coupled with a bad side-effect of the workshop and pedagogical technique of encouraging beginners uncritically, through constant praise, even when their technique is imperfect and inept. In the early stages of a writer's maturation, this is the right thing to do, but sometimes the practice persists to the point where the writer never learns anything about technique. A writer can become convinced that all talk of technique is just negativity and boasting.

For poets, the language of craft includes the language of prosody, a difficult subject to master unless you teach it, whose vocabulary is obscure and whose underlying principles are rarely clearly stated.

These all conspire to make any deeper-than-superficial discussion of craft difficult in a workshop setting without an expert workshop leader. Knowing this, attend to craft as best you can.

∽

The "suggestions for improvement" phase of workshops is where less-experienced moderators might find that the group is getting out of control. Some groups—usually technical groups—tend to get into a contest in which the winner is the one who is most clever in pointing out the most damaging problem. This is a way to get attention for oneself rather than helping the author. The writers' workshop setup and ritual is designed to both invoke and evoke the spirit of gift giving and to create a feeling of shared ownership—at least for the duration of the workshop—of the work and a feeling of responsibility for the work.

The moderator needs to keep tight control of the workshop at this point. Sometimes the moderator can spot someone simply lying in wait—perhaps that person had not said anything during the positive feedback phase, perhaps the person even says something like "Good, now we can get to the real stuff." Blanket comments like "This sucks" cannot be tolerated; the moderator must step in immediately and gently reprimand anyone who simply puts down a piece. The moderator at least needs to insist for every comment made that there be a corresponding suggestion for improvement. Some workshop moderators require reviewers who want to make a comment without a suggestion to ask permission.

More practiced moderators have a set of guidelines and require the group to stick to them. Once the workshop format and ritual are understood and the individuals have some practice with it, groups rarely spin out of control.

At the suggestion phase of the workshop, the moderator needs to be paying close attention to the author's reactions, both by observing the author and by putting himself or herself in the author's place. The moderator has to be prepared to take control of the workshop, to reprimand people, or even to stop the workshop if things are bad enough. The moderator must have enough self-confidence to stand up to anyone in the workshop.

The ultimate nightmare scenario for a workshop in this phase was the product launch workshop I mentioned earlier in which I was the only experienced moderator and two of my own pieces were among those to be workshopped. I had hoped that someone would have picked up on the relatively firm hand on the tiller I demonstrated. My first piece went over well, with essentially no suggestions for improvement. The second, though, was in for nasty weather.

The first hint came when one reviewer who had been effusive during the positive feedback phase for my first work was totally silent, sitting there smiling during the positive feedback phase for this work. When the moderator—who was merely a marker of the phases—announced we were entering the section in which we could provide the author with suggestions for improvement, the reviewer said, "Good, now the real thing." She immediately opened with, "I'm not sure how to say this, but it just plain sucks." No one pressed her for any suggestions or reeled her in. I decided, though my anger was rising, that the best thing would be to demonstrate that the author should not defend his or her work. But the negative comments just kept coming and soon turned vicious.

At the end I remarked that I was obviously not qualified to write the piece in question—which was some collateral material for the product launch. She agreed, not surprisingly, and offered to have one of her hired outside writers tackle it.

My mistake was thinking that I could take time off from moderating to let my own work be reviewed. I should have either explicitly trained another moderator from the group or else gone outside, perhaps to the creative writing community, for a moderator. Another mistake was thinking that the culture and gift nature of the writers' workshop could be internalized over the course of one day.

The strong critic in question should have probably merely suggested the piece be taken over by someone else since it was clearly a genre I didn't understand, but she wasn't familiar with the workshop process. Before this piece was workshopped, I would have said that I was the least likely person to feel humiliated by criticism since the genre of the piece really was foreign to me, but even so I became quite angry at first and later had a hard time revising my other, well-received piece.

When I asked the critical reviewer later why she had been so harsh, she said that she thought that unless her remarks were over the top, I would not pay attention to them, which is typical of the culture she was used to doing reviews within.

Nevertheless, the overall workshop was a success. We had about twenty pieces written by ten people (including an important public presentation on computer-projected slides), and in one long day, we did a review that normally would have taken two weeks using the standard process. Participants remarked they got better and more usable comments than they can recall ever having gotten before.

∼

This section of the workshop—suggestions for improvement—can be tough on everyone, at least at first. Therefore, between the previous section, positive feedback, and this one, the workshop moderator might want to remind the participants of the ground rules for behavior.

The moderator could remind participants to couch their comments as concrete suggestions for how to make the work the best it can be, to refrain from talking directly to the author, and to treat the work as fiction. The moderator could also remind the author to remain silent and not defend the work.

A question that comes up is what to do when it is clear that the author is not prepared to make the piece work—that it is beyond that author's current capabilities. Cases like this don't occur when there is a shepherding or selection process guiding and filtering workshop membership. First, although the workshop members might consider the author not capable, they could be wrong. Second, there is no telling how an author will approach revising a piece given the comments made—perhaps the author will turn it into a piece he or she can write. Third, this is a judgment outside the purview of the workshop, so there is no real point to making it.

I once workshopped a poem of mine about Leonardo da Vinci working on the *Mona Lisa* while visiting the French Court. The comments I received talked about how the poem needed more about the details of painting—the implements, the types of paints and how they were made, how the paints interacted on the canvas, and how the three dimensions of the actual paint contributed to the lighting effects. Well, yes, I could have approached it that way, were I able to find out enough about the mechanics of painting. But this was only one way. Some poems are about the details of making something that not many people know about—they are akin to list poems. After the workshop, I did some research into painting along the lines suggested and quickly found it was not going to be so easy to find the sorts of pretty-sounding facts that would help me write the poem the workshop wanted me to, so I turned it into a love poem between Leonardo and the canvas he was working on, a dodge no one anticipated.

∼

Asking questions can be a way to make a pure, critical comment without harshness. It is a sort of raising of the question in the hopes that someone else can come up with a suggestion for improvement. However, it is not easily practiced, and should be tried only by those who can phrase things well.

An example was provided by a workshop member when my poem "Jimmy, Jimmy, O Jimmy Mc" (see Creative Workshop, on page 191, in Appendix A, Examples) was workshopped. In it there is some dirty language. A reviewer said something like, "I wasn't too sure about the use of foul language in this poem. Can any of you explain to me how it moved the poem forward?" This led to some suggestions on how to accomplish the same thing with less offensive terms. (I ignored them.)

Expert workshop leaders use this technique all the time: "What do you all think of the last couplet? Is it too neat?"

Tread with care here.

∼

As a member of a workshop, endeavor to offer no criticisms without an accompanying and balancing positive suggestion for how to improve the work. Remember that you are an author too and your turn will come, in this workshop or in another.

As an audience member, remember you're a guest. Do nothing to inflame.

As a moderator—especially with technical workshop novices—view this phase of the process as the time that you need to be vigilant and quick to restrain. Watch the author for signs of distress. Listen attentively for any hint of insult to the author. Don't hesitate if you suspect things are going awry. As a last resort, halt the workshop and talk to the author about what he or she wants to do. Above all, remember that throughout a review, you are the advocate for the author. He or she cannot speak, cannot defend himself or herself—it is up to you to do that. Whether you succeed or fail as a moderator depends on how well you represent the author's interests and feelings. When things are going well, keep track of the time and move the discussion along. Create a balanced dynamic of participation. Ask those who think quickly and tend to speak up first to hold back. Encourage those who are quiet to give themselves a push and jump into the discourse. Let people know that everyone's opinion counts. Listen very carefully and be prepared to give thoughtful, insightful feedback on every piece of writing.

As an author, try to recall the good things said about the piece in the positive feedback phase and, most importantly, try to remember that you are not your piece. It is simply something you are trying to write, it is not finished, it is your work in progress. Every writer has his or her lesser works, it is not you they are talking about, just the words on the pages in front of them. If you are worried about it being too much, establish a signal with the moderator with an agreement about what to do if you give the signal.

Suggestions made to the author by the reviewers are pure gifts—the author may use whatever is suggested without quoting or credit. If a reviewer revises a passage, the author should, out of politeness, ask whether it's OK to incorporate the material, but you can expect that the answer will be yes.

The suggestions for improvement phase is where the best work of the workshop can take place. Remember xenia and the idea of gifts. When the workshop works best, people have shined while offering suggestions.

I rarely see breakdowns in workshops with experienced moderators and leaders. Workshops with experienced participants also seem to keep an even keel. You will be surprised at how much good advice can come out of the writers' workshop and in so little time.

CHAPTER SIXTEEN

Clarifications

The workshop is now essentially over, and with some attention the setting has remained safe for the author sitting like a fly on the wall. The balance of "power" in the room has tilted toward the reviewers while the author has remained passive. Lots of comments may have been made, some or most of them in discussion format and generated on the fly. The author last spoke when he or she read from the piece. Now it is time for the author to return to the circle, perhaps literally but certainly figuratively.

The author at this time can ask questions, request clarifications, or, depending on the culture developed within any particular workshop, ask for comments about specific passages or aspects of the piece. Almost always, this part of the workshop is quite short—most of the time only a few minutes are reserved for it. Though the ethos of the workshop is still in force, the clarifications phase is where one of its fundamental preconditions is dropped: The author and reviewers are interacting directly. A typical request for clarification is a request to repeat a poorly heard comment or to explain what was meant by a certain suggestion; sometimes it can be in the form of a question about whether an unmentioned approach to solve a problem with the work seems like it could work.

The author still must not defend the piece or explain what he or she was trying to do except insofar as this is in pursuit of a suggestion of how to improve the work. The author does not need to apologize or defend the piece—it stands on its own as what it is, imperfect as it may be. The workshop may in fact later be asked to review a revision of the work.

Typically the author takes this opportunity to thank the reviewers and workshop. If the review has run well, it always seems to be the natural thing to do at this stage.

~

When an experienced workshop leader or moderator is working with a mature group of authors using an explicit set of guidelines, all parts of the workshop go well. Unfortunately, as the use of the workshop spreads to new disciplines and as people not used to having their writing critiqued bring their work to workshops, the possibility of defensive and sometimes aggressive behavior arises. Writing is hard to do; an author must do a lot of work to become good at it. Creative writers seem, on the whole, to understand this better than writers in other disciplines who write as part of their profession. Sometimes a scientist will believe that being an expert in his or her field is sufficient credentials to be a good scientific writer. Most doctoral programs for computer science, for instance, have no workshop or other writing instruction and no writing requirement other than have their doctoral advisers approve the dissertation. Other times a technical person gains a reputation among his or her colleagues for a particular style of writing or stance toward certain types of material. Not used to criticism, such writers sometimes face difficulties with the workshop.

If you are a workshop moderator facing a workshop with authors who might not have had extensive experience with criticism of their work or who come from a discipline or culture in which hard-edged criticism is common, then you should be prepared in case things go wrong in this section of the workshop.[33] There are two modes of getting off track. The most common is for the author to start to defend and explain. Here the solution is obvious: The moderator simply reminds the author not to do that.

The other common mode is for the author to seek revenge. This can be in the form of a diatribe or a point-by-point rebuttal to perceived insults to the work and to the author. Even when the moderator has been careful to keep comments in check, an author who is perhaps too sensitive can go over the edge.

I have witnessed two such outbursts by an author in this stage. In both cases I was not moderator and watched as the author was allowed to go through all the comments and hurl insults back to the group. Both times, the level of invective dropped off quickly and the speech seemed to stop short of its intended length. No one seemed damaged by it, and a sort of balance was restored. Authors in the workshop should nevertheless try to ignore such outbursts.

∼

In essentially all cases, the author first thanks the workshop members and asks one or two simple clarifying questions. This is a mark of a good workshop. You can see and feel any tension drop away at this stage, the writer and the reviewers begin to engage, and the formality of the session loosens in favor of ordinary give and take.

∼

The workshop is an envelope that begins with the author's reading and ends with the author's requesting clarifications. The review is now nearly over; the special rules have ended. Only one formal ritual remains. Any criticism of the work or, accidentally, of the author is over with.

CHAPTER SEVENTEEN

Wrapping Up

In terms of the work of the workshop, things are done—all the comments that should have been made have been made; there has been a balance of comments; helpful feedback has been offered and received; no one has visibly become upset; decorum has dwelt in the circle for about an hour.

But beneath the surface, emotions have perhaps been less settled. The players have confronted one another where the tender edges of self-confidence and self-doubt rub up against each other. The emotional arc is possibly unbalanced—the most remembered spate of comments has likely been the suggestions for improvement. The positive comments came first, as they needed to in order to lay the groundwork for the suggestions to be heard. But to almost any author, the order has been this: good followed by bad.

... And here we sit with the echoes of the bad ringing round and round the circle. The freshest memories to the author are about the shortcomings of the piece, and that discussion is likely to have been the most animated, with the most give and take between members of the workshop.

Certainly the order could not have been reversed, because having the suggestions for improvement come first would have had the nature, perhaps, of a firehose of negativity as perceived by the author. We need to have something positive to close the process for the author so that the emotional arc is more balanced—something that is tied more directly to the author than a thank you or another highly formal, pro forma closing.

The moderator should make a positive comment or ask someone else to do so—something about the work that could encourage the author to continue with the work. The remark can be small, but preferably it should be large (though not lengthy) or about something distinctive about the work, something that makes it unique and valuable or enjoyable or deserving to be in the world's literature, as well as something that implies that the author's unique position, skills, and talents are required to bring this work to its best form. In short, a small dose of both acceptance and approval.

Though this is a small upturn at the end of the process, it is significant because it echoes the positive comments made at the outset, reminding the author of them, of their genuineness, and of the fact that the suggestions for improvement were made about a work the group sees as valuable. If the entire workshop is a gift, then this last bit of positive feedback is the beautiful ribbon which in itself is a gift that can be reused on another package later.

~

Despite the positive comment at the end—which can be given either expertly or ineptly, depending on the person—the workshop must give a real gift back to the author, who has to an extent put his or her reputation and emotional self in some jeopardy by allowing a group to critique work that is not finished. This gift to the group by the author needs to be returned in kind in a form that is unmistakable and not subject to quality of performance.

How the gift is returned depends on the nature of the workshop and its culture. In creative workshops where six people's works are reviewed in three hours, perhaps each author is simply thanked. In Western cultures if not universally, a round of applause is the traditional way to give thanks for a performance. At the end of most technical and some creative (full-length) workshops, the participants do the same thing. Sometimes the workshop members stand to applaud the author and his or her gift. If the work were merely performed either as a presentation or a reading, this would be the expected response.

As for performances, applause is a cue that causes the author to let down his or her guard. It discharges pent-up emotions, relaxes the body, mind, and spirit. Whereas during the workshop the author may have felt that he or she was under the microscope, being criticized, all his or her shortcomings laid out on the table and analyzed, applause signals the gratitude of the members of the workshop to the author, who has let them into the creative process to help out. It reminds the author that the most complete and coherent part of the workshop was provided by the work that was carefully prepared beforehand, that the author's piece, and not the comments sometimes made completely off the cuff, was the center of attention. At this point the author can be sure nothing more will happen to him or to her.

∽

The workshop is the nexus of the crisis, the origin of storms. A steady stream of workshops all day for several days without some relief for everyone can deaden the spirit of even the most enthusiastic of workshoppers. Just like at a fancy meal, the palate needs cleansing between courses, something that takes the taste of the previous piece and discussion off the tongue no matter how pleasant that taste might have been. The tension needs to break.

Some workshops just have people stand, have a drink of water or juice, or change seats. Others ask someone to make an irrelevant comment, tell a story or a joke. At one software patterns workshop in Europe, the moderator asks someone to tell a dirty joke, which is likely to be about as far away a topic as anything could be. A puzzle, a quick game, a song sung, a short dance—whatever the moderator's taste encourages. Some believe it's better to shift from the left (analytic) brain to the right (wholistic) brain—even in creative writing workshops the process of critiquing is a left-brain activity.

That and a bio break.

∽

Some workshops encourage reviewers to return their copies of the piece, which contain their written comments, back to the author. This can serve two purposes. One is to give the author more comments, perhaps things that the reviewer didn't get to in the discussion. The other is that the copies of the piece are returned to the author, acknowledging that the piece is a work in progress and that the members of the workshop should wait for the new or final version of the work. This also gives the author some assurances that the flawed gift is not passed around where it might not be appreciated as a gift.

Members of the workshop should resist the temptation to interact heavily with the author right away. The author is likely not in a mood or situation in which he or she can even understand the conversation, and whatever emotions—positive or negative—the author had during the workshop are likely to return or continue.

Unless the author is used to encores.

∽

Formal but purposeful. It ends all the rituals of the workshop. Everyone is off the hook, and people can behave as usual. The author should be left alone unless he or she seeks you out.

Remember, the workshop can be traumatic for authors regardless of how calm and collected they seem. Everyone is human.

CHAPTER EIGHTEEN

Revising the Work

Once the workshop is over and people have gone home, the next step is for the author to revise the work. If the workshop has worked as well as it can, the author has extensive notes that he or she took at the workshop, additional extensive notes taken by a friend who shared the burden of note-taking, and marked-up copies of the work from each of the workshop members—there may be less than this, but this is the best case.

The premise of the workshop was that the group was going to assume temporarily group ownership of the piece and offer suggestions for improvement. Now things are different.

The first important difference is that the author owns the work exclusively once more. It is totally and solely the decision of the author how to revise, how much to revise, and whether to revise. The author may feel that the total feedback of the workshop showed that the piece was simply ready as is. Not every comment needs to be taken into account, not every suggestion taken. No suggestions need to be taken or only a small number of them. Here are some observations from an experienced poet:

> *I have found myself responding to a workshop's critiques of work in a lot of different ways, over the years, in different kinds of workshops, and with different stages of work I brought in. Usually the entire experience is not especially revelatory, but if only a few comments or questions offer an insight about the work, it can be*

extremely helpful. I might discover that the piece was one I wasn't really willing to have workshopped—a mistake in my choosing. Most helpfully, I might discover where in the piece I had been imprecise, confusing, or fainthearted. I also might discover that the poem is headed down a track I don't want to take my work. I might discover that a new poem would be a more hopeful revision of the piece than a revision that looks much like that version.

In addition to the group not delving into what one needed commentary about, the group might be divided on certain issues, or the group might misread. Responsibility of where the piece goes next inevitably falls back on the author who must sort out the feedback, gleaning what is really useful and considering as well questions about what in the work led the group down the path they took.

An author's prerogative stems from two considerations: The author will inevitably judge whom to listen to during the workshop, and revision is a matter of preference, style, and experience for the author and not something attached to the workshop per se.

The author sat through a number of reviews at the workshop, heard the sorts of comments each reviewer made, and was able to judge the abilities and style of each reviewer. It would be unusual for the author to conclude that they all had the same abilities and approached pieces with enough similarity of purpose that each should be afforded the same credence. Some members of the workshop are more like the intended audience for the piece than others. Some members are more experienced as writers and readers than others. The author may respect some more than others.

The author should attend to all these clues to decide whose comments to pay attention to; otherwise, there may be simply too many comments and some may contradict others anyway. Therefore, the author should explicitly in his or her own mind judge the reviewers during the workshop process. Maybe one reviewer is good for style, another for content, a third for grammar, another for emotional vectors, and so on. The author should figure out how to annotate his or her notes to know which comments to pay attention to or should endeavor to capture only the comments that the author will probably want to work on. On the other hand, sometimes this judgment can't be accurately made until later, when the emotions of the moment have passed. Sometimes it takes discussing things with a trusted adviser.

For many writers, it helps to put some time between first encountering comments and acting on them. This is good advice regardless of where the comments come from. For workshop comments, perhaps you should go over the comments soon after the workshop to make sure you have written them down clearly, and then you should let them sit for a few days. For comments on your manuscript—by workshop members or other people—you should read them all, then put them aside for a couple of days. This way you are not reacting to the comments only from your gut, but also from your head and heart.

The goal of the postworkshop experience is revision, and approaches to revision differ. Some revise lightly whereas others obsess over it. At one extreme was James Dickey, the poet and novelist. Dickey believed it was crucial to always produce better and better work, and he was terrified of the idea that his work one year would be worse than that of the year before.

Dickey had numerous methods of revision. His favorite was redrafting, in which he would create new drafts of a poem until there were literally hundreds from which he could choose. Another was to experiment with word order and placement in hopes of finding the best words—through putting pressure on them by occupying different positions in the poem—along with their best order. He was interested not only in the meanings of words but their sounds, connotations, and rhythms.

Sometimes he would cut out words or phrases and physically try them out in different orders and arrangements rather than making different drafts with only simple changes. I have used a similar technique for long prose works. Sometimes I draft in the order in which I think of things, each in its own section; later I print out the piece and cut it into those sections and then lay them out on the floor, judging the effectiveness of dozens of different presentation orders. Once I have selected one, I reorder the draft and then make the transitions between sections appropriate.

Dickey viewed his process as one of experimentation. In the end, when he had hundreds of versions and drafts of a piece, he was able to choose from them. Surely some of them were better than others, and if he chose one of those, he was better off than he could have been.

His choice was selection; others choose perfection. That is, in writing, one can adopt the approach of producing lots of drafts and selecting the best, and at the other extreme one can adopt the approach of producing a single draft and then systematically perfecting it as much as possible, producing the final result. Many writers choose a balance of selection and perfection—writing a lot, choosing the best work, and then perfecting it. Dickey perhaps took revision, editing, and selecting too seriously, but his approach shows it is hard to be too extreme in approaching the process of revision.

How novelist Richard Schmitt writes is an example of the traditional fiction writers' way of revising, though he practices it on a computer rather than with a typewriter. Like many fiction writers, he keeps the novel manuscript double-spaced. Once he gets his work to a stage at which he feels it needs a good looking at, he prints it out. Then he retypes the piece. He puts the draft to the left of his monitor and transcribes it back into the computer, retaining the previous version.

Why does he do this? When he is writing, he is living in the story at typing pace. It's a fast pace because he can't see and take into account the entire story, but it is a slower pace than the pace at which the reader experiences it—it is the pace of writing, not reading. While at that pace, the story has its rhythms, and the words and phrases have their textures, which he is used to feeling through his arms and fingers. The story unfolds one line at a time on the screen. It is a physical feeling, not just emotion or intellect.

While retyping, he can see that the story is not already on the page he is typing, demanding to be followed, but at every turn he can take it in another direction—perhaps in a small way by rewriting a paragraph or a section, but also perhaps in a large way, taking the story in another direction entirely. Retaining the original words and making small revisions take the same typing effort, so there is no obvious bias in favor of keeping what's already been written. If he does go in a different direction, he has both drafts to look at and judge—it's a way to get some diversity and choose which is best, much as Dickey has done.

The short story writer, Grace Paley, revises her work by reading it aloud over and over. The sound of the words, the ease and difficulty of saying them, hearing the piece, and the physical experience of reading combine to show her where a work is weak and where it's strong.

It's easy to think of revision as a simple process or skill that an author needs to know and exercise, something a little mindless in a sense, though not a thoughtless or automatic activity—somewhere between raking the lawn and grading homework problems. That is, some think of revision as a skill or process that once "learned" is not forgotten and that does not improve with time. Revision feels, to a lot of people, like a simple kind of reading followed by a simple sort of touching up, though sometimes a larger revision is necessary and, at that point, the mechanics of it seem to overwhelm. Others, of course, consider revising hard, and when one is trying to fully realize the work, it can be.

There is a secret to writing—and to revision. It is this: practice. Writing, including revision, is a skill that gets better with practice, like playing a musical instrument or tightrope walking. You do it over and over, and you get better at it. Perhaps the level you can achieve and the pace at which you get better depends on talent, but everyone gets better at writing by writing. Writers don't seem to know this the same way that musicians do. Practice seems to be something that has to do with "muscle memory," but isn't there a muscle memory involved in writing, in the pathways between where the ideas and words are and their confluence into sentences—or things like sentences—on the page? Perhaps it is because we learn to speak almost unconsciously and language is so deeply buried within us that the concept of practicing makes no sense. Do we need to practice walking and running? Well, yes, if we are athletes or dancers focusing on movement.

When I first met the poet Mark Strand, he thought I was pretty good for someone who had written only twenty-five poems or so at a relatively old age. He said I must have written lots of stuff before that, but I couldn't think of what it was. He eventually asked about email, and I said that for fifteen years I averaged twenty-five longish emails a day along with twenty-five short ones. He remarked that this must be where I got the practice. Practice.[34]

The best predictor of how good the next piece you write will be is the number of words you have already put on paper. The same is true of revision. The more you revise, the better you will be at it. In fact, the two go together—as you practice writing and practice revising, some of the revising skill you gain will be transferred into your drafting process, usually subconsciously. That is, your drafts will require less revision later because you are revising as you draft without thinking about it.

The following is an observation a poet I know made about drafts and practicing:

> *I think we as writers sometimes devalue our drafts more than painters, say, value their sketches. A painter and printmaker friend of mine used to go home from his crappy office job years ago to sketch for at least two hours as soon as he got back to his little apartment. I don't recall him fretting about whether a certain sketch was going to become a perfect painting one day. The sketching was a fluid process he relished. His paintings and intaglio prints came out of—evolved from—that process, but he didn't regard the sketches as failed works or ugly stepchildren, the way writers may. I'm not sure whether workshopping always supports valuing drafts as much as it should. Sometimes it seems too focused on the achievement of the proverbial perfect poem.*

A poet friend told me this story about the poet Linda Gregg:

> When Linda Gregg was in Greece, for five months she wrote and worked on and finished a poem every day. She didn't insist that each poem be good—she worked on ones she knew she would later reject until they were done, anyway.

When I first started writing (technical prose) seriously, I would spend about a day writing each page or two of text—about the same amount as two or three pages of this book. It would take weeks or months to prepare a first draft of a long paper. Then I would read and reread each draft numerous times, making sometimes major revisions, but usually tinkering with the structure of paragraphs and sentences. When a sentence or paragraph didn't yield to small changes, I would ask myself what that passage was trying to say and then I'd redraft.

Once I had a good draft, I would ask others to read it. I usually made every suggested change, thinking that I could eliminate their objections to the piece that way. Then I would do my own rounds of revision again, trying to let the draft sit for a few days so that I would have a fresher take on it next time. For my first major technical paper publication, I did thirty different major drafts with several subdrafts in between—it took me one month of drafting and three solid months of revision.

During my early years of writing I read and tried to digest dozens of books on writing, particularly on revision. It wasn't until fifteen years into my technical writing career that I discovered the writers' workshop while retrying my hand at poetry and fiction. By then I had made two major changes in how I wrote nonfiction.

The first change had to do with how I drafted. Originally I would try to draft with great artistry—complex and clever sentences, unusual wording, erudition. After ten years of that, I somewhat suddenly started writing in my *natural voice*, which is the voice I use in email and casual writing. At the same time, I started reading poetry and serious fiction, which moved my writing in an artistic direction. The move from a conscious, directed style of writing to a more natural voice was repeated in my fiction and poetry writing over the next ten years.

The second change had to do with revision. Once I made the move to my own unadorned voice, I found that the revisions I needed to do mostly concerned global organization—I still sometimes cut out sections and rearrange them on the floor—and compression (simplifying sentences through more efficient wording). I would characterize the revision I generally do these days as light or very light. Two revisions usually does it, and the revisions take little time—perhaps a day each for twenty-page pieces. As with the change of voice, the change in revision started with nonfiction, moved to fiction writing, and ended with poetry. It seems likely that each change in revision style was caused by my adopting my natural voice.[35]

Both of these changes had to do with losing the fear that unless I used a faked voice, I would not be taken seriously as a writer. Not only did I eventually become more confident as a writer, but I think my writing gained a confident sound. Along with this, the amount of effort to start and complete a project of the scope of the one that previously took four months has been reduced to a couple of weeks. I believe the change was aided by the effects of practice on writing—that the more I wrote and revised, the easier it became and the better I became at these tasks.

These four examples—the way the writers James Dickey, Richard Schmitt, Grace Paley, and Richard Gabriel approach writing and revision—show that each person has his or her own style or process to both drafting and revision. No one of them is better than any other. With experience, practice, and talent, each person can become more comfortable with writing and with reduced fear of failure.

Each person's arc in a writing career—be that person a poet, a proser, or a scientist—is his or her own, but as long as the person takes writing seriously and practices it, it is an arc and not a single point or short line.

∼

Steal.

Doesn't sound like good advice offhand, does it? If you can write one sentence, you have already demonstrated that you are a thief. Idioms, figures of speech, common metaphors, cultural references, and the basics of the language you speak itself—you got these by theft. You didn't make them up. Almost anything you can think of saying has been said before. Stealing is not plagiarizing. Plagiarizing is stealing large portions of another author's work verbatim. The kind of stealing I'm talking about is this: phrases, metaphors, lines, approaches to description or explanation, stylistic quirks, anything distinctive that catches your fancy short of plagiarism.

When I was studying with Stephen Dobyns, he asked me to list for each poetry collection or poet I read what exactly I planned to steal. At first I thought he meant just approaches or general qualities, but I finally realized he meant very concrete things.

Read to see how other writers work. Read for style, for what's on the page. If you're a scientist or an engineer, read great explainers to see how they do it. Don't break the law or your code of ethics, but steal what you can.

In *The Sacred Wood: Essays on Poetry and Criticism*, T. S. Eliot discussed theft:

> *Immature poets imitate; mature poets steal; bad poets deface what they take, and good poets make it into something better, or at least something different. The good poet welds his theft into a whole of feeling which is unique, utterly different from that from which it was torn; the bad poet throws it into something which has no cohesion.*

You can see throughout this short book what I have stolen—the words and ideas of my writing colleagues. I stole, except that in most cases what they said or wrote was so much more articulate than what I could write that I quoted rather than incorporated (and I asked them if it was OK). In the first sentence of this paragraph and again in this one, you can see something concrete that I have stolen—the dash. I use the dash to separate thoughts that are related in a vague or variable way to each other, but whose relation is not so easily put into subordinate or coordinate clauses or any other syntactic relationship—I'm not even willing to commit to an "and." Lots of writers have used it before, especially Emily Dickinson, or at least we often typeset it that way now. Her dashes are really an unknown and complex punctuation.[36]

I stole them from Rick Bass, who in his early career used them all over. The way he used them was a porthole into his thought processes—you could see him thinking, gathering the pieces and parts together. But rather than glue his thoughts together in a finished, polished whole, he would leave them a little rough and scattered, with their logical connections implied by their contents and by the better rhythms his writing displayed. In some ways his sentences were like the periodic sentences of Samuel Johnson, but without the heavyweight syntax and punctuation. In fact, about the same time I stole this from Rick, I stole the idea of no or minimal punctuation from W. S. Merwin and Cormac McCarthy. It seemed to me that just as English had shed many of its inflections, so it might start to shed some of its punctuation and syntax. Anyhow, I adopted the thefts like any punk growing muttonchops.

Experienced writers tend not to take a lot of detailed comments away from a writers' workshop. The reasons have to do with their experience levels—an experienced writer knows not only that he or she is basically writing well but also what he or she sounds like. Typically, only surprising comments or a number of remarks aimed at the same general failure of the piece are taken seriously. Perhaps only a few reviewer's comments will be taken into account if it feels right.

Many experienced writers use the workshop as a deadline to get work done and as a community to be part of. They will read their work aloud to the workshop to test it out.

Another reason seasoned writers ignore most workshop comments is that they fear the "workshop piece." A workshop poem, for example, has a indistinct cast to it, the result of lopping off its extremities. Any rough piece written by a unique voice has parts that stick out. For each part that sticks out, there undoubtedly is someone who doesn't like it. In a workshop, there's a reasonable chance that somebody will speak out against the extremity. If the author acts on all these comments, then many or all those extremities will be chopped off and the piece will have fewer flaws but perhaps nothing that makes it worthwhile. Like a burr that sticks to an animal's fur, a good piece of writing needs something sticking out and maybe a little sharp or awkward to hook onto a reader's mind and be dropped somewhere inside and grow up to be a powerful force. When all the stickers are worn off, you get a slick ball that just keeps rolling by. Hence, the workshop poem, the workshop story, the workshop novel, and the workshop essay—nothing wrong, but nothing exceptional.[37]

Patterns can suffer the same fate. A pattern is a solution to a (design) problem in a context. When a pattern is sharply and succinctly stated, it has an impact on the reader, who might internalize it quickly. But such a statement of the pattern is likely to miss a lot of subtle details and special cases; there are considerations and equivocations about when it applies. The forces potentially in place that could make some difference in how the pattern could be implemented can multiply. A typical outcome is for an eager-to-please author to add all this stuff and make a fluffy, large mudball of a pattern that causes no reaction when read. The workshop pattern.

An experienced writer knows or intuitively feels what makes his or her works work, and avoids paying attention to comments that void or nullify those strengths, even when they are heavily commented upon. A perfect piece is not simply one with no faults. This is a process of selective listening, and as one becomes more experienced with workshops, the better one becomes at knowing whom and what to listen to, and the more courage and less doubt one has about not listening.

Beginning writers, on the other hand, might want to adopt an approach that maximizes the amount of practice they get. Therefore, I recommend that beginning writers try to implement lots of suggestions, even if the piece starts to sound like a workshop piece. This gives the writer revision practice, and the result may not be distinctive, but it will almost certainly not be objectionable. The writer gets experience revising a wider variety of problems—even if in the end these problems are actually the writer's style. At worst, the writer gets to see what it feels like to write something another way—a way he or she eventually might not agree with. A writer who adopts this approach should carefully try to judge the outcome of each change and not feel uncomfortable backing out of it. As the writer gains more experience, he or she can start to rely more on personal judgment. Remember: A writer should never take a suggestion unless he or she can see that it makes some sense.

A good way to practice for a creative writer is to imitate. Try to sound like Jack Gilbert; try to revise toward his voice and noise.

When you're starting out with the workshop, pay special attention to comments you don't agree with or even understand. Often they are coming from someone with a lot more experience and that's why their suggestions don't make sense to you. If you don't agree, try making the change anyway, or try to think of when and why it might be good advice. If you don't understand it, write it down somewhere in a little notebook of mysterious writing secrets—someday you will understand it.

∽

The range of comments in a workshop depends on the sort of material workshopped. In poetry workshops, comments range from the choice of topic* and the images and figures used, to ordering, length, genre, and other craft elements such as meter, rhythm, noise, line breaks, and word selection—for example. In fiction workshops, the focus is more on plot and character development than on the more word- and sentence-centered craft elements of poetry. In technical and scientific writing, the content of the work comes into play more.

---

* Although commenting on this is annoying and passé.

In other nonfiction workshops, the emphasis can be on the content, people and how they're treated, the organization of the piece, and the presentation approach. In any writing workshop, though, any and all of these topics could come up.

In technical and scientific workshops, comments having to do with the accuracy and completeness of the content have to be addressed one way or another. If an author discussing an approach to a technical problem in a technical paper has missed some important prior art in his or her literature search, this needs to be addressed. Similarly if a reviewer finds a fatal flaw in a key proof of a claim, the author needs to take this very seriously and perhaps abandon the work.

In this sense, even the most experienced writer and researcher can benefit from the writers' workshop—factual and logical flaws and weaknesses in an argument can be uncovered because more eyes are looking at the work in a cooperative frame of mind than would be if the author used only a few trusted reviewers or none at all.

∼

Many comments made by reviewers in the workshop can be dismissed as the result of poor reasoning or as matters of opinion. But there is one comment that cannot be dismissed except as a matter of choice: "I didn't understand." Someone might be mistaken about a craft element or whether an earlier piece of research is relevant, but not about whether he or she understood. The comment "I didn't understand" cannot be contradicted.

A good workshop moderator will try to elicit from a reviewer why a passage wasn't understood—were there misleading clues, was the writing ambiguous at the wrong place, did a tantalizing alternative pop up, did the material require more subject-area expertise than the reviewer had, were some assumptions not made explicit? Sometimes all that can be gotten is the interpretation or reading the reviewer took, if there is one. Sometimes the moderator can clarify (or ask the author to do so) in order to find out where the reviewer went wrong. During the clarification section, the author can perhaps ask some questions that get to the bottom of the problem of understanding. The author can try to trace back a bad reading to where it started and clarify there.

And sometimes workshop reviewers say they don't understand unless it's dead simple, as this poet explained: "I've been in poetry workshops where several of the writers did not understand anything unless it was simple and direct—linear.

They didn't get implied meaning, nuance, etc. The danger of workshops is that poetry will be dumbed-down to the lowest common denominator."

∽

When is the work finished—how do you know when revising is over? Diminishing returns? Sense of satisfaction? Nothing significant changed? The poet Paul Valéry said, "A poem is never finished, only abandoned." William Butler Yeats said a successful poem will "come shut with a click, like a closing box"—some strive for a kind of perfection, others for release.

When you don't feel compelled to work on a piece or when other things seem more pressing, and abandoning it seems OK, then it is probably as finished as you can make it.

Abandon it. It has taught you all it can.

∽

Recognize where you are in your maturation as a writer; practice drafting and revising, even unnecessarily. Adopt an attitude while drafting that encourages experimentation and practice. Try selecting; try perfecting.

Realize that as you gain more experience and practice, you might be able to adopt different ways of working, that you can be more selective in terms of which suggestions to follow. Adapt your use of the workshop to match your experience and comfort levels. Get from it what you need, not simply what it gives.

Coda: The Work of Making Things

> I asked how can you ever be sure
> that what you write is really
> any good at all and he said you can't
>
> you can't you can never be sure
> you die without knowing
> whether anything you wrote was any good
> if you have to be sure don't write
>
> —W. S. MERWIN, FROM "BERRYMAN"

The secret to the work of making things is courage—the quality of mind or spirit that enables us to face fear. What we fear when we try to make a thing is that we don't have the ability to do it, that we're not good enough, that no matter how hard we try, we might come up short. To combat this we naturally turn toward overachieving: adding to what we would normally and naturally do in making the thing. Or we fear revealing too much, and we carefully watch what we write to stay within the boundaries we've made up to keep ourselves safe.

When I was writing in my artful, ornate, complex, sophisticated, edgy, intellectual phase, the mistake I made was to think that in my first attempt I could achieve suddenly what a master could only after unimaginable practice and reflection. This is the mistake we all can make at any point along our arcs of learning and development of skill.

But there are no masters. Only people moving along their own arcs, making what they can and all along just practicing. With practice we improve. By being attentive to what we make when we make things and how we make them, we learn what works and doesn't—we improve. By reading those who are further along on their arcs of writing, we can see how they have achieved what seem to us as masterworks, and we improve.

When we watch someone acting courageously, we don't know whether that person is facing fear or simply facing what's in front of him or her. What writers face is the blank page with an abstract picture of the perfect piece in their head and no idea how to make their version of that perfect piece on that piece of paper.

What we cannot make alone, we can make together. No one can make a cathedral, but many people together can. This is the premise of the writers' workshop. The author gives the gift of a work in progress to a group of writers each just as afraid as the other, and that group will own the work for a while and give back the gift of suggestions. By carefully crafting the setting and ritual of how those authors work together, the gift exchange can be made to work beautifully, and no matter how inept each of the authors around the circle may be, if some of the suggestions are taken, the work can't help but get better, and the author who takes the suggestions can't help but get more practice putting one word after another and seeing how it comes out.

Some beginning writers fear that they might not have as complete a plan as they need to complete the work adequately. Many people were taught to write longer pieces by writing long essays using the approach of doing research and writing outlines and then filling them out. It is possible to work like this, but many if not most writers do not. This doesn't mean you shouldn't make a plan. But this fact should reduce your fear that your plan is inadequate—if someone can write without a plan, then you should be able to write with the plan you have.

Many write to find out what they think about a topic—many essays are exactly this. One of the definitions of the word *essay* is "an initial attempt or endeavor, especially a tentative attempt."*

---

* *American Heritage Dictionary of the English Language*, 4th ed.

When Samuel Johnson was writing his essays for *The Rambler* or *The Idler*, he would wait until the last minute to start: He would write the first half of the essay while the boy courier waited—writing just enough for the first typesetting plate. The boy would run off with the first pages, and Johnson then could think more about the essay and what he had already written and what it taught him about the topic. Then he would complete it. We can see this in his essays, and now it's a style: The first half is the one hand, and the second half is the other. Johnson was one of the finest essayists who ever lived. He didn't think too much about plans for essays.

In the end it comes down to trust—trusting that we have within us all we need to write well and beyond our fear. Audre Lorde wrote, "We can learn to work and speak when we are afraid in the same way we have learned to work and speak when we are tired."

∽

A writer makes a tentative attempt, revises it as best as he or she can, and gives the work in progress to the workshop. Each iteration of this cycle along with the drafting and revising gives the writer more skills and more confidence.

The workshop brings together a variety of people with varying skills and knowledge. For creative writers the workshop can help hone craft element skills, and for technical and scientific writers the workshop can additionally help the content, accuracy, and precision.

The author of a work reviewed in a workshop gets to observe, while in the workshop, a group of peers who have assumed a degree of ownership of his or her work react to that work—as if the author were a fly on the wall in a room with no fly swatters. Just as an audience or readership would or will react to the work out in the world.

Often what appears on the page to a reader is not the same as the combination of what's on the page and what was in the author's mind when the piece was written. When the writer reads his or her own work, the initial trigger typically comes to mind. Such trigger traces in the writer's mind can cause two failures of seeing that plague writers: obscuring what's missing and displacing possibilities. Because the initial trigger pops into the writer's mind and completes what's only partially on the page, the author is less likely to notice that the reader has too few clues to grasp the piece. Or, the trigger added to what's on the page makes it too hard for the author to see other directions the piece could go—if only the trigger wouldn't appear, other associations would, and the author could take the piece in another—better—direction.

Writing is about seeing—seeing what is on the page, seeing what is important and essential about a topic, what is relevant, what is in the heart, what is in the world. We are taught to see by people kind enough to point things out. We can learn to see from our teachers, from our experiences, and from our colleagues.

~

As we progress as writers of whatever genre, what we need from the workshop changes. First it is basic help and an answer to the question, "Can I write?" We learn a bit about revision and what the reader can see in our work and what cannot be seen. We get used to the idea of people reading our work. We practice talking about work and craft. If there's a knowledgeable moderator, we learn some of the language of literature and writing. We hear about other authors' experiences with drafting and revising. We learn that there is a community of writers that maybe we never knew existed.

In the technical world, we might be surprised that there are other people struggling to write just as we are; in the creative world, we might be surprised that the community of writers is as supportive as it is. We learn that giving gifts can work in a selfish world. We toughen our skin and begin to learn that we are not our work. We learn that the workshop world and the community of writers are gift realms, whose gifts of help, advice, suggestions, and support are abundant, that giving this gift doesn't diminish our ability to create, write, or give further gifts. In a world of abundance, excess thrives.

Later as our skills grow and we gain more practice, we need more targeted help: Does this character seem to have the right motivation? Can I really seem to paste this stanza in right here? Isn't this line break too corny? Is the problem statement in this pattern too close to the solution? What about the pacing of this presentation here, or do any of you know of a garbage collection algorithm like this one I think I invented? We have discovered what we need to hear and how to ignore what is not important to us. Our skins are tough and callused, but we also know how to be gentle and constructive with our suggestions. With some luck and observation, we learn how new authors react to sharp words and thus we soften ours and teach others about teaching writing. Drafting becomes easier and so does revising. We finish pieces faster. And more often.

Even later as we become good writers with successful pieces behind us, perhaps we attend workshops for very limited purposes: to check an experimental work, to try out a new genre, to solve a particular problem. Our requests for targeted comments become precise and limited. We take fewer notes. We moderate more because we are experts at workshops and writing. We rarely feel any disturbed emotions while sitting on the wall as a fly. Drafting and revising are easier except when the writing problems are hard, and we want the harder challenges. We wish to create, as Eliot suggested, "a whole of feeling which is unique, utterly different" from anything written before; and our thefts are deliriously undetectable and unnoticed.

We're starting to develop what Keats called *negative capability*, a state "when a [writer] is capable of being in uncertainties, mysteries, doubts, without any irritable reaching after fact and reason."[38]

Writing causes no fear—it isn't that we have a quality of mind or spirit to face fear, but that what we face is simply the page waiting to be filled.

Writing is hard, and it sneaks up on us sometimes so that we write to have a page to quickly turn, to see how it comes out.

We write in our natural voices which have been tuned through feedback and learning but also deepened and sweetened by maturing. There is something confident about our writing. Readers follow.

One of the surprising things I learned when I entered the creative writing community was that the well-known or experienced writers who were our workshop moderators generally didn't use workshops or used them for limited purposes for specific problems. Most who didn't attend workshops said that they had friends or trusted colleagues who would read their work. In very advanced poetry workshops, I found that the author wasn't a fly on the wall, and that the workshop was more like a conversation among peers. No one was defensive; reasons for choices were discussed but never defensively. Suggestions for edits or revisions were easily passed along.

The ritual of the writers' workshop had fallen away or been dismantled like a scaffolding no longer necessary. There weren't any fights or emotional outbursts, as if the spirit of xenia had blanketed the workshop members and the work was simply there to be discussed as if it had a life of its own.

Often even when a writer has moved past needing the workshop, that writer sees something of value in it. An experienced writer talked about when workshops help most:

> I found workshops to be most useful when I was younger and considerably less experienced. In later life, due to the vagaries of several folks discussing your work at a time, all trying to make a decent impression and/or truly to give a sound presentation of their opinions regarding the work at hand, it seemed that the group often was discussing aspects that were not my main concern, which is not to say that they weren't interesting, but in an oral, group setting, [they were] often too diffuse or not immediately aimed at the areas I considered problematic. On the other hand, the handwritten comments of workshop members often provided more practical and insightfully focused remarks.

In fact, experienced writers who have a down view on workshops also wonder at their magic:

> There's a time and place for the workshop in an apprenticeship or developmental stage to be sure. And after that the white noise (diffused ideas) can become just a nattering to shake off. But when the chemistry and seriousness match (a rare thing), learning happens on both sides—writer and readers—and that's invigorating.

Many experienced writers stick with the workshop even though they've gained the confidence and the chops to work on their own. Deadlines can encourage a veteran writer to use the workshop to rapidly improve the work. And for writers who don't regularly interact with an audience, the workshop can provide a good substitute. But more often, those who stay are interested in the gift and the community, a sense of sharing and growing with others, the joy of being able to talk to others enthusiastic about writing—a connection to other writers to buoy up doubts about drifting.

~

The arc of becoming a writer—whether a scientist, engineer, technical person, proser, essayist, novelist, or poet—has many transitional places, requires special techniques for people to move forward, has many gates.

Even though the workshop can still be a resource for problem-solving and for help with research-related questions, for most writers of whatever stripe, it is a gate that enables them to pass through their barriers of fear and uncertainty to the next level of writing maturity. For many writers, the ability to look dispassionately enough at one's own work to make progress and to get in enough practice at writing to get better requires gifts from other writers who have chosen—sometimes for selfish reasons—to be generous with their time and expertise.

We need help finding ways out of problems; we need the suggestions to know what to do next. We need affirmation that we can write and that what we write about is worthwhile. Once we have those things, we can get busy putting one word after another on the page and making things happen. We can pass through the workshop gate.

Sometimes when we pass through the gate and look back, there is no fence, just the gate, or the fence is little and we could have stepped over it, it seems. But, as I said, there are no masters, and we will continue to encounter fences and we will need to find gates to get past them. For many, the workshop is a gate that, once passed through, is no longer needed. For many, a few writing companions are all they need to move on. And sometimes we might need or wish to realign our direction or get inspiration or join in the community of gift-giving once more, but we probably don't need exactly the workshop gate—it simply is one that will do and do quite nicely.

One of the consequences of our economic structure is that poets and fiction writers don't make much money, and so for a small fee many first-rate writers act as moderators for creative writing workshops. I, for example, have been in poetry workshops with two poets laureate—Mark Strand and Robert Hass—not to mention a dozen other poets whose names are household words in the community of poets.

There really are no circumstances in which people in other fields such as computer science can take a writing workshop with the best writers in those fields—in fact, those writers perhaps aren't even aware of the existence of the writers' workshop and the teaching that can go on there. And many of them don't even consider themselves writers.

Students in those fields work with those writers only during graduate school, and rarely do their mentors teach writing, only the contents of the fields themselves. Perhaps some of you in fields like computing, physics, biology, marketing, and manufacturing who have become excellent writers after attending writers' workshops will give your own gifts to your community of writers and teach and moderate writers' workshops, creating gates where before there were only imaginary fences.

But the poets and writers who teach in workshops don't do it only for the money. Because money is not a strong factor in the lives of poets and other first-rate writers, money is also not a strong motivator. Poets and writers live in two economies at once: the gift economy and the monetary economy. If you think that every piece of writing has a secret or hard-to-find meaning or theme, seek it here.

The writers' workshop is a rare confluence of gift-giving, teaching, the imagination, and the spectacle of many minds writing and creating, for a short time, a single work. Poets, prosers, and software developers—and perhaps others I don't know about—gather evenings, maybe at conferences or at work during lunch or in the off hours to sit in a circle and follow the little ritual I've explained here.

Many do it for free for their own education or to help others. They work on writing and ideas, two of the most personal activities a person can do. Regardless of the subject matter, this is work of the imagination, it is creation, and what is created has value.

So much value they'd do it for free—it's simply joy in the work of making things.

Notes

1. (PAGE IX) Before I started writing this book, the only book I found that talked about how writers' workshops ran was Pat Schneider, *The Writer as an Artist: A New Approach to Writing Alone and with Others*. Later I found some other books that could be useful in understanding how the writers' workshop works. See note 27.

2. (PAGE XIV) For the benefit of creative writers, I will briefly explain patterns. A pattern, very generally, is a statement of a particularly effective way to resolve a (design) problem in the construction or design of buildings or software. The pattern suggests concrete actions for building part of the artifact. It's called a pattern because the things constructed to effect the fix are readily observed in many excellent artifacts in which the stated problem or problems needed to be addressed. A pattern is also the written description of the physical configuration, the problem it solves, and the forces and considerations that go into the choice to build this configuration over others. A pattern, then, is both something in the world—the configuration found in excellent artifacts—and a literary form, that is, the written description of the physical configuration and why it should be built.

    The literary form of a pattern has both a problem and solution statement. The problem and solution statements occur in a context, which is roughly the state of design or construction. A pattern language is a set of patterns that combine to design or construct a particular category of things. In a pattern language, each pattern's context is the set of patterns from the language already having been applied.

    Here is a pattern taken from *A Pattern Language* by the architect Christopher Alexander:

179. Alcoves

... many large rooms are not complete unless they have smaller rooms and alcoves opening off them. ...

No homogeneous room, of homogeneous height, can serve a group of people well. To give a group a chance to be together, as a group, a room must also give them the chance to be alone, in one's and two's in the same space.

This problem is felt most acutely in the common rooms of a house—the kitchen, the family room, the living room. In fact, it is so critical there, that the house can drive the family apart when it remains unsolved. ...

In modern life, the main function of a family is emotional; it is a source of security and love. But these qualities will only come into existence if the members of the house are physically able to be together as a family.

This is often difficult. The various members of the family come and go at different times of day; even when they are in the house, each has his own private interests. ... In many houses, these interests force people to go off to their own rooms, away from the family. This happens for two reasons. First, in a normal family room, one person can easily be disturbed by what the others are doing. ... Second, the family room does not usually have any space where people can leave things and not have them disturbed. ...

To solve the problem, there must be some way in which the members of the family can be together, even when they are doing different things.

Therefore:

Make small places at the edge of any common room, usually no more than 6 feet wide and 3 to 6 feet deep and possibly much smaller. These alcoves should be large enough for two people to sit, chat, or play and sometimes large enough to contain a desk or table.

Alcoves

Give the alcove a ceiling which is markedly lower than the ceiling height in the main room. ...

The following is a software pattern I wrote, aimed at the design of the internal coding of a program, particularly with the design of local variable architecture. I chose it for its simplicity.

Pattern: Local Variables Re-assigned above Their Uses

this pattern helps complete the Simply Understood Code pattern [not included]. This pattern helps solve the problem of making code understandable when you need to re-assign the values of variables.

Sometimes a piece of code needs to re-assign local variables more than once. If this is done without paying attention to a person reading the code who is unfamiliar with it, misunderstandings are easy.

Sometimes a piece of code requires that a local variable have its value changed several times, perhaps in a loop. When this happens the problem is how to know which use or reference of the variable goes with which assignment. In cases of complex control structure, there might be no way to have each reference or use correspond to exactly one assignment.

People normally read code from top to bottom, so their inclination is to recall the assignment that is textually above the reference or use.

Of course, if the code is complex, it will be difficult to understand and the code chunk ought to be well-documented other ways than by making the code plain, though it rarely hurts to do both.

Therefore:

A local variable that must be re-assigned should be re-assigned in a place that is textually above where it is used or referenced.

Sometimes a local variable that is re-assigned could be turned into two variables where each assignment is actually a definition of a local variable, one inside the scope of the other. This is preferable to assigning twice.

3. (PAGE 1) In 1896, George Cook gave a course called Verse Making, in which the emphasis was on how poetry is made, how the words on the page make the poem work. Later, Clark Fisher taught a similar course on the short story. These two courses led to Edwin Piper's course called Poetics, in which students' work was discussed critically. This course was the direct precursor to the writers' workshop format as we know it, and also to the practice of granting a degree for creative writing. The history of writers' workshops at the University of Iowa and beyond to other writing programs is detailed and fascinating in its own way. A good resource is D. G. Myers, *The Elephants Teach: Creative Writing Since 1880*.
4. (PAGE 2) The list of regional PLoPs includes or has included PLoP, EuroPLoP, UP (Using Patterns), ChiliPLoP (Arizona), Mensore PLoP (Japan), KoalaPLoP (Australia), and SugarLoafPLoP (Latin America).
5. (PAGE 16) The programming language is Common Lisp, and the colleague was Kent Pitman. His point was valid in the situation we were in, because we were not trying to encourage new implementation strategies—we were trying to codify existing practice.
6. (PAGE 18) This story is taken from Daniel L. Schacter, *Searching for Memory*. That the source of writing seems to come from a different source than for speaking is subjectively

confirmed by my own experience of writing a poem a day for over two years. As my experience in writing poems grew, the more it felt that the work was being pushed out by a mechanism very different from the pulling I used to do while writing poems. This feeling is akin to "flow" as described by Susan K. Perry in *Writing in Flow*.

7. (PAGE 25) The two phrases use the word *making* rather than *construction* or *building* to indicate any kind of act in which a person makes something, whether it's a physical object, a song, a poem, a piece of software, or a comment. *Repetitive* implies drudge work, but I intend both drudge work and highly skilled, difficult, and challenging work. I wanted to use two similar phrases in order to indicate that it might be hard to tell whether an activity falls into one or the other category.

8. (PAGE 33) Duende is hard to explain. It is a kind of passion-filled creative inspiration or muse or trickster that has a little bit of darkness mixed in. If you look it up in a dictionary, you will see it means something like "the ability to attract others through personal magnetism and charm." Perhaps the magnetism and charm is the result of being "infected" by the duende as defined by Federico García Lorca, who wrote this in *In Search of Duende:* "The duende . . . is a power, not a work. It is a struggle, not a thought. I have heard an old maestro of the guitar say, 'the duende is not in the throat; the duende climbs up through the soles of the feet.' Meaning this: It is not a question of ability, but of true, living style, of blood, of the most ancient culture, of spontaneous creation."

9. (PAGE 38) Both pieces of information about photography came from the World Wide Web: Joanna Pinneo, "Working for National Geographic Magazine," *Digital Journalist* #105 (n.d.); and Kim Hachiya, "Focus, Focus, Focus," *Nebraska Magazine*, n.d.

10. (PAGE 39) I heard these figures in an interview of Walter Murch by Terry Gross, on *Fresh Air*, National Public Radio, 15 April 1996 (rebroadcast 3 August 2001). Murch was the film editor and sound designer for *Apocalypse Now*.

11. (PAGE 39) But what of Michelangelo, the Sistine Chapel, and *David?* An artist who has practiced extensively accumulates lots of techniques and "tricks" for creating "art." Enough that even early drafts or impromptu performances are quite good. An improvised lead by Eric Clapton is likely to be quite good—to a typical audience, though it might disappoint Eric and other guitarists. Even Jimi Hendrix's famous live leads are filled with mistakes and odd string, tube, and speaker-cone effects that highlight the musicality of most of his gestures. We learn by listening that Hendrix often missed notes but would bend them or slide the mistake into something musical. The overall musicality of Hendrix's leads overwhelms us and we see all the other accidentals as intentional and part of his musical repertoire. (It's not an accident that *accidental* is a musical term.)

With this analysis of nonclassical artists behind us we can approach Michelangelo. In *David*, Michelangelo used sculptor's "tricks" and broad gestures to produce a perceived perfection that we fill out to the whole statue. Michelangelo used distortions for certain visual effects: David's head and right hand are too large for his body; his furrowed brow protrudes from his forehead in an anatomically impossible way. Everyone is familiar with the three-quarter profile of the right side of David's head. If we were able to observe his left profile from a fair distance away—which we can't now because the museum wall is in the way—we would see it would make a perfect Roman coin. To achieve this, Michelangelo made David walleyed. We could see this from a head-on view had Michelangelo not put David's upraised left arm in the way as seen from the intended viewing angle.

Michelangelo, like other sculptors before and since, used tricks like these all the time. If the Virgin as depicted in his *Pietà* in St. Peter's Basilica were to stand up, she would be mostly legs. Her right arm, which supports Christ's shoulders, is too long. Michelangelo used these distortions to depict a grown man lying in a woman's lap.

Michelangelo made mistakes, too. He started a pietà for his own tomb, but stopped when he broke off Christ's left leg. Michelangelo was also known for not finishing many projects. Renaissance artists, particularly sculptors, used teams of assistants and students to get work done. Since Michelangelo regularly refused to use assistants, perhaps he stopped projects when they proved too difficult, or when he took on too many projects, or they seemed not to be progressing well. Perhaps he abandoned projects that were not "keepers."

The Sistine Chapel presented problems because frescoes are painted on freshly laid plaster, and there is little or no opportunity for repainting and repairing mistakes. Michelangelo painted nine history panels, twelve prophets and sibyls, and a number of spandrels, lunettes, medallions, and pendentives. Of these, most people could recognize just a few or only the one—the *Creation of Adam*. And perhaps because it was "defaced" by Daniele da Volterra, who was commissioned to paint draperies over the offending nudity, the *Last Judgment* fresco at the front of the chapel is not very well known.

Of all the work Michelangelo did, most people know very little of it, and these two examples—the Sistine Chapel and *David*—stand out. The "quality" of work from artists and writers typically displays something called a *normal distribution*, which is depicted in the figure on the next page.

The way to interpret this picture is as follows: The *x*- axis (horizontal axis) represents some measure, for example the height of a person, and the *y*- axis (vertical axis) represents the number of items exhibiting this measure. The vertical line is the mean, or average. For example, the average height of men in the United States is about 5'8". If the figure represented the distribution graph for American male heights, then the height of the vertical line in the middle of the graph would represent the number of men in the United States who are exactly 5'8" tall. Just to the left or right of this vertical line would be the number of men whose heights are just shorter or just taller than 5'8", and we could see that there are almost as many men of those heights as those who are 5'8". But we notice that this graph would tell us there are not very many American men 4' and 7' tall.

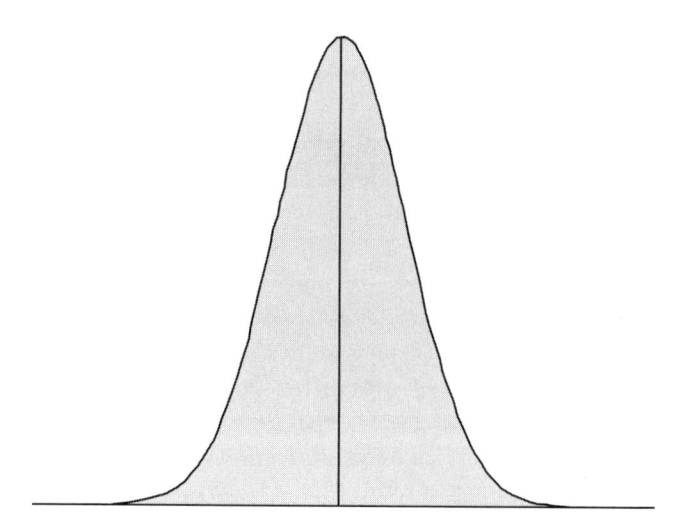

The vertical line in the figure marks the *mean*, or average, and the term *standard deviation* describes the distribution's width. For most artists, their total life's work will fall in a normal distribution: most of it average (for them), some of it not as good, and some of it excellent. For Michelangelo, the panel of God creating Adam in the Sistine Chapel and the statue of David are out to the right on this curve: They are masterpieces that were unusual even for Michelangelo.

The use of normal distributions is not theoretical. The computer industry uses it for a very specific and important purpose. A central processing unit (CPU) is the chip that is the heart of a computer. When a computer is doing something, it is the CPU that is executing or running operations programmed by someone. Each CPU functions by means of a clock that injects electrical pulses at some predetermined rate. When someone says that a computer has a 500 MHz Pentium, that means that the clock in the computer's Pentium CPU chip pulses 500 million times per second. A chip is made of electrical conductors and insulators etched into and deposited onto a silicon substrate. These etchings and deposits are accomplished by complicated chemical and physical processes. CPUs are designed to operate at some clock rate, but the actual rate any particular chip can run depends on how clean and nice the etching came out.

Suppose that a chip was designed to run about 700 MHz; if you look at all the chips made on, say, Monday, they would form a normal distribution around some clock speed—let's say it's 713 MHz. That means that most of the chips would be able to run at 713 MHz, but some would be faster, and some considerably faster. Moreover, most if not almost all of them would run at 500 MHz, for example (all the numbers are made up since such details aren't important to the example). The manufacturer would test the chips to see how fast they can run and put them into bins: ones that run at 500 MHz in one bin, ones that run at 600 MHz in another—700 MHz, 800 MHz, 900 MHz, 1 GHz, and so on. As the clock speed goes up, the number of chips in the corresponding bin drops, so the manufacturer charges more for the faster chips. When you see computers using the same CPU chip advertised running at various speeds, it isn't because the manufacturer designed or made the chips any differently, but because they selected the speeds at which they happened to be able to operate. (Note that designing a chip to run at high clock rates is unimaginably hard to do, so harvesting for clock rate is a way to take further advantage of an already difficult process requiring talent and skill—just as with any art.)

The same is true of fruit, vegetable, and meat quality. Prime beef is noticed and selected, not planned—though some diets and other living conditions can shift the distribution to the right, toward better quality.

This discussion is not meant to diminish Michelangelo's genius and the masterpieces he or any other artist has produced. The idea of distribution and selection is important to how writers write and how they feel about their writing over time. I've found that when we look at artists carefully, even great ones, we learn that they seem to work a lot like the rest of us in our humble ways.

12. (PAGE 39) Making art is not magic, but the experience of writing *in flow*—where the writing seems to come from somewhere else either deep inside or from the cosmos—can feel like magic, a sort of spiritual magic, which can be experienced by both creative writers and technical writers.

13. (PAGE 39) The other "best" way to learn to write well is to closely read and critique perfected, finished work. A combination of methods including workshops, classes, mentoring, and critical reading is used at the Warren Wilson MFA program for writers. See note 17.

14. (PAGE 42) The abstraction of money into intrinsically valueless tokens is actually a step quite distinct from the choice of a scarcity/trading culture over an abundance/gift culture; to see this, one need only consider barter economies. Moreover, there is the concept of a gift certificate for a particular gift (not a substitute for money limited to a particular vendor)—children often give such tokens as gifts in the form of a promissory note for services such as washing dishes.

15. (PAGE 42) The law of diminishing returns talks about the return on fixed investments. Suppose there is a limited supply of some substance, for example, and that retrieving it takes some expenditure. The law states that as time goes on, the same expenditure retrieves less and less of the substance. With a limited supply, it's worthwhile to corner the market, which is what a lot of corporations try to do.

16. (PAGE 42) This definition of *xenia* comes from Gabriel Herman, "Ritualized Friendship and the Greek City." Xenia is discussed quite thoroughly in Ann Carson, *Economy of the Unlost*. Though he doesn't use the term *xenia*, Lewis Hyde, *The Gift: Imagination and the Erotic Life of Property*, explores the topic of gifts in the same vein and very thoroughly.

17. (PAGE 45) At Warren Wilson College, the MFA Program for Writers is a low-residency program with four major teaching components: workshops, the supervisor, classes and lectures at the residencies, and annotations. The supervisor is a successful writer and teacher of writing who acts as a mentor (shepherd) for a student. The supervisor directs the student's critical reading, helps the student complete work, and provides an understanding of the creative life of writing. Critical reading is done via the annotation. An annotation is a narrowly focused, short essay on the use of a craft element in the work of a poet—for example, the use of puns in Heather McHugh's poems.

18. (PAGE 46) This is one of the paradoxes of the writers' workshop. In the creative writers' workshop, the moderators are almost always paid. Poets and fiction writers who are good enough to be excellent moderators typically do not earn much money or are not wealthy. But the gift nature of the workshop is not hindered, because the exchange of money is outside the workshop setting, and helps balance an exchange that would perhaps favor the workshop participants because the moderator brings much more experience than do the participants.

    Most importantly, many creative workshop leaders prepare extensively for workshops—reading pieces thoroughly enough to carry the discussion of each piece, and sometimes preparing teaching material. To such leaders, the workshop is a classroom.

19. (PAGE 49) Some family members look for autobiographical parts and talk about them ("it didn't happen like that"), not realizing the event was a trigger. Others won't feel they understand the writing and won't offer much support. In dysfunctional families, support of any sort might be hard to come by. Nevertheless, a good workshop can be like a good, supportive family.

20. (PAGE 50) This quote comes from Pablo Neruda, "Childhood and Poetry," in *Twenty Poems*, translated by James Wright and Robert Bly, and quoted in Lewis Hyde, *The Gift*.

21. (PAGE 64) At some national conferences, the total hierarchy can be quite deep: Besides the authors as usual—often referred to as *contributors*—there may be novice observers who do not or rarely speak. Above the contributors but below the fellows are the *waitstaff*, writers with a published work (but no book) and whose tuition to the workshop is paid in exchange for their acting as kitchen crew and food servers. From top to bottom, the order is this: faculty, junior faculty, fellow, waitstaff, contributor, observer. Members of each level can be members of the same workshop group, sometimes getting in each other's way a bit.

22. (PAGE 65) The poem I presented to the workshop is in Appendix A, in Examples, along with the notes I took at the time. By the time I put it in the workshop, it had been revised seven times and had shrunk down from a loose two pages to what you see—the poet Thomas Lux acted as my shepherd. See Richard P. Gabriel, "Jimmy, Jimmy, Oh Jimmy Mack," *Ploughshares* 24, no. 4 (1998–1999).

23. (PAGE 72) Opinions differ on where the moderator should sit. An experienced creative workshop leader told me the following: "I think the moderator should sit in one of the strong places in the circle. For example, [the moderator should sit in one of the circled seats

shown in the figure]. This creates balance: If the moderator sits in the other places, the circle feels wobbly. However, I agree with your thoughts on light from the window."

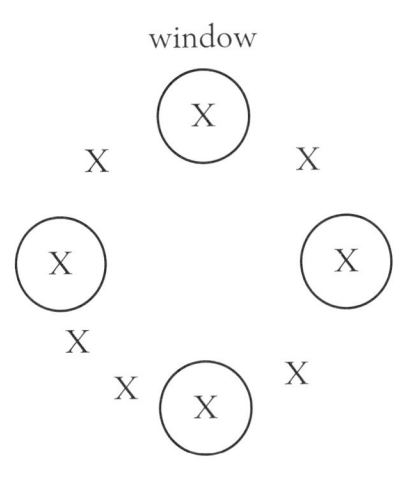

window

```
        X
    X       X
  X           X
    X       X
        X
```

24. (PAGE 76) See the guidelines in Appendix B for giving feedback.
25. (PAGE 79) Not all national workshop participants choose to join in completely. Sometimes older or more experienced writers or veterans of many workshops choose to find private accommodations. Some national workshops discourage participants from writing while attending, but some attendees wish to continue their daily writing routine. Others find that they don't need the shared accommodations to get into the culture of the workshop or are not accustomed to the dormitory scene. The danger is that by not accepting the usual accommodations, a workshop participant is partially excluding himself or herself, and therefore should adjust his or her expectations so as to not feel excluded by the workshop.
26. (PAGE 80) What can seem like a gentle shared culture can also become a wedge of cliquishness or ostracism. If some participants happen to have never heard of the shared stories or myths, then those stories can serve as a paintbrush that colors the insiders differently from the outsiders. Someone not in on the stories and myths can easily feel excluded and hence not get as much out of the experience. Some software patterns workshops therefore hold "newbie" meetings at the start and sometimes every day so that questions and comments about culture and practice can be addressed.
27. (PAGES 84, 175) Three books about learning theories and other takes on the writers' workshop are the following: Carol Bly, *Beyond the Writers' Workshop: New Ways to Write Creative Nonfiction*; Robert E. Brooke, *Writing and Sense of Self: Identity Negotiation in Writing Workshops*; and Wendy Bishop, *Released into Language: Options for Teaching Creative Writing*.
28. (PAGE 97) Shepherds exist in the creative writing world—some help writers prepare their work for the workshop, but much more often they help writers who have "outgrown" the workshop and are creating mature work for a thesis or professional publication.

29. (PAGE 100) So valuable are shepherds considered to the software patterns community that each PLoP bestows the Neil Harrison Shepherding Award on the best shepherd for that conference. The award states, in part, that each winner "exemplifies the observant, helpful, and insightful characteristics that are crucial to quality shepherding."

30. (PAGE 132) A good illustration of the inability of authors to hear and appreciate positive feedback is the following, which is an excerpt from the notes taken during a workshop reviewing a pattern language on teaching technical concepts in computing. The excerpt contains all of the positive feedback comments noted by the authors:

- Concept explanation
- Problem and activity structuring
- Should be published to a broader audience
- Important especially for new teachers
- Wish that all teachers would read it
- Problem statements are helpful. These are real problem statements.
- Alexandrian form is appropriate for the contents
- Examples, make the patterns very practical
- The names work
- Importance of the refactoring approach
- Number of authors shows that this is a community, which means it's credible even without known uses
- Good examples for other domains
- Literal poetry
- Uniform (although many authors)
- Summaries and extra commentary
- Names of the patterns (except "Understanding Abstraction")

Notice how terse and general each entry is. I attended this workshop, and the positive feedback phase of the workshop provided very detailed comments about particular sections and paragraphs, specifics about the writing, and many comments not reflected in this précis. The notes for the suggestions for improvement section are considerably more detailed: Whereas the notes on positive feedback are about 100 words long, the notes on suggestions for improvement are 1500 words long. To me, that indicates that the authors did not hear the praise with the same attention to detail as they heard the criticism.

31. (PAGE 135) Though suggestions are preferable, sometimes all a reviewer knows is that the piece did not work, was confusing, wasn't understandable, or was unsatisfying. In most cases with a mature group of writers and other people, and when the culture and atmosphere of the workshop are right, comments stating and describing these flaws without suggestions for improvement are fine. In technical workshops, it is usually easier to come up with avenues for exploration to fix problems than in a creative workshop, where sometimes a person only has unease and disquiet to go on.

32. (PAGES 140, 185) John Keats, letter to Benjamin Bailey, 22 November 1817.
33. (PAGE 148) Seasoned creative workshoppers are usually shocked to read about outbursts in the workshop at this or any stage. But the scientific and technical cultures harbor very aggressive pockets in which insults are part of daily life. Some corporate cultures can also be very harsh. When a workshop is formed at a company and the goal is reviewing and revising collateral material, for example, the workshop participants might include people who adamantly believe they exclusively "own" all aspects of the material—the rest are "outsiders." In such cases, the comments of the outsiders might be dismissed and even resented or worse.

    Moreover, some people who have heard of the writers' workshop or been to one once are trying it out on their own without finding a strong moderator or experienced workshoppers as guides. Experienced moderators know about the failure modes and take steps all along the way to prevent them, whereas a self-operated workshop may not stay on track on its own. This book is designed to help such folks anticipate and recover from blunders.
34. (PAGE 159) Does writing without revising constitute practice? Perhaps, if the writer does so deliberately, choosing words carefully, considering different strategies, sentence structures, and phrasings. But even simply putting something onto the page is worth something, maybe as a way to ward off blockage later.
35. (PAGE 161) My experience with technical writing is unusual. I write and revise fiction and poetry more rapidly than most writers do, but the results are not as good, either. I am exploring my writing process and the range of work I can do. Being able to get hold of a strong trigger and having the material flow (relatively) easily from some hidden source seems to be part of an artistic process that could produce better work with less revision.
36. (PAGE 162) Emily Dickinson used dashlike marks of varying lengths, some turned up, some down, some level. They seem to be a combination of dash, comma, period, and mimetic tap. She used them not only in her poems, but in her recipes and when transcribing others' poetry.
37. (PAGE 163) Some writers learn to write poems that the "crowd" likes—that's the workshop poem. But a similar problem, perhaps larger, has to do with a writer's coming to rely on the workshop community to provide the reason to write. The writer thereby becomes unable, effectively, to write without it. In particular, if a writer goes to just one workshop, which is the writer's entire world of writing, that group can effectively narrow the creative and aesthetic choices for the writer, perhaps even to the point of crippling him or her, by limiting exposure to other writers, aesthetics, cultures, and populations.
38. (PAGE 171) See note 32.

APPENDIX A

Examples

These are examples of workshop material—pieces that were workshopped, revisions, summaries, positive feedback, and suggestions for improvement.

Creative Workshop: Positive Feedback and Suggestions for Improvement

Ellen Bryant Voigt is perhaps the most gifted workshop leader I have encountered. In the winter of 1997, at one of my MFA residencies at Warren Wilson College in Swannanoa, North Carolina, I was in a workshop with her and Carl Philips as workshop leaders. While I was writing this book, I found among my papers the notes on a minor poem I had workshopped with them. The notes I took are illustrative of the sorts of comments one can get from a good workshop focusing only on craft elements and not on content. Later in the spring of 1997, I revised the poem based on these comments, with Thomas Lux as adviser. The final poem is still a minor poem, but it probably has become the best it could be.

The original was written during the semester that I wrote a long critical essay on James Wright; you can see the clear influence from his later work. The primary comments—from the whole workshop, really—had to do with the flatness of the language in key places, the use of didactic, or "preachy," statements, the location of important information in syntactically unimportant places in the

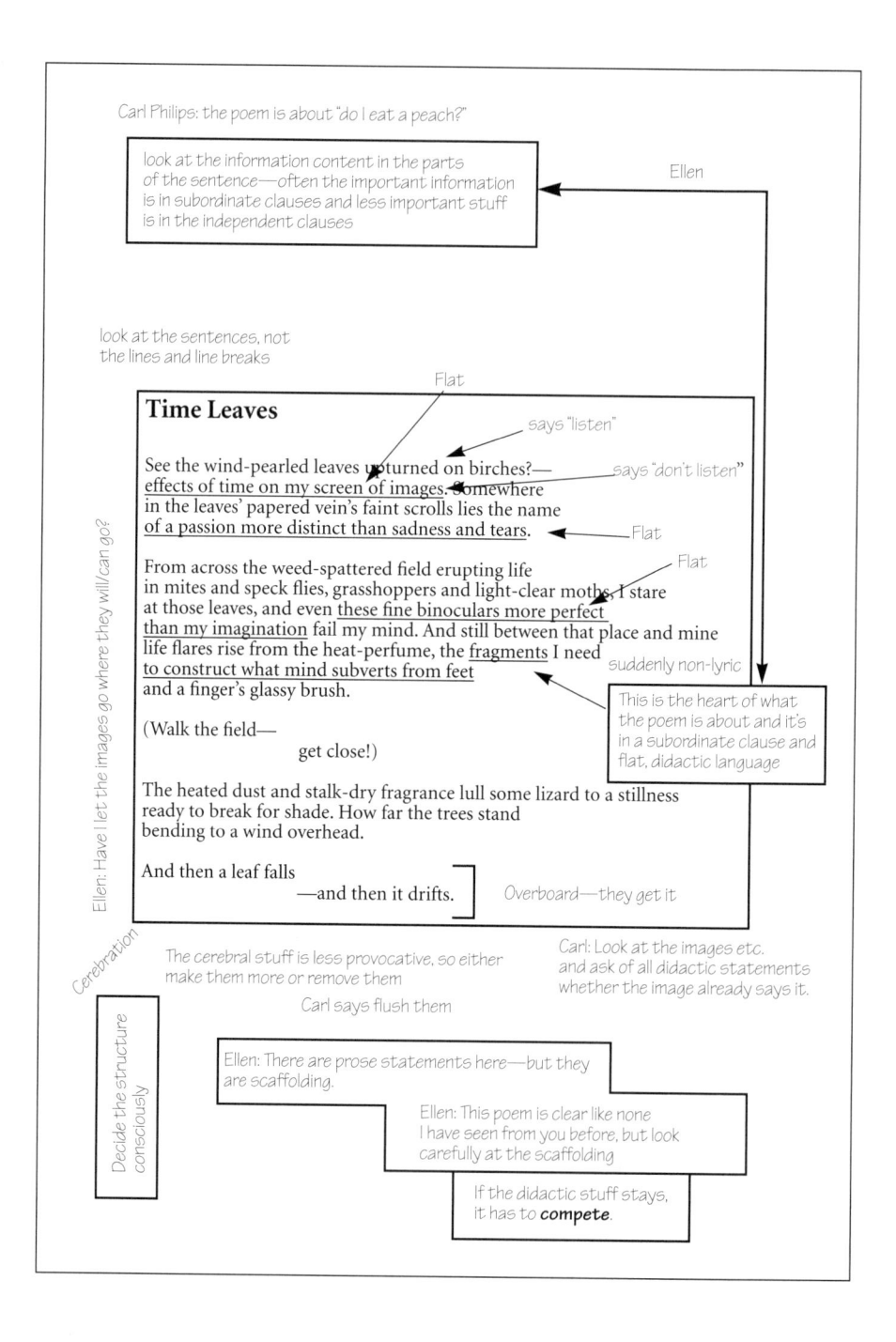

188 · WRITERS' WORKSHOPS & THE WORK OF MAKING THINGS

Carl Philips: the poem is about "do I eat a peach?"

> look at the information content in the parts of the sentence—often the important information is in subordinate clauses and less important stuff is in the independent clauses ← Ellen

look at the sentences, not the lines and line breaks

Flat

Time Leaves

says "listen"

See the wind-pearled leaves upturned on birches?— ← says "don't listen"
effects of time on my screen of images. Somewhere
in the leaves' papered vein's faint scrolls lies the name
of a passion more distinct than sadness and tears. ← Flat

From across the weed-spattered field erupting life — Flat
in mites and speck flies, grasshoppers and light-clear moths, I stare
at those leaves, and even these fine binoculars more perfect
than my imagination fail my mind. And still between that place and mine
life flares rise from the heat-perfume, the fragments I need   suddenly non-lyric
to construct what mind subverts from feet
and a finger's glassy brush.

> This is the heart of what the poem is about and it's in a subordinate clause and flat, didactic language

(Walk the field—
            get close!)

The heated dust and stalk-dry fragrance lull some lizard to a stillness
ready to break for shade. How far the trees stand
bending to a wind overhead.

And then a leaf falls
            —and then it drifts.   Overboard—they get it

Ellen: Have I let the images go where they will/can go?

Cerebration

The cerebral stuff is less provocative, so either   Carl: Look at the images etc.
make them more or remove them   and ask of all didactic statements
                                whether the image already says it.
        Carl says flush them

Decide the structure consciously

> Ellen: There are prose statements here—but they are scaffolding.

> Ellen: This poem is clear like none I have seen from you before, but look carefully at the scaffolding

> If the didactic stuff stays, it has to **compete**.

sentences (ignoring the lines), and whether the images could or should be made to do the heavy lifting.

Although my notes do not indicate the order I took the notes, we can still see the workshop order. Carl Philips started out by commenting that the poem is about "Do I eat a peach?" That is, the poem, according to him, is a celebration of nature of a sort. We can see that someone, probably Ellen, noted that the poem is mostly a lyric, though later she pointed out that it turns nonlyric at a key point. So we started with talking about genre and what it was about.

Ellen commented that the poem is clear, unlike earlier poems of mine—which were indeed maddeningly obscure. There is a hint that someone said that the images were at least a little provocative. These are statements about what worked about the piece.

Next, we see the suggestions for improvement: Look at the flat and didactic statements, and either make them as provocative as the images or find some way to eliminate them and have the images do the work. Ellen commented that the use of scaffolding seems to have paid off in constructing a clearer poem than I had ever written before. The term *cerebration* was coined by the group as a light-hearted way of referring to the sort of poem it was: a celebration filtered a little too much through the intellect.

The workshop also pointed out how the images ask to be listened to while the didactic statements ask the opposite. Ellen also asked whether the images have been given their head enough—that is, did I ever let the images take hold of the poem while I simply watched and recorded? At the time I was in this workshop, this was a statement I was unable to understand except intellectually.

Also notice that none of the comments have to do with the choice of content or of aesthetic—all the comments are craft related.

This is what the poem became after a number of revisions:

Time Leaves
Wind-pearled leaves upturned on birches,
and leaves' papered veins' faint scrolls carry
dropped lines in mid-kiss, lips from old films,
lies spurting in the fine print.

From across the weed-spattered field erupting life
in mites and speck flies, grasshoppers and light-clear moths, I stare
at those leaves, and even these binoculars, perfect and fine,

fail. And still between us, the fragments I need—life flares—
rise in the heat-perfume. Feet and fingers stop, lips
stop their glassy brush.

Dust and stalk-dry fragrance lull this lizard to a stillness
ready to break for shade. How far the trees stand
bending to a wind overhead.

The poem entitled "Jimmy, Jimmy, O Jimmy Mc" was also workshopped while I was at Warren Wilson College. There were two workshop leaders—call them α and β. The leaders disagreed strongly on the poem (the story is recounted in Chapter 6). When the poem was workshopped, it had already been extensively revised under the supervision of Thomas Lux, so I changed only the title to make it easier to pronounce ("Jimmy, Jimmy, Oh Jimmy Mack").

Creative Workshop: Summary

Outside of Master of Arts (MA) and Master of Fine Arts (MFA) programs and their graduates, it might seem hard to come up with narrative structures, lyric moments, or images and figures. This might be true. But people writing stories and poetry can likely observe more than they realize, and there are ways to convey those observations. The following is a difficult poem by Federico García Lorca, from his collection *Poet in New York*.

Scream to Rome
(From the top of the Chrysler Building)
Apples lightly wounded
by the fine little swords of silver,
clouds scraped by a hand of coral
that carries on its back an almond of fire,
fishes of arsenic like sharks,
sharks like tears to drown a multitude,
roses that wound
and needles installed in the tubes of the blood,
enemy worlds and loves covered with worms
will fall on you. They will fall upon the great dome

APPENDIX A *Examples*   191

commas only

α thought commas
would help because it takes
the reader out of the poem

or just enough commas
so they don't leave the poem

lack of punctuation
obscures tone

Jimmy, Jimmy, O Jimmy Mc
James Michael Maguire 1954–1980

not enjambed / stay consistent

Jimmy's grave is flat and nothing
in the cemetery grove of fat maples
blowing electric green not a mile from the river
wind blowing like the background sound
of highspeed tires on the highway not far away
nearby toy trucks and a 2-month-old's grave
playing dead but it's Jimmy I found
curled black Jimmy in his box
whose head thrown through sheetrock
was a missile aimed at his mother's cunt bursting out black Jimmy's

too confusing?

shifts rhythm here, enjambment begins here

?

enjambed

voice knocked from his head Jimmy bare
in the trees by the stonewall we tried
being girls by the side of the road we lay
on each other and he whispered lust my name
and Buddy and Jimmy and me with the girls
in the sandpit Buddy a man
almost and Jimmy and Buddy bare jumping from the sand cliffs
for the girls to watch Buddy hard
and I told them it's ok it's ok
but they hunched in a circle thinking God Jimmy
in a school for the deaf for imbeciles coming home
Jimmy in the shootout
with cops in his car to escape his head
through the windshield the oak
bark the meat through the otherside
past the sandpit the highway the river Jimmy
laughing Jimmy
whose voice was bunched on one side of his head the cracks in his skull
like the hammer in her cunt Jimmy
under ground his stone flat and nothing only the baby
can laugh under ground in his box full of toys
in the electric green cemetery by the river wind
blowing the sand over grass in my eyes with no cracks

?

build up to turn of speaking to Jimmy

in my head to see with
no cracks in my head
direct to you
Jimmy

β. put it in sections
maybe need a
break to make enjambment start/stop
more palatable

Dean Young

that the military tongues anoint with oil
where a man urinates on a dazzling dove
and spits crushed coal
surrounded by thousands of bells.

Because now there is no one to share the bread or the wine,
nor anyone to cultivate grasses in the mouth of the dead man,
nor anyone to open the linens of repose,
nor anyone to weep for the wounds of the elephants.
There is nothing more than a million blacksmiths
forging chains for the children that will come.
There is nothing more than a million carpenters
that make coffins without a cross.
There is nothing more than a crowd of laments
that open their clothes to await the bullet.
The man who deprecates the dove should speak,
should cry out naked amid the columns,
and give himself an injection to infect himself with leprosy
and let out a sobbing so terrible
that his rings and telephones of diamond may be dissolved.
But the man dressed in white
does not know the mystery of the wheat,
does not know the moan of childbirth,
does not know that Christ may still give water,
does not know that the coin burns the kiss of the prodigy
and sheds the blood of the lamb on the idiot beak of the pheasant.

The teachers show the children
a marvelous light that comes from the mountain;
but that which comes is a collection of sewers
wherein cry the dark nymphs of cholera.
The teachers point out with devotion the enormous improved domes;
but beneath the statues there is no love,
there is no love beneath the eyes of hard crystal.
Love is in the flesh torn open by thirst,
in the tiny hut that fights the flood;
love is in the ditches where the serpents of hunger fight,
in the sad sea that rocks the dead bodies of the sea gulls

and in the dark penetrating kiss beneath the pillows.
But the old man with translucent hands
will say: Love, love, love,
acclaimed by millions of dying ones;
will say: love, love, love,
amid the quivering tissue of tenderness;
will say: peace, peace, peace,
amid the shiver of knives and melons of dynamite;
will say: love, love, love,
until his lips become silver.

Meanwhile, meanwhile, oh!, meanwhile,
the blacks that take out the spittoons,
the boys that tremble beneath the pale terror of the directors,
the women drowned in mineral oils,
the crowd of hammer, violin, or cloud,
will scream although their brains may blow out on the wall,
will scream in front of the domes
will scream maddened by fire,
will scream maddened by snow,
will scream with their heads full of excrement,
will scream like all the nights together,
will scream with a voice so torn
that the cities tremble like little girls
and the cities of oil and music break,
because we want our daily bread,
flower of the alder and threshed tenderness,
because we want to be fulfilled the will of the Earth
that gives its fruits for all.

The following summary is adapted from an essay written by Ian Wilson. Notice that despite how incisive this summary appears, it really is just a recitation of observations about what is in the poem and how parts of the poem relate to one another. There is no poetic or literary jargon, just penetrating observation.

> There is no narrative that leads us through. The poem starts small with a single image of apples "lightly wounded" which could be part of a pastoral. But their wounding by one of the technologies of war, "swords of silver," begins to dispel

connection to the bucolic. This is not only our starting point in nature but also the finishing point of the poem. The image in the first line has more complexity than what appears on the surface. "Apples lightly wounded," when considered on the literal level, is not easy to picture. A small bruise? A wormhole? A little piece cut off? Eden and The Fall are some of the first associations that come to mind. As the poem goes on, the wounding grows in scope and ferocity. García Lorca creates phrases whose parts do not fit in ordinary concert, making such metaphors as: "clouds scraped by a hand of coral," an "almond of fire," "fishes of arsenic like sharks," "needles installed in the tubes of blood." These phrases have a Surrealist quality to them. These images, which come early in the poem, also have a wildness to them; they are not civilized nor controlled. Death is implicit in the images of the sharks and drowning. A deep rumbling of the sinister is set in motion.

García Lorca conducts us to a bad place through the imagery whose power accrues by virtue of number. Beginning with a single image we progress to multitudes. More and more images come as if "piled on." Long before the end of the stanza, any trace of the pastoral in the simple image of "apples" vanishes.

There are a number of certain similarities of sound in the first stanza. "Dome," "doves," "coal," and "thousands" are "o" sounds which move through a range of cries, from various groans—oh, uh, oh—to outright pain—the "ow" in "thousands." All of this pain comes at the end of a stanza of bizarre and strange terrors, horrors that will come crashing down—on Rome.

The passionate address continues in the second stanza along with additional enumerations and accumulations. The speaker begins cataloging loss: "No one to share the bread or the wine," "nor anyone to cultivate . . . ," "nor anyone to open . . . ," "nor anyone to weep. . . ." The human is absent from human activities. No one to share, cultivate, open linens, weep. Beyond the enumerations and accumulations, García Lorca catalogs and repeats. The scale of the enumerations both contracts and expands in the next lines. In the beginning of the first repetition we have: "There is nothing more." At the end of the line we return to multitudes: "a million blacksmiths / forging chains for the children . . ." This pattern repeats twice more: "There is nothing more" expanding to "a million carpenters / that make coffins . . ." Finally, "There is nothing more than a crowd of laments. . . ."

In stanza three there is a sharp contrast between the highly idealized images presented by "The teachers"—"a marvelous light that comes from the mountain" and "the enormous improved domes" (a blackly humorous phrase that recalls some kind of bureaucratic discourse)—and those of the blasted true world—"a collection of sewers / wherein cry the dark nymphs of cholera."

The final stanza rises in pitch with the seven lines each beginning with "will scream" that can be likened to chanting in a religious service. The lines, except the first one, are mostly short and have great punch. The stanza, the whole poem, rises to a crescendo and climax on the word "break," and then there is a huge emotional letting go in the resolution of the final four lines. The letting go is achieved because the repetition—stops; we've risen as high as we can go, while at the same time, we've reached the bottom of the slide and the ride smoothes out.

Finally, there is a calming in the poem, the relief of the more placid pastoral images recalling the poem's first image of apples: "daily bread," "flower of alder," "fruits to all." García Lorca continues his technique of repetition here in the phrase "because we want" which echoes all that has come before. Ending with an earth "that bears fruit to all," after all the frenzy, peace comes to the poem.

Technical Workshop

The following is a draft pattern I wrote for a pattern language to design textual electronic communications systems. Textual electronic communications systems include email, instant messaging, chat, mailing lists, and any other form of textual interaction between or among people—video, audio, and multimedia are excluded. All aspects of such systems are considered, including message archiving, cataloging, composition, and so forth.

The pattern language operates at the level of user-visible design rather than at the architectural, design, or implementation levels. Moreover, the pattern language does not assume limitations or requirements imposed by current implementation of such systems, though implementability is crucial.

Short, bold phrases are pattern names.

The summary, positive feedback, and suggestions for improvement that follow this draft pattern were written by Ron Goldman.

Sharing Feelings or Being Clear or Communicating Subtlety

... people want to convey emotions because **No Man Is an Island**, especially when writing an **Intimate Communication**, but even were they to take the time for a **Slow Letter**, some are unable to show their emotions well. In **Workgroups** (**Small Groups Come and Go**) there needs to be a way to keep misunderstandings under control....

Every person needs to convey emotions, share emotions. Ideally you should talk to the other person face-to-face or by telephone, but sometimes circumstances prevent this. Tone of voice, facial expressions, body movements and stances—these are the language even the most inarticulate person learns to convey emotions accurately.

But in words? Conveying emotions well using words takes skill and patience, and even talent. Sometimes even the best writers are unable to convey sincerely what they feel or what they want to say that they feel. For many, the act of trying to convey emotions in words takes them out of those feelings, making it even harder to convey them.

Language is about information, surely, but also about the human condition and spirit. It's our blessing and curse to have to heap so much into language. There are some emotions we are afraid to express directly in front of others: some forms of love, hatred, disgust. It depends on each of us.

Even in a slow letter expressing emotions can be difficult, but especially in short notes or letters when you need to write quickly it is still important to get the emotions right. If, for example, you want to show you are not angry in a hurried letter, this could be hard to do because rapid writing is often curt and sounds to the reading mind like the sentences are cut off. If the recipient is expecting a long letter and receives a short one, what is she to make of this? If she had a clue to the real emotion behind it . . .

In the early days of textual electronic communication, misunderstood sarcasm often sparked fierce disputes, and wisecracks too often prompted avalanches of response postings.

Therefore,

Use emoticons (emotional icons) and avatars (graphical, sometimes animated characters) to convey emotions. As an alternative, establish an emotional communication mechanism that is like a meta-statement—perhaps as parenthetical statements.

Emoticons can express only crudely how we feel, but they can be used to avoid communication blunders. This is especially true if you are writing sarcastically— the use of a friendly glyph can convey the sarcasm that the ineptness of overfast composition belies. These are some simple emoticons:

:-)	Expresses happiness, sarcasm, or joke
:-(	Expresses unhappiness
:-]	Expresses jovial happiness
:-[	Expresses despondent unhappiness
:-D	Expresses jovial happiness
:-I	Expresses indifference
:-\	Indicates undecided, confused, or skeptical
:-Q	Expresses confusion
:-S	Expresses incoherence or loss of words
:-@	Expresses shock or screaming
:-O	Indicates surprise, yelling or realization of an error ("uh oh!")

The emoticon was first used in email in 1982 by the computer scientist Scott Fahlman. He was trying to find a more aesthetically pleasing way to convey that a statement or passage was to be taken as a joke. Earlier, the word "joke" was added after such a passage, but it seemed to Fahlman to be a poor way to convey the emotion.

Build systems that recognize the strengths and weaknesses of people, as well as which fit into the way they work and the tasks they do every day. Carefully observe the failures and breakdowns of our tools and endeavor to improve them over time.

Technical Workshop: Summary

Here is Ron Goldman's summary of the draft pattern from the preceding pages:

> This is a draft of a pattern from a pattern language for designing programs like email and instant messaging in which people communicate textually with each other via computer. The pattern is written in Alexandrian format.
>
> This pattern comes from a part of the pattern language that focuses on the quality of conversation and, in particular, intimate communication and the need to convey the writer's emotions. This happens naturally through body language and tone of voice when two people talk face-to-face. The problem is that conveying emotions is difficult to do in words alone and takes a special skill that many writers are not good at. It is especially hard in quickly written or short notes—media in which the clear expression of the writer's mood may be most needed to avoid a misunderstanding.
>
> The solution given is to indicate emotions via graphics by drawing a "smiley face" like :-) using characters from the regular keyboard, or by drawing an animated character with different expressions, or via regular text set off somehow to indicate its meta-nature.
>
> Eleven sample emoticons are shown along with their meaning. The first use of a smiley face in email is attributed to Scott Fahlman in 1982.
>
> The pattern concludes with a remark that we need to build computer systems appropriate for the human condition and that we should observe where our tools fail and improve them.

Technical Workshop: Positive Feedback

Ron Goldman supplied this feedback for the aforementioned draft pattern:

> The pattern is very well written. It is quite clear and easy to understand. The problem statement flows out of the context and nicely contrasts the richness of nonverbal communication with the purely textual nature of words. The use of the short phrase "But in words?" is a wonderful device to emphasize the contrast. All of the previous sentences are long and somewhat complex, so the short question really punctuates the shift.
>
> The two forces of needing to express emotions to clarify the message and the difficulty of doing so with words are described well. The description of the possible problems of short notes was good.
>
> I especially appreciated the paragraph stating that language is "also about the human condition and spirit." It reinforces the pattern language's intent of creating humane software by focusing on what it means to be human.

It was really nice to have the history of the first use of a smiley included; I hadn't known that anyone could claim credit for them. Including the list of smileys was also good.

Technical Workshop: Suggestions for Improvement

The following are Goldman's suggestions for improvement for the draft pattern piece.

A shorter pattern name would be better: maybe "Conveying Feelings"?

The first sentence seems to wander and is hard to follow. Maybe break it into two shorter sentences: "People want to convey emotions because **No Man Is an Island**, especially when writing an **Intimate Communication**. Even were they to take the time for a **Slow Letter**, some are unable to show their emotions well."

Also in the context, would it be more appropriate to refer to the pattern "Group Discussions" rather than "Workgroups," that is, "In **Group Discussions** there needs to be a way to keep misunderstandings under control . . ."?

How about using some synonyms for "convey"? The third paragraph of the pattern's body uses "convey" four times in as many sentences. Wouldn't "express" or "communicate" also work? For example: "For many, the act of trying to communicate emotions in words takes them out of those feelings, making it even harder to express them."

The sentence "It depends on each of us" doesn't seem quite right. Why "depends"? How about something similar like "It is different for each of us"?

There seems a tendency in the software patterns community when writing a pattern in Alexandrian format to put the problem statement before the "therefore" and the solution after it. I prefer the way Chris Alexander includes a full discussion of the problem and possible solutions in the body and reserves the section after "therefore" for the instructions on how to solve the problem that summarizes the earlier discussion. (For example, see the pattern "Alcoves" where the use of alcoves is fully discussed in the body of the pattern.)

So for this pattern I would move the history of the emoticon to just before the "therefore." I would follow it with the paragraph that starts "Emoticons can express" and the sample emoticons. Then some additional material explaining how avatars have been used in interactive chat systems would be welcome. Maybe even include some images of different avatars expressing various emotions? It would also be good to include some examples of meta-statements, like "<flame on> xxxx <flame off>," and maybe explain how they came from early text formatting commands. It might even be good to include two short text messages, one just plain text and the other with emoticons to temper the message.

Maybe everyone is now familiar with smileys, but it might be good to mention to view them sideways.

Also it might be worth mentioning that people have created thousands of different smileys but only a few are in common use. Maybe mention that there's even a 93-page print emoticon dictionary with 650 examples (Doherty and David Sanderson, *Smileys*, Sebastopol, Calif.: O'Reilly and Associates, 1993).

Once one includes graphics, why not multimedia too? A short voice clip can set the tone for a message, while a background sound track of incidental music can also help establish a mood.

The final remark seems very general and it's not clear how it relates to this pattern in particular. Maybe it belongs in the introduction to the pattern language?

Is this pattern completed by some other patterns in the language? Does it tie into the cultural part of the pattern "Host and Introductions and Culture"?

APPENDIX B

Writing Workshops Guidelines for Feedback

This set of guidelines is used by Linda Elkin, a poet friend who leads workshops in San Francisco. Note that she refers to the author whose work is currently being reviewed as the *reader* and the other workshop participants at that moment as *listeners*.

Writing Workshops
Guidelines for Feedback
by Linda Elkin

Receiving positive feedback on your work is an excellent way to learn and highly underrated. We will *always* begin with a round of positive feedback. Before you begin to revise, it is essential to know what works in your writing: what your strengths are, what is memorable, moving, and interesting.

Readers:
- Take a deep breath before you begin. Continue breathing while reading and while listening to your feedback.
- Tell us where the idea for the piece came from, if you like. For example: "This came from the homework assignment/didn't."
- *Don't apologize* but tell us what stage the writing is in, if you like (rough, second draft, and so on).

- Listen to the feedback comments and assume they are meant to help you. *Do not defend or explain your work.*
- When you are finished reading, there appears to be a thirty-minute silence. Actually, this is about five seconds. This pause will feel longer than it really is. We are gathering our thoughts. Don't worry. Someone *will* speak up soon!
- Take notes. It is very easy to forget what has been said.
- Feel free to ask questions about your work. However, please wait until you have received a full round of feedback. You may wish to come to the workshop with questions in mind or, instead, ask questions sparked by the group's comments.

Listeners:
- Always keep in mind that the purpose of feedback is to help the piece to grow more fully into itself, not to change it into something else.
- We will treat everything we hear as fiction. When you comment on a piece, refer to the character as the woman, the man, the speaker, or some variation of this. Do not refer to the character as "you."
- Give feedback as you'd like to receive it. Quips, jokes, or sarcastic comments, even if kindly meant, are inappropriate.
- It's all right to comment on either the entire piece or on smaller sections.
- Is there a part you didn't understand? What?
- Be specific—is there anything you'd like to hear more of? What is it? Why?
- Tell the writer things you especially liked—write the words or phrases down as you hear them.
- Tell the writer what stayed with you after she finished reading, what you remember most clearly, what was most vivid.
- Is there some important information missing? Did this take you out of the writing?
- Is there any part that stands out as being different in rhythm or tone? (In your opinion, this section might make the piece more powerful, or it might not fit in.)
- Did the writer leave a smoking gun on the mantle? In other words, is something provocative or mysterious mentioned once, but not

again? Point it out, give your opinion on whether it should be left out or expanded on.
- If you've noticed any patterns or themes in this piece, tell the writer. She might have put them in unconsciously and might not be aware of them.
- Don't ask questions, for example, "How do you and your mom get along now?" Instead, tell us how the writing works, or does not work, for you.
- Be brief. If someone else already said what you wanted to say, it's important to let the writer know you agree, but don't repeat the whole thing.
- Feel free to say nothing if you like. It's not mandatory to speak.
- *Feel free to disagree.* This often is where the writer receives the most important information.
- Remember, *your opinion counts*. If you are someone who does not speak up easily, give yourself a push and jump in. For those who comment frequently, be mindful of giving others a chance to speak.

References

Alexander, Christopher. *A Pattern Language.* New York: Oxford University Press, 1977.

———. *The Timeless Way of Building.* New York: Oxford University Press, 1979.

———. "The Perfection of Imperfection." In *Roots and Branches: Contemporary Essays by West Coast Writers*, ed. Howard Junker. San Francisco: ZYZZVA, 1979.

Bayles, David, and Ted Orland. *Art & Fear: Observations on the Perils (and Rewards) of Artmaking.* Santa Barbara, Calif.: Capra Press, 1993.

Bishop, Wendy. *Released into Language: Options for Teaching Creative Writing.* 2nd ed. Portland, Maine: Calendar Islands Publishers, 1998.

Bly, Carol. *Beyond the Writers' Workshop: New Ways to Write Creative Nonfiction.* New York: Anchor Books, 2001.

Brooke, Robert E. *Writing and Sense of Self: Identity Negotiation in Writing Workshops.* Urbana, Ill.: National Council of Teachers of English, 1991.

Carson, Anne. *Economy of the Unlost (Reading Simonides of Keos with Paul Celan).* Princeton, N.J.: Princeton University Press, 1999.

Craige, Betty Jean. *Lorca's Poet in New York: The Fall into Consciousness.* Lexington: University Press of Kentucky, 1977.

Dickey, Christopher. *Summer of Deliverance.* New York: Simon and Schuster, 1998.

Dickey, James. *Self-Interviews.* Edited by Barbara and James Reiss. Baton Rouge: Louisiana State University Press, 1984.

Eagleton, Terry. *Literary Theory: An Introduction.* Minneapolis: University of Minnesota Press, 1996.

Eckstein, Jutta. Interview with author. 6 November 2001.

Einstein, Albert. "What Life Means to Einstein: An Interview by George Sylvester Viereck." *Saturday Evening Post*, 26 October 1929.

Eliot, T. S. *The Sacred Wood: Essays on Poetry and Criticism*. London: Methune, 1920.

Elkin, Linda. Interview with author. 30 November 2001.

Farr, Judith. *The Passion of Emily Dickinson*. Cambridge, Mass.: Harvard University Press, 1992.

Feyerabend, Paul. *Against Method*. 3rd ed. London: Verso, 1993.

Gabriel, Richard P. "Jimmy, Jimmy, Oh Jimmy Mack." *Ploughsharess* 24, no. 4 (1998–1999): 85–86.

Gamma, Erich, et al. *Design Patterns: Elements of Reusable Object-Oriented Software*. Reading, Mass.: Addison-Wesley, 1995.

Goldman, Ron. Interview with author. 30 January 2002.

Hachiya, Kim. "Focus, Focus, Focus." *Nebraska Magazine*. N.d.

Harrison, Neil, Brian Foote, and Hans Rohnert. *Pattern Languages of Program Design 4*. Boston: Addison-Wesley, 2000.

Herman, Gabriel. "Ritualized Friendship and the Greek City." *Classical Journal* 85, no. 2 (1990): 357–358.

Hugo, Richard. *The Triggering Town: Lectures and Essays on Poetry and Writing*. New York: W. W. Norton, 1979.

Hyde, Lewis. *The Gift: Imagination and the Erotic Life of Property*. New York: Vintage Books, 1979.

Johnson, Samuel. *The Rambler*. 4 vols. London: n.p., 1809.

——— . *The Idler*. 2 vols. London: n.p., 1810.

Lorca, Federico García. *In Search of Duende*. New York: New Directions, 1955.

Lorde, Audre. "The Transformation of Silence into Language and Action." In *Sister Outsider: Essays and Speeches*. Freedom, Calif.: Crossing Press, 1984.

Merwin, W. S. *Flower & Hand: Poems 1977–1983*. Port Townsend, Wash.: Copper Canyon Press, 1997.

Morris, Ian. "Gift and Commodity in Archaic Greece." *Man* 21 (1986).

Murch, Walter. Interview by Terry Gross. *Fresh Air*. National Public Radio, 15 April 1996 (rebroadcast 3 August 2001).

Myers, D. G. *The Elephants Teach: Creative Writing Since 1880*. Englewood Cliffs, N.J.: Prentice Hall, 1995.

Neruda, Pablo. *Twenty Poems*. Translated by James Wright and Robert Bly. Madison, Wis.: Sixties Press, 1967.

Perry, Susan K. *Writing in Flow: Keys to Enhanced Creativity*. Cincinnati, Ohio: Writer's Digest Books, 1999.

Pinneo, Joanna. "Working for National Geographic Magazine." *Digital Journalist* 105 (n.d.).

Porter, Browning. Interview with author. 9 October 2001.

Preminger, Alex, and T. V. F. Brogan, eds. *The New Princeton Encyclopedia of Poetry and Poetics*. Princeton, N.J.: Princeton University Press, 1993.

Sanderson, Doherty, and David W. Sanderson. *Smileys*. Sebastopol, Calif.: O'Reilly and Associates, 1993.

Schacter, Daniel L. *Searching for Memory*. New York: Basic Books, 1996.

Schmitt, Richard. Interview with author. 29 June 2001.

Schneider, Pat. *The Writer as an Artist: A New Approach to Writing Alone & with Others*. Amherst, Mass.: Amherst Writers and Artists Press, 1993.

Stafford, William. *Writing the Australian Crawl: Views on the Writer's Vocation (Poets on Poetry)*. Ann Arbor: University of Michigan Press, 1978.

Stevens, Wallace. *The Palm at the End of the Mind*. Edited by Holly Stevens. New York: Vintage Books, 1972.

Thomas, Frank, and Ollie Johnson. *Disney Animation: The Illusion of Life*. New York: Abbeville Press, 1981.

Tufte, Edward R. *The Visual Display of Quantitative Information*. Cheshire, Conn.: Graphics Press, 1983.

———. *Envisioning Information*. Cheshire, Conn.: Graphics Press, 1990.

———. *Visual Explanations: Images and Quantities, Evidence and Narrative*. Cheshire, Conn.: Graphics Press, 1997.

Warren Wilson College, *MFA Program for Writers Handbook*. Rev. ed. Swannanoa, N.C.: n.p., September 1995.

Williams, Joseph M. *Style: Toward Clarity and Grace*. Chicago: University of Chicago Press, 1990.

Wilson, Ian. "Improvident Collision: Strategies of Expression and Formal Containment in the Work of Three Spanish/Spanish-American Poets—Federico García Lorca, César Vallejo, and Antonio Machado." MFA diss., Warren Wilson College, 2000.

Index

"179. Alcoves" pattern by Christopher Alexander
    (quotation), 176
1880
    University of Iowa writers' workshops, 177
1896
    George Cook's "Verse Making" course, 177
1994
    Hillside Group introduction to writers'
        workshops, 5
    software patterns community, writers'
        workshop start, xiv, 4
1998
    technical writers' workshop used for product
        launch, 8
2000
    writers' workshop used for Hillside Group
        evaluation, 9

Acceptance
    See Also Approval; Validation
    fears based on, 29
    of formal workshop setting by software
        community, 47
    process for writer's workshop, shepherd's role,
        97, 100
    summarization as source of, 124

(term description), 29, 124
    as writers' workshop gift, 39
Accommodations (shared)
    as culture component, 79
    danger of not participating in, 183
Accuracy of the claims
    as technical writers' workshop subject, xvi
Actions
    See Also Attitudes and attributes; Emotions;
        Evaluation; Reviewers/reviewing
    negative
        debates among workshop members, 60
        insults, protecting authors from, 112, 144
Active listening
    See Also Listening; Skill(s)
    (term description), 63
Adam and Eve
    transparency and understandability issues, 119
Aesthetics
    See Also Appearance; Style
    concerns
        as creative writers' workshop subject, xvi
        of user-visible patterns, 93
    as danger to appropriate comments, 92
    of "Sentences My Father Used" by Charles
        Bernstein, 120
"Against Method" by Paul Feyerabend, 206

209

AI (artificial intelligence)
    in "Is Jack Gilbert's Mind a Computer" story, 83
Aleshire, Joan
    meaning of poem, reader expectations, 95
Alexander, Christopher
    See Also Pattern(s)
    "179. Alcoves" pattern, (quotation), 176
    as canon member, 80
    Hillside Group relationship to, 5
    "A Pattern Language," 205
        as canon component, 80
        Hillside Group influenced by, 5
        purpose and characteristics, 5
        (quotation), 176
    "The Perfection of Imperfection," 205
        (quotation), 129
    philosophy, user-visible patterns relationship to, 93
    "The Timeless Way of Building," 205
        as canon component, 80
    vocabulary, technical writers' workshop use, 78
Allerton Conference Center
    See Also Conferences; Location
    characteristics of, 79
    as setting for PLoP, 74
Amateur
    vs. professional, practice as differentiator, 37
Amphitheater
    natural, (term description), 73
Anderson, Bruce
    conversion to pattern writers' workshop, 8
Annotation
    See Also Critical, writing; Teaching
    (term description), 182
Anonymous peer review
    See Also Review(s)
    advantages and disadvantages of, 43, 109
    as fly-on-the-wall strategy, 114
    (term description), 43
"Apocalypse Now" film
    preparation and practice activities, 38
Appearance
    See Also Aesthetics; Style
    impact on discussion, 87
    of piece to be workshopped
        issues, 86
        neatness and modesty as a value in, 87
Applause
    as workshop gift to author, in response to author's gift of work-in-progress, 152
Apprehension
    denotation vs. connotation, 119
Approval
    See Also Acceptance; Validation
    fears based on, 29
    (term description), 29, 124
    as writers' workshop gift, 39
Arc
    See Also Cycle
    conflict-crisis-resolution, as fiction craft component, 136
    content classification, ordering of pieces consideration, 85
    emotional
        balancing at end of workshop session, 152
        of the creative cycle, xv
    of maturation
        changes in writers' workshop benefits, 170
        learning from those further along, 168
        ordering of pieces consideration, 85
    in risky making, 161
    transitions characteristic of, 172
    uncertain course, 30
    writers' workshop role in, 173
Art
    See Also Craft; Creativity; Music; Poetry; Writing
    end-point vs. work-in-progress, impact on artist, 33
    making
        commonalties with software making, 28
        flexibility vs. creativity in, 26
        skill development, 39
        triggers role in, 26
    projects, as creativity-loosening exercise, 81
    as source of quality, for positive feedback, 129
"Art and Fear: Observations on the Perils (and Rewards) of Art-making" by David Bayles and Ted Orland, 205
Art of the Wild conference (Squaw Valley)
    See Also Conferences
    Gary Snyder's readings, 82

Attention
    See Also Listening
    fear's deleterious effects on, 30
    by moderator, on author during fly-on-the-wall
        role, 113
    during practice, importance of, 168
    practice combined with, as hallmark of
        professional, 38
    specific requests for, placing after the initial
        reading, 107
    on the work, as antidote to focusing on fear, 30
    value for improving skill in making things, 26
Attitudes and attributes
    See Also Emotions; Negative, attitudes and
        attributes; Positive, attitudes and
        attributes; Work-in-progress
    author, separation from work, 145
    brilliance, as rare commodity, 59
    clarity, creative vs. technical writers'
        workshops, 119
    compassion for one's self, as consequence of
        spirit of generosity, 80
    competitiveness, 42, 58, 141
    of experienced writers, See Experienced
        writers
    generosity, 80
    gentleness, 102
    gift-giving, 80
    of graphics and artwork, as positive feedback
        component, 129
    jealousy, as anonymous peer review
        complication, 43
    kindness, 99
    mean-spiritedness, 59
    of moderator, See Moderator(s)
    negativity, as problem for moderator, 67
    of novices, See Novice(s)
    politeness, workshop success dependent on,
        114
    separation of self from work, importance for
        author, 114
    territoriality, 45, 61
    towards workshop process, creative vs.
        technical community, 41
    of work, that contribute to quality, 129
    work-in-progress as, consequences of, 41
    xenia, 80

Audience(s)
    See Also Role(s)
    in creative vs. technical writers' workshop, 53
    Hillside Group design of rules to permit, 8
    ideal, 55
    impact on setting of workshop, 73
    natural amphitheater arrangement of, 73
    non-participatory, 55
        (term description), 54
    participatory, 55
        preparation for writers' workshops, 85
        (term description), 54
    position and stance, as creative writers'
        workshop subject, xvi
    preparation for workshops by attending as,
        96
    responsibilities of, 55
        during suggestions for improvement, 144
    target
        of book, xvii
        crucial role in assessing technical writing
            comprehensibility, 123
        writing for, obtaining feedback on success
            of, 117
    (term description), 53
    types of, 54
Auditor
    as Bread Loaf term for audience, 73
Author(s)
    See Also Gift(s); Role(s); Safety; Work-in-
        progress
    alternatives to, in initial reading, 106
    audience allowed by, 73
    co-authors, handling of, 54
    creative, benefits of book, xvii
    defensiveness
        avoidance during clarification stage, 147
        disadvantages of, 111
        moderator handling, 112, 148
    development, software pattern community
        practices for, 6
    emotional needs and expectations
        aligning with culture of workshop, 94
        handling during suggestions for
            improvement stage, 144
        impact on success of workshop, 61
        moderator tactics for handling, 132

Author(s) (*cont.*)
   end-point vs. work-in-progress, impact on artist, 33
   experienced
      writers' workshop dangers for, xvii
      writers' workshop impact on, xv
   as expert
      focus on writing, not content a consequence of, 60
      impact on suggestions for improvement stage, 135
   feedback guidelines, (appendix), 201
   as final judge of how to use workshop comments, 156
   fly-on-the-wall role
      difficulties with, 110
      mechanisms for creating illusion, 111
      origins, 3
      role violations, 113
      room formations that support, 72
      workshop success dependent on, 114
      during workshopping, (chapter), 109
   gifts, of work-in-progress, 35
   hopes, in return for gift of work-in-progress, 37
   importance of summary for, 118
   intended reading, notetaking about differences between reader perception and, 118
   introductions of, guidelines for, 75
   limitations, in revising a piece, handling, 143
   location, importance for effectiveness of the workshop, 72
   moderator relationship to
      author's advocate, 144
      during fly-on-the-wall role, 113
      monitoring author's state, 131, 141
   as most important players in writers' workshops, 54
   motives, focus on, as failure cause in creative writers' workshops, 48
   new, writers' workshop impact on, xv
   novice, writers' workshop dangers for, xvi
   obstreperous, moderator handling, 112
   participation, during endpoints of workshop, 149
   posture, importance for effectiveness of the workshop, 72

   preparation for writers' workshops, 85
   questions, during clarifications stage, 147
   reading by, as initial phase of workshop, (chapter), 101
   references to, during workshop, 111
   responsibilities
      deciding if workshop with be of benefit or not, 95
      take what is food for you and leave the rest, 139
   safety
      as consequence of work-in-progress attitude, 41
      protection from insults during workshop, 112
      requirement for success of workshop, 110
      setting importance for, 69
   separation of self from work
      as benefit of writers' workshop, 37
      importance of, 114, 145
      role in art making, 39
      as skill aided by working on other people's work, 16
   special instructions from, placing after the initial reading, 107, 130
   specific workshopping goals, 86
   suggestions for improvement, as pure gifts from the reviewers, 145
   summarization value, 125
   support for, in good suggestions for improvement sessions, 138
   surrogate, situations where needed, 67
   technical, benefits of book, xvii
   termination of fly-on-the-wall role, 147
   thanks, during clarifications stage, 148
   workshop, culture determination in advance by, 94
   as writers' workshop role, 2
Authority
   See Also Moderator(s)
   of author
      respect for in good workshops, 138
      to "take what is food for you and leave the rest," 139
   difficulties with
      when moderator's boss is a workshop participant, 112

when project leader is workshop
participant, 67
of voice, as craft term, 78
Autonomous
See Also Fly-on-the-wall author role
critic, limitations, 34

Background
role in art making, 28
Bailey, Benjamin
John Keats letter to, 185
Balance
as consequence of range of comment types, 133
real power as shepherd, with effective review, 99
Barter
gift economy use, 42
Bass, Rick
dash use by, 162
Bavaria, Germany
as setting for EuroPLoP, 75
Bayles, David
"Art and Fear: Observations on the Perils (and Rewards) of Art-making," 205
Beck, Kent
Hillside Group relationship to, 5
Behavior
See Also Responsibilities
boundaries, interaction with gift ethos, 58
family-like, in writers' workshops, 58
humane, ritual setting support for, 46
norms
establishment of in on-going workshops, 69
impact on the experience, 2
patterns of, as culture component, 77
rules
importance in suggestions for improvement stage, 143
as shared culture component, 37
stylized, of writers' workshop, 2
swarming, writers' workshop compared with, xiv
Bell-shaped distribution
of experience levels, recommendations, 56
of writing levels, 130

Benefits
See Also Gift(s); Xenia
for author, responsibility of author to determine, 95
of diversity, for experienced writers, 68
of group practices, (chapter), 11
of listening, applying to one's own work, 15
for novices, of experienced moderators, 32
psychological, of separation of author from work, 37
of release early phenomenon, 17
writers' workshops, xvii
affirmation, 173
to author, (quotation), 35
craft understanding and skill improvement, 15
education in selection and critical skills, 39
experience level changes in, 170
for experienced writers, 39, 165
of novice moderator training, 63
(quotation), 95
reflection on craft issues, 16
separation of author from work, 37
Bernstein, Charles
"Controlling Interests," (footnote), 120
"Sentences My Father Used," (quotation), 120
"Berryman" by W. S. Merwin
(quotation), 167
"Beyond the Writers' Workshop: New Ways to Write Creative Nonfiction" by Carol Bly, 205, 183
Bibliography
(chapter), 205
"big picture"
shallow and broad review handling of, 91
Biological breaks
inter-session ritual use, 153
Bishop, Elizabeth
as canon member, 80
Bishop, Wendy
"Released Into Language: Options for Teaching Creative Writing," 205, 183
Bly, Carol
"Beyond the Writers' Workshop: New Ways to Write Creative Nonfiction," 205, 183
Bly, Robert
translation of Pablo Neruda's "Twenty Poems," 182

Bobrow, Daniel
   reference-counting garbage collector work, 135
Bonds
   See Also Culture
   exercises that build, as software pattern community practice, 6
   of the gift economy, 41
   gifts role in forming, 49
Boss
   See Authority
Boulder Creek meeting
   development of software pattern community practices at, 6
   of Hillside Group, 5
Brain
   emotionally disturbed children, writers' workshop-like work with, 19
   writing mechanisms within, 18, 178
Brainstorming
   See Also Group(s), types of activities
   as fertile source of rituals for writers' workshops, 81
   as group activity that assists the individual, 11
   as group practice that aids individual creativity, 1
   -like mode, dynamic comment process like, 91
   as short-term collaboration, 14
   (term description), 11
   writers' workshop compared with, xiv
Bread Loaf Writers' Conference
   See Also Conferences; Location
   Alan Shapiro denotative gloss advocacy, 104
   audience
      as part of, 53
      permitted at, 73
   characteristics of, 78
   as creative writers' workshop, 2
   culture of, 69
   as established creative writers' workshop, 77
   getting there, as part of the culture, 78
   workshop leader characteristics, 64
   as workshop with relatively uniform expertise and expectation level, 61
Brilliance
   See Also Attitudes and attributes
   as rare commodity, 59

Brogan, T. V. F.
   "New Princeton Encyclopedia of Poetry and Poetics," 206
Brooke, Robert E.
   "Writing and Sense of Self: Identity Negotiation in Writing Workshops," 205, 183
"but"
   deleterious effects of, in positive feedback stage, 131

Canon
   See Also Culture
   readings as instrument for building a, 81
   writers' workshops, 80
Carson, Anne
   "Economy of the Unlost," 205
   xenia definition in, 181
Cezanne, Paul
   art as selected details, 15
Chaos
   See Also Order; Pattern(s); Structure(s)
   emergence of order from, writers' workshop compared with, xiv
Charrette(s)
   See Also Group(s), types of activities
   design
      face-to-face interaction in, 14
      as group practice that aids individual creativity, 1
   as group activity that assists the individual, 12
   (term description), 12
Chemistry
   See Attitudes and attributes
"Childhood and Poetry" by Pablo Neruda, 182
ChiliPLoP (Arizona) conference
   See Also Conferences
   as established technical writers' workshop, 78
   Neruda, Pablo, (quotation), 49
   as regional PLoP conference, 177
   writing practice in, 83
Chip
   CPU, normal distribution in manufacture of, 180

Circle
    See Also Structure(s)
    as ideal layout for room, 71
Circumstances
    See Also Triggers
    role in art making, 28
Clapton, Eric
    impromptus, 178
Clarification/clarity
    See Also Attitudes and attributes; Stages of the writers' workshop
    creative vs. technical workshop issues, 119
    as goal of work summary, 117
    request by moderator, as exception to author silence rule, 111
    stage, of writers' workshop, (chapter), 147
    thought, as writing improvement component, xv
Classification
    See Also Structure(s); Types of
    of pieces, by moderator, as part of review order determination, 93
Classroom-style organization
    deleterious effects on writers' workshops, 71
Cliques
    as shared culture danger, 183
Clock rate
    of CPU chips, normal distribution of, 180
Close reading
    See Also Tools
    as pedagogical tool, 181
    writers' workshop as a form of, 2
Closure
    emotional, as work of wrapping up stage, 151
Co-authors
    See Also Author(s)
    handling of, 54
Co-ownership
    See Also Author(s); Ownership; Shared; Work-in-progress
    suggestions for improvement stage threat to, 141
    temporary, as hallmark of best workshops, 138
Coda
    the work of making things, (chapter), 167

Code review
    See Also Review(s); Writers' workshops, format
    writers' workshop format use with, 18
Collaboration
    See Also Face-to-face interaction; Group(s); Interaction(s); Shared evaluation
    advantages, 13
    open source as example of value, 14
    in making things, power of, 168
    pair writing, as activity that assists the individual writer, 12
    practices that benefit individuals, (chapter), 11
    role in writers' workshop "midwife" job, 20
    work-in-progress evaluation, value of, 34
Colleagues
    as review resource, 43
Color
    of graphics and artwork, as positive feedback component, 129
Comments
    See Also Feedback; Improvement; Responsibilities; Teaching
    appropriate
        aesthetics not a subject for, 92
        ignorance as danger to, 92
    content as subject for, creative vs. technical writers' workshops, 139
    contradictory reviewer, subjective nature of writing indicated by, 139
    creative vs. technical writers' workshops, 87, 88
    different types depending on stage of the piece, 86
    dynamics, of workshop process, 90
    effective, in suggestions for improvement stage, 138
    from experienced writers, importance of, 164
    framing as questions, 100
    inappropriate, dangers of, xvii
    interrelated, as skilled moderator tool, 62
    moderator preparation and use, 94
    negative, during positive feedback, deleterious impact on safety, 132
    order of, importance for maximizing authorial comfort, 70

Comments (*cont.*)
    positive
        bad effects of requiring reviewers to provide, 132
        Sandra McPherson door-to-door comments, 102
        as tactic for providing emotional closure, 151
    by shepherd, importance of establishing the right tone, 98
    shorthand, for repeated phrases, 133
    types of
        author preferences, 87
        in suggestions for improvement stage, 138
        understanding of the work impact on, 118
        work-focused, as goal, 92
        workshop, handling in post-workshop revision process, 155
    written
        giving to author, 153
        value for experienced writer, 172
Commitments
    See Also Attitudes and attributes
    importance of shepherd keeping, 98
Commodity economy
    See Also Economy; Gift(s)
    vs. gift economy, 42
    law of diminishing returns in, 181
    operations in parallel with gift economy, 42
    (term description), 42
Commonalties
    See Also Culture
    of purpose, safe setting created by, 71
    in risky making, 25
    in software and art making, 28
Communication
    See Also Creative writers' workshops, vs. technical writers' workshops
    crucial importance in technical writing, 116
    reading out loud reinforcement of, 102
Communities
    See Also Conferences; Creative writing; Culture; Group(s); Pattern(s); Shared
    bond-buidling exercises, in software pattern community, 6
    creative writing
        Community of Writers Workshop in Poetry (Squaw Valley), 77, 82
        cross fertilization with software community insights and practices, xviii
        history of writers' workshops, xiv
        history of writers' workshops, 1, 2
    culture, as consequence of work-in-progress attitude, 41
    gift economy
        dynamics in, 41
        failure to recognize, as source of workshop failure, 41
        as writers' workshop salient characteristic, 39
    initiation of, as consequence of work-in-progress attitude, 41
    literature-building, writers' workshop as ritual within, 80
    open source, "release early, release often" maxim, 17
    software
        cross fertilization with creative writing community insights and practices, xvii
        formal setting acceptance by, 47
        patterns, Hillside Group introduction to writers' workshops, 5
        patterns, literature building efforts, 6
        patterns, writers' workshop history, xiv, 7
    supportive, writers' workshop as, 172
    of trust
        enhancement by authors staying together for duration of workshop, 70
        safe setting created by, 71
    work-in-progress, shared purpose and culture of, 37
    writing arts, shepherding limitations, 46
Community of Writers Workshop in Poetry (Squaw Valley)
    as established creative writers' workshop, 77
    See Also Conferences
    writing on location at, 82
Companies
    See Organization(s)
Compassion
    See Also Attitudes and attributes
    for one's self, as consequence of spirit of generosity, 80
Competition
    See Also Economy
    commodity economy role, 42

deleterious impact on gift ethos, 58
within technical workshops, as danger in suggestions for improvement stage, 141
Completion
See Also Work-in-progress
knowing when work has reached, 166
level of work, determining when ready to be workshopped, 17
Comprehension
context dependence, in technical writing, 123
creative vs. technical workshop issues, 119
failure of, eliciting reasons for, 165
Computer chips
normal distribution in manufacture of, 180
Computing
vocabulary, technical writers' workshop use, 78
Conferences
See Also Art of the Wild conference (Squaw Valley); Bread Loaf Writers' Conference; ChiliPLoP (Arizona) conference; EuroPLoP (European Pattern Languages of Programs) conference; KoalaPLoP (Australia) conference; Mensore PLoP (Japan) conference; Napa Valley Writers's Conference; PLoP (Pattern Languages of Programs) conference; Sewanee Writers' Conference; Squaw Valley; SugarLoafPLoP (Latin America) conference; UP (Using Patterns) conference; Writers' workshops
anonymous peer review process, 44
crowded accommodations, as technical writers' workshop practice, 8
multi-workshop
genres as partitioning mechanism in, 82
leader rotation in, 82
software pattern community, 6
writers' workshop, as alternative to, xiv
Confusion
See Also Attitudes and attributes; Emotions
creative workshop handling of, 120
handling
creative vs. technical writers' workshops, 122
in suggestions for improvement, 184
implicit presence of triggers as cause of, 117

masking of, work summary as tool for avoiding, 123
uncovering, as role of work summary, 120
Connotations
vs. denotation, 119
vs. literal meaning, 119
unintended, work summary uncovering of, 117
Constructed works
structure and craft, as creative writers' workshop subject, xvi
Content
See Also Craft; Structure(s); Writing
as appropriate topic for discussion, tension around, 139
author as expert on, 59
classification arc, ordering of pieces consideration, 85
craft focus vs., author as expert attitude support of, 60
experience, impact on writers' workshop, 56
focus on
as failure cause in creative writers' workshops, 47
as failure cause in technical writers' workshop, 48
not responding to, importance in emotionally-disturbed children story, 19
strategies for deflecting discussion on, 66
technical, handling of, 59
in technical writing, privileged over writing quality, 140
well-explored, handling in creative workshops, 140
when appropriate to discuss, 66
writing as releaser of, 19
Context
See Also Setting
dependence, for comprehension, in technical writing, 123
establishing
initial reading role in, 104
opening remarks guidelines, 75
pedagogical
examples of, 84
fly-on-the-wall strategy can work with anonymous review, 114
impact on participant qualifications, 56

Context (*cont.*)
    interaction of craft lectures and
        workshopping process, 62
    setting of workshop, 84
    remote and rural, as part of the culture, 78
    safe, creating a context that enhances, 25
    of specific work, workshop benefits, 16
"continuous integration"
    as extreme programming maxim, 17
Contributions
    benefits of, in creative writers workshop, 15
Contributors
    in creative writers' workshops, (term
        description), 182
"Controlling Interests" by Charles Bernstein
    (footnote), 120
Cook, George
    "Verse Making" course, 177
Courage
    as secret to work of making things, 167
    (term description), 167
Craft
    See Also Art; Creativity; Music; Poetry;
        Skill(s); Teaching; Tools; Writing
    discussions, creative workshop difficulties
        with, 140
    elements
        as creative writers' workshop subject, xvi
        example of workshop focus on, 187
        examples of, 89
        of software patterns, 139
    expertise, impact on writers' workshop, 56
    focus on, as releasing mechanism, 20
    improvement
        critique based on craft importance, 31
        suggestions for improvement stage, 135
        tools for, 89
        tools for, practice and reflection as, 21
        writing about craft elements, 84
    issues, in context of specific work, 16
    knowledge, role in art making, 28
    language for poets, 141
    lectures
        as component of national workshops, 81
        in creative writers' workshops, 62
    mastery
        habits of professionals, 37
        workshop moderators, in creative vs.
            technical writers' workshops, 64
    Maxine Kumin's approach to, 65
    of Michelangelo, 178
    pedagogical principles, for effective
        development, 141
    vs. Romantic preference for nature, 140
    skills, revision, (chapter), 155
    terms, 78
    topics, in creative writers' workshops, 164
    trigger transformation, workshop help with, 136
    understanding, as benefit of workshopping, 15
    writers' workshop applicability, 2
Craige, Betty Jean
    "Lorca's Poet in New York: The Fall into
        Consciousness," 205
Creative writers' workshops
    See Also Teaching; Technical writers'
        workshops; Writers' workshops; Writing
    advanced workshop characteristics, 171
    Alan Shapiro denotative gloss advocacy, 104
    audience generally not part of, 55
    author as expert implications, 60
    benefits, studying with experts as, 173
    canon, 80
    craft
        discussions, difficulties with, 140
        topics in, 164
    dumbing down danger, 123
    examples
        of well-known, 77
        of workshop experiences, 187
    experienced moderators, gift economy and, 182
    failure causes, 41, 47
    feedback guidelines, (appendix), 201
    fly-on-the-wall role violations in, 113
    history of, xiv
    intimacy of, 35
    leaders
        skills, 61
        strategies for deflecting content discussion, 66
        as teachers, 67
    listening, benefits of, 15

participating in discussions, benefits of, 15
rewriting poems in, 14
   dangers of, 93
shepherding limitations, 46
strategies for maintaining focus on work, 70
subjects and concerns of, xvi
summarization example, 190
vs. technical writers' workshops
   aggressiveness in, 185
   attitudes towards workshop process, 41
   audience, 53, 55
   benefits of workshop, 170
   clarity and understanding of work, 119
   comment range, 164
   comparison, xvi
   content as subject for comments, 139
   craft expertise of workshop moderators, 64
   expert writers as moderators, 173
   explanations in initial reading of work, 105
   family-like behavior in, 58
   fly-on-the-wall role, 72
   formal setting adherence differences, 57
   game types, 81
   handling confusion in, 121, 122
   initial reading, 101
   shallow review advantages, 92
   suggestions for improvement tactics, 136
   summarization of piece as area of greatest difference, 3
   summary of work, 115, 116
   teaching role of moderator, 94
   things to look for in suggestions for improvement stage, 137
   transparency and understandability in, 119
   types of comments appropriate to, 87
   types of feedback from, 88
   value of good writing in its own right, 90
(term description), xiv, xviii
vocabulary of, 78
where to find, 2
workshop leader characteristics, 64
Creative writing
   See Also Technical, writing; Writers' workshops; Writing
   benefits of book for, xvii

communities
   cross fertilization with software community insights and practices, xviii
   informality preferences, 47
craft expertise, impact on writers' workshop, 56
detail selection, personal vs. needs of the piece, 15
vs. software writing, writer vulnerabilities, 48
(term description), xiv, xviii
transparency and understandability in, 119
Creativity
   See Also Gift(s); Practice(s); Triggers
   Albert Einstein quotation, 27
   criticism risks, creating a context that reduces, 25
   duende relationship to, 33
   enhancement of, by craft discussion in the context of a specific work, 16
   flexibility vs., role in art making, 26
   games as stimulant to, 81
   group practices that aid, 1
   process cycle, writer's workshop role, xv
   triggers relationship to, 26
Critical
   reading
      annotation as tool for, 182
      pedagogical value, 181
   skills, role in art making, 39
   writing, about craft elements, as pedagogical tool, 84
Criticism
   See Also Comments; Feedback; Responsibilities
   avoidance, importance in emotionally-disturbed children story, 19
   craft-based, importance for improvement, 31
   damage control importance, 68
   effective, writers' workshop facilitation of, 2
   experience with, impact on writers' workshop, 57
   group, vs. private act of writing, as writers' workshop paradox, xv
   guidelines, experience level buffering by, 57
   harsh, impact on novices, 32
   initial concerns about, by Hillside Group, 7
   New Critics, philosophy, 3

Criticism (*cont.*)
  positive suggestions importance as companion to, 144
  requirement that possible fix be included along with, 4
  risks of, creating a context that reduces, 25
  during suggestions for improvement stage, dangers of, 135
  as tool for discovering avenues of improvement, during suggestions for improvement stage, 135
Critiques
  See Also Group(s), types of activities
  as group activity that assists the individual, 11
  as short-term collaboration, 14
  (term description), 11
Cross-fertilization
  See Also Creative writers' workshops, vs. technical writers' workshops
  of both technical and creative writing communities, as goal of stories and examples, xviii
  of technical writing community, with creative writing workshop insights and practices, xvii
Crowd
  See Group(s)
Crucible
  See Also Gift(s), economy; Metaphors for writers workshop; Transformation
  as metaphor for writers' workshop, xvii
Culture
  See Also Bonds; Canon; Communities; Context; Games; Gift(s); Group(s); Ritual(s); Setting; Shared; Xenia
  author support, in "Is Jack Gilbert's Mind a Computer" story, 83
  of community, as consequence of work-in-progress attitude, 41
  daily newspapers, as component of, 79
  differences, between Europe and US, 72
  existing workshops, known setting as advantage of, 69
  games role in creating, 81
  geographical setting for workshop impact on, 77
  impact
    of setting on, 74
    on type of preparation required, 85
  reasons why it works, 80
  route for getting there as component of, 78
  shared
    accommodations as component of, 79
    cliques as danger of, 183
    stories as component of, 80
    of work-in-progress community, 37
  shepherd as part of, 97
  summary of its value, 84
  (term description), 77
  vocabulary as part of
    in creative writers' workshops, 78
    in technical writers' workshops, 78
  of Warren Wilson MFA program, 79
  workshop, shepherd as representative of, 98
  of writers' workshop
    ascertaining in advance, 94
    impact on the experience, 2
Cunningham, Ward
  as first author to be workshopped in the software patterns community, 8
Cycle
  See Also Arc
  creative process, writer's workshop role, xv
  of shepherd/author interactions, 97

da Vinci, Leonardo
  "Mona Lisa," poem about, illustration of author limitations issues, 143
da Volterra, Daniele
  as defacer of Michelangelo's "The Last Judgment," 179
"The Daily Crumb" newsletter
  as Bread Loaf daily workshop newsletter, 79
Damage
  See Also Criticism; Emotions; Moderator(s), responsibilities; Ritual(s); Safety
  control of
    failure, in product launch workshop story, 67, 142
    importance for effective listening, 68
  of lazy reviewing, 90
  to members, of criticism, 68

Dangers
   See Also Benefits; Gift(s); Negative; Responsibilities; Safety; Setting
   of approval- and acceptance-based fears, 30
   criticism
      people just waiting to criticize, 132
      during suggestions for improvement stage, 135
   of dependence on writers' workshop for motivation, 185
   destructive
      dynamics, generosity amelioration of, xv
      dynamics, in product launch workshop story, 142
      workshop leaders, 103
   dumbing down
      of accepting comments from writers who don't understand what you said, 166
      in creative workshops, 123
      (quotation), 165
   ignorance, to appropriate comments, 92
   of inappropriate comments, for both experienced and inexperienced writers, xvii
   of intimacy of writers' workshop, 41
   of not participating in shared accommodations, 183
   about question-asking tactics, 144
   reviewer rewriting, dangerous and inappropriate nature, 93
   of self-organized workshops, 66
   of shared culture, cliques as, 183
   of suggestions for improvement stage
      competitive attitude, 141
      focus on criticism, 135
   of work-in-progress, ameliorating, 69
   workshop pattern, 163
   of writers' workshops, as initially viewed by the Hillside Group, 7
Dante
   "Inferno," moderator compared to the guide Virgil, 72
Dash
   Emily Dickinson use, 162, 185
   Rick Bass use, 162
   semantic value of, 162
"David" by Michelangelo
   skills and "tricks" used to create, 178

Deadline
   workshop use as, by experienced writers, 163, 172
"The Death of the Last Centaur" statue
   as Allerton Park feature, 79
Debates
   See Also Actions; Dangers; Negative
   among workshop members, drawbacks of, 60
Defensiveness
   See Also Attitudes and attributes; Negative, attitudes and attributes
   by author
      moderator handling, 112, 148
      technical culture role in producing, 185
   avoidance during clarification stage, 147
   disadvantages of, 111
Degree programs
   See Also Teaching; University of Iowa; Warren Wilson College MFA program
   impact on participant qualifications, 56
Delight
   See Also Positive
   identifying parts of work that, in positive feedback stage, 127
Denotation
   vs. connotation, 119
   gloss, Alan Shapiro advocacy, 104
Depth review
   See Review(s)
Design
   See Art, making; Craft; Structure(s)
Design charrette
   face-to-face interaction in, 14
   as group practice that aids individual creativity, 1
"Design Patterns: Elements of Reusable Object-Oriented Software" by Gamma et al., 206
   See Also Pattern(s)
   as canon component for software patterns community, 80
   "Gang of Four" as name for, 78
   Hillside Group role in development of, 5
Destructive
   See Also Dangers; Negative, attitudes and attributes; Safety
   dynamics
      generosity amelioration of, xv
      in product launch workshop story, 142

Destructive (*cont.*)
 workshop leaders, hard judgmental poetry workshop leader story, 103
Details
 irrelevant, detecting and handling of, 15
 role in summary of work stage, 115
 selection of, creative writing, personal vs. needs of the piece, 15
Determination
 See Also Actions; Responsibilities
 of acceptance, as shepherd's power, 100
 of culture, by workshop authors, 94
 of finished appearance level, impact on work-in-progress impression, 86
 of piece review order, by moderator, 93
 of when a work is ready to be workshopped., 17
 of workshop
  appropriateness, as author responsibility, 95
  style, 94
Deutsch, Peter
 reference-counting garbage collector work, 135
Deviance
 positive, (term description), 130
Dickey, Christopher
 "Summer of Deliverance," 205
Dickey, James
 revision practices, 157
 "Self-Interviews," 205
Dickinson, Emily
 as canon member, 80
 dash use by, 162, 185
Difficulties
 See Also Attitudes and attributes; Dangers; Skill(s); Tools
 authority
  when moderator's boss is a workshop participant, 112
  when project leader is workshop participant, 67
 of building a literature, software pattern community solutions to, 6
 with craft discussions, creative writers' workshops, 140
 discussion, deeply buried nature of language as source of, 140

of experienced writers, 131
with fly-on-the-wall role
 for author, 110
 for author, (quotation), 114
in hearing, during positive feedback, 184
in listening, during positive feedback, 132
of notetaking, recommendations, 88
of work, as property of risky making, 25
of writing, xiii
Dignity of author
 See Also Attitudes and attributes; Dangers; Gift(s); Moderator(s), responsibilities; Safety
 enhancement by focus on work, 70
 preservation of, as requirement for success of workshop, 110
Direction
 See Also Author(s)
 writers' workshop role in finding, xv
Director
 weak moderator viewed as, 64
Discovery
 See Also Creativity
 writing as tool for, 19, 168
Discussion(s)
 See Also Feedback; Teaching
 benefits of participating in, 15
 content
  strategies for deflecting, 66
  tension around, 139
  when appropriate, 66
 craft
  creative workshop difficulties with, 140
  generative aspects, 16
  postmodern relativism as barrier, 140
 difficulties, deeply buried nature of language as source of, 140
 groups, as component of national workshops, 81
 impact of appearance on, 87
 poetry
  "Is Jack Gilbert's Mind a Computer," 83
  "Of Mere Being" by Wallace Stevens, 121
  "Sentences My Father Used" by Charles Bernstein, 120
 "Disney Animation: The Illusion of Life" by Frank Thomas and Ollie Johnson, 207

Dissociation
    See Separation of author from work
Distinctive environment
    See Also Context; Setting
    as source of strength in writers' workshops, 81
Distortions
    See Also Craft; Tools
    as Michelangelo craft tool, 178
Distribution
    See Also Arc; Cycle
    of experience levels, recommendations, 56
    normal
        role in manufacture of computer chips, 180
        (term description), 179
    of quality, within a piece, differentiating, 130
    role in art making, 181
    statistical, quality assurance use of, 181
Diversity
    See Also Attitudes and attributes
    of experience
        bridging, as moderator role, 58
        value for group of experienced writers, 68
    of reviewers, strong advantage of, 91
    of revision strategies, in good suggestions for improvement sessions, 138
"Do I eat a peach"
    as interpretation of "Time Leaves," 187
Dobyns, Stephen
    stealing recommendations, 161
Documentation
    review of, writers' workshops as replacement for, 4
Dogs
    See Also Stories
    two skinny dogs in plaza of Taos Pueblo story, 102
        followup experience, 104
Doing
    See Practice(s)
Domain(s)
    See Also Author(s); Content
    author as expert on, 59
    expertise issues, technical writers' workshops, 56
Donne, John
    as canon member, 80
Door-to-door comments story, 102

Drafts
    See Also Piece(s); Revision; Work-in-progress
    early
        drawbacks of workshopping when too rough, 17
        as inappropriate for some workshops, 85
        when to workshop, 86
        workshopping length for, 86
        workshops designed to handle, 17
    written at the workshop, workshops designed to handle, 17
Dubus, Andre
    craft elements, 89
Duende
    belief about creativity's relationship to, 33
    semantics of, 178
    (term description), 178
Dumbing down as danger
    of accepting comments from writers who don't understand what you said, 166
    in creative workshops, 123
    (quotation), 165
    in uncritical acceptance of all comments, 163
Duration
    impact on nature and depth of involvement, 14
    of stay, importance for building community of trust, 70
    of workshop sessions, 4
        as indicator of workshop style, 70
Dynamics
    See Also Attitudes and attributes
    of comment process, 90
    destructive
        generosity amelioration of, xv
        in product launch workshop story, 142
    gift economy, 42
    group
        inter-session rituals importance for managing, 153
        moderator balancing, 144
        moderator impact on, 64
        moderator sensitivity requirement, 63

Eagleton, Terry, 205
Eckstein, Jutta
    interview with the author, 205

Economy
  See Also Culture
  commodity
    vs. gift economy, 42
    law of diminishing returns in, 181
    operations in parallel with gift economy, 42
    (term description), 42
  gift
    as code of ethics source, 80
    vs. commodity economy, 42
    experienced moderators and, 182
    as factor in lives of poets, 174
    failure to recognize, as source of workshop failure, 41
    group transformation through magic of, 49
    operations in parallel with commodity economy, 42
    vs. paid moderators, as writers' workshop paradox, xv
    (term description), 41
    as writers' workshop salient characteristic, 39
"Economy of the Unlost" by Anne Carson, 205
  xenia definition in, 181
Education
  See Teaching
Effective
  See Also Benefits; Tools
  author strategy, in handling multiple review comments, 138
  comments, in suggestions for improvement stage, 138
  craft discussions, deleterious effect of postmodern relativism on, 140
  criticism, writers' workshop facilitation of, 2
  families, writers' workshop comparison to, 49
  improvement
    standard review vs. writers' workshop, 4
    suggestions, question-asking tactics, 144
  leaders, Maxine Kumin's style, 65
  practice
    selection as strategy for, 166
    writing poems every day, 160
  review process, balancing power of shepherd with, 99
  work, fear's deleterious effects on, 30
  writers' workshops
    arrangement of people importance for, 71
    author location importance for, 72
    factors that influence, 2
    hallmarks of, 149
    room layout importance for, 71
    sound environment importance for, 74
Einstein, Albert
  (quotation), 27
  "What Life Means to Einstein: An Interview by George Sylvester Viereck," 206
"The Elephants Teach: Creative Writing Since 1880" by D. G. Myers, 206
  history of writers' workshops in, 177
Eliot, T. S.
  (quotation), 171
  "The Sacred Wood: Essays on Poetry and Criticism," 206
  (quotation), 162
Elkin, Linda
  interview with the author, 206
  "Writing Workshops: Guidelines for Feedback," (appendix), 201
Email
  See Also Communication; Structure(s); Tools
  relationship, style of, between shepherd and author, 99
  shepherd interaction use, 97
Emergent
  See Also Teaching, writing; Work-in-progress
  expertise, as writers' workshop characteristic, 69
  order, in writers' workshops, xiv
Emoticons
  Scott Fahlman as inventor of, 196
  workshopping example, 196
Emotions
  See Also Actions; Attitudes and attributes; Confusion; Fear; Response; Trust
  bringing to closure, during wrapping up stage, 151
  creative cycle arc, xv
  disturbed children
    importance of focus on writing, not content, 60
    writers' workshop-like work with, 19
  and expectations of authors, impact on success of workshop, 61

jealousy, as anonymous peer review
  complication, 43
 in risky making vs. repetitive making, 29
 workshop members as experts with respect to
  their own, 60
 writers' workshop evocation of, xvii
Emptiness
 See Also Attitudes and attributes
 of self, as characteristic of gift giving, 49
Encouragement
 See Also Attitudes and attributes; Setting
 for author, in good suggestions for
  improvement sessions, 138
 of humane behavior, ritual setting support for,
  46
 of novice, in writers' workshops, 39
 of trust, work-in-progress gift support for,
  47
End-points
 See Also Clarification/clarity, stage; Initial
  reading stage
 of work, beliefs about importance of, 33
 of workshop
  author participation in, 149
  value of ritualization, 108
Environment
 See Setting
"Envisioning Information" by Edward R. Tufte,
  207
Equivocation
 See Also Attitudes and attributes
 potential negative aspects, warding against in
  positive feedback stage, 131
Errors
 See Also Improvement; Safety; Suggestions for
  improvement; Work-in-progress
 collaborative evaluation advantages for
  locating, 13
 factual and literature-review, handling, in
  suggestions for improvement stage,
  135
Essay
 (term description), 168
Ethics
 See Also Attitudes and attributes; Dangers;
  Gift(s); Responsibilities
 gift economy as source of, 80

EuroPLoP (European Pattern Languages of
  Programs) conference
 See Also Conferences
 audiences permitted at, 73
 as established technical writers' workshop, 2, 77
 as regional PLoP conference, 177
 setting for, 74
 writing on location at, 82
 writing practice in, 83
Evaluation
 See Also Actions; Improvement;
  Reviewers/reviewing
 collaborative, advantages, 13
 Hillside Group, technical writers' workshop
  use for, 9
 organizational
  of Hillside Group, initial reading in, 105
  questions that might be asked, 9
  writers' workshop use for, 8
 public, in writers' workshop, vs. act of writing, xv
 shepherd's role in, 97
 work-in-progress
  value of collaboration in, 34
  writers' workshop participants investment
   in, 15
Examination
 See Also Craft; Teaching; Tools
 of craft masters, as tool for learning writing, 89
Examples
 See Also Quotations; Stories; Tactics;
  Teaching
 (chapter), 187
 of collaborative evaluation advantages for
  identifying problems, 13
 of creative writers' workshop
  positive feedback and suggestions for
   improvement, 187
  summarization, 190
 of difficulties in listening during positive
  feedback, 184
 example of software pattern, (quotation), 177
 patterns, "179. Alcoves" pattern from "A
  Pattern Language," 176
 purpose of, xviii
 of question-asking tactic in suggestions for
  improvement stage, "Jimmy, Jimmy, O
  Jimmy Mc," 144

Examples (*cont.*)
　of summarization, in creative writers' workshops, 190
　of tactics for approaches to suggestions for improvement
　　creative writers' workshop, 136
　　technical writers' workshop, 136
　of technical writers' workshop
　　Hillside Group introduction to notion of, 4
　　for product launch in 1998, 8
　　for product launch in 1998, as example of nightmare scenario, 142
　　workshopping a software pattern, 195
　of writers' workshop, for organization evaluation in 2000, 9
Exemplars
　See Also Examples; Stories; Teaching
　teaching role in software patterns community, 6
　of writing and writing process, as goal of Part 1-"The Work of Making Things," xvii
Expectations
　See Also Attitudes and attributes; Emotions
　author, aligning with culture of workshop, 94
　emotional needs and, of authors, impact on success of workshop, 61
　impact of piece's appearance on, 86
　of workshop, unexpected riches, 95
Experience(s)
　See Also Culture; Guidelines; Responsibilities; Setting
　with content, impact on writers' workshop, 56
　with criticism, impact on writers' workshop, 57
　desired, reflection on, as preparation for the workshop, 92
　diversity of, value for group of experienced writers, 68
　levels
　　impact on workshop, 55
　　recommendations, 56
　　workshop leader role in bridging and teaching, 58
　preparation for, as part of author preparation, 89
　shared, as binding force for workshop participants, 78
　similarity of, importance for a new group, 68

　types of
　　craft or technical expertise, 56
　　with criticism of one's work, 57
　　with workshops, 57
　　writing ability, 57
　of workshop moderators, range of, 61
　　with workshops, impact on writers' workshop, 57
　writing ability, impact on writers' workshop, 57
Experienced writers
　See Also Novice(s)
　attitudes towards writers' workshops, 171
　difficulties experienced by, 131
　diversity benefits for, 68
　revision tactics, 163
　types of comments useful for, 87
　workshop
　　benefits, 39, 165
　　piece avoidance, 163
　　use, 163
Expertise
　See Also Novice(s); Teaching
　in alternative areas, as advantage of collaborative evaluation, 13
　of author
　　advantages, 61
　　impact on suggestions for improvement stage, 135
　contact with, as writers' workshop benefit, 173
　distinguishing among types of, 60
　emergent, as writers' workshop characteristic, 69
　as gift of non-author leaders, 68
Explanations
　See Also Guidelines; Moderator(s), responsibilities; Teaching
　in initial reading
　　guidelines, 102
　　guidelines, for how much to say, 104
Exploration
　See Also Tools
　of mind contents, writing as tool for, 19
Extreme programming
　See Also Open source; Pair, programming
　"continuous integration" maxim, 17

Face-to-face interaction
    See Also Collaboration
    absence in anonymous peer review, 44
    brainstorming, 14
    design charrettes, 14
    pair programming, 14
    in reviews, disadvantages of, 109
Fact(s)
    See Also Content; Craft
    handling errors of, in suggestions for
        improvement stage, 135
    as technical writers' workshop subject, xvi
Fahlman, Scott
    as emoticon inventor, 196
Failure(s)
    See Also Emotions; Guidelines;
        Responsibilities; Safety; Setting
    in creative writers' workshop, causes of, 41, 47
    MFA workshop, 48
    of Michelangelo, 179
    to observe safety rules, as workshop danger, 57
    practice as antidote to, 31
    probability of, as property of risky making, 25
    in product launch workshop, 67, 142
    as real possibility in risky making, 25
    in shepherding relationship, causes of, 46
    in technical writers' workshops, 48
    value of, 66
    in writers' workshops
        examples of, 7
        explosive possibilities, 41
Faint praise
    See Also Actions; Attitudes and attributes;
        Negative; Responsibilities
    avoiding in positive feedback stage, 131
Family(s)
    See Also Culture; Gift(s), economy;
        Relationships
    behavior that resembles, in writers' workshops, 58
    effective, writers' workshop comparison to, 49
    gift economy, dynamics in, 41
    good workshop like supportive, 182
    group transformation into, through gift
        economy magic, 49
    writers' workshop, for a novice, 39
    writers' workshop as, 35

Farr, Judith
    "The Passion of Emily Dickinson," 206
Fear
    See Also Attitudes and attributes; Emotions;
        Responsibilities; Safety; Setting
    antidotes to
        focus on work as, 30
        risk-sharing as, 32
    as component of presenting risking making
        products, 28
    deleterious effects on attention, 30
    facing, as definition of courage, 167
    overcoming, impact on writing speed, 161
    trust as tool for overcoming, 169
    types of, 29
    writers' workshop as mechanism for
        addressing, 29
Feedback
    See Also Comments; Guidelines;
        Improvement; Negative; Positive;
        Responsibilities; Suggestions for
        improvement
    guidelines for, (appendix), 201
    paucity and limited number, as drawback of
        anonymous peer review, 45
    positive
        (chapter), 127
        difficulties in hearing, 132, 184
        workshopping example, 197
    on type of work, as initial review stage, 115
    in writers' workshop, experienced writers use
        of, xv
Feyerabend, Paul
    "Against Method," 206
    (quotation), 91
Fiction
    See Also Poetry
    piece-as-fiction approach, fly-on-the-wall role
        compared with, 111
    things to look for, in suggestions for
        improvement stage, 137
    treating work as, in suggestions for
        improvement stage, 143
    workshops, craft topics, 164
    writers' workshops for, history of, xiv
Filmmaking
    preparation and practice activities, 38

Finished
    knowing when work is, 166
Fisher, Clark
    short story course, 177
Flexibility
    See Also Actions; Attitudes and attributes; Improvement
    creativity vs., as role in making art, 26
Flow in writing
    magic of, 181
    "Writing in Flow" description of, 178
"Flower and Hand: Poems 1977-1983" by W. S. Merwin, 206
Fly-on-the-wall author role
    See Also Separation of author from work; Stages of the writers' workshop
    creative vs. technical writers' workshop attitudes, 72
    illusion, mechanisms for creating, 111
    importance, in suggestions for improvement stage, 143
    origins of, 3
    role violations
        in creative writers' workshops, 113
        in ongoing workshops, 113
    room formations that support, 72
    as stage of writers' workshop, (chapter), 109
    (term description), 113
    termination of, during clarifications stage, 147
    workshop success dependent on, 114
Focus
    See Also Attitudes and attributes; Separation of author from work
    specification requests, placing after the initial reading, 107
    on work
        as antidote to focusing on fear, 31
        author's dignity enhanced through, 70
        vs. focus on maker and reviewer, 35
"Focus, Focus, Focus" by Kim Hachiya, 206, 178
Foote, Brian
    "Pattern Languages of Program Design 4," 206
Forces
    See Also Pattern(s)
    as term used by technical writers' workshops, 78

Formalist(s)
    paradigm
        vs. software patterns, 6
        (term description), 6
    Russian, philosophy, 3
Formality
    See Also Guidelines; Ritual(s); Setting
    purposeful, as hallmark of workshop rituals, 154
    ritual setting
        value of, 49
        writers' workshop, advantages of, 46
    variations in workshop cultures, 69
    of writers' workshop, importance for effectiveness of, 2
Format
    See Also Guidelines; Setting; Structure(s)
    of room layout, importance for effectiveness of the workshop, 71
    writers' workshop
        code review use, 18
        overview, 3
        purpose of, 4
"Fresh Air" (NPR program)
    Walter Murch interview, 178
Fresh thinking
    See Also Attitudes and attributes; Creativity
    games as resource for evolving, 81
Friendships
    See Also Collaboration; Relationships; Setting; Xenia
    gift economy embedded in, 42
    gifts role in forming, 49
    as review resource, 43

Gabriel, Richard
    background, xvi
    "Is Jack Gilbert's Mind a Computer," discussion of, 83
    "Jimmy, Jimmy, O, Jimmy Mac"
        as alternate spelling of title, 190, 206
        background on poem, 182
        workshop story about, 64

"Jimmy, Jimmy, O Jimmy Mc," 144
  (quotation), 191
  workshopping of, 190
  Local Variables pattern example, 177
  product launch workshop story, 142
  revision practices, changes in, 160
  technical vs. creative writing experience, 185
  "Time Leaves"
  (quotation), 189
  as workshopping example, 187
Games
  See Also Creativity; Culture; Ritual(s)
  creative writers' workshop, vs. technical writers' workshop, 81
  as creativity-loosening exercise, 81
  inter-session ritual use, 153
  playing, as software community rule acceptance influence, 47
  technical writers' workshop, 8, 81
Gamma, Erich
  as "Design Patterns" author, 78
  "Design Patterns: Elements of Reusable Object-Oriented Software," 206
"Gang of Four"
  as canon members, 80
  as name for "Design Patterns," 78
Gate
  writers' workshop as, 172
Gender differences
  canon-building issues, 82
  positive feedback difficulties of women writers, 132
Generative aspects
  See Also Creativity; Improvement
  of craft issue discussions, 16
Generosity
  See Also Attitudes and attributes; Gift(s); Positive; Xenia
  as attribute of writers' workshop, 80
  as code of ethics source, 80
  vs. destructiveness, in workshop dynamics, xv
  importance in successful writers' workshop, 8
  in two skinny dogs in plaza of Taos Pueblo story, 102
  as workshop expression, 78
Genres
  See Also Organization(s)

  as multi-workshop conference partitioning mechanism, 82
  uniformity of, pros and cons, 58
  unusual, presentation needs, 105
Gentleness
  See Also Attitudes and attributes; Positive
  in two skinny dogs in plaza of Taos Pueblo story, 102
Geographical setting
  See Also Culture; Setting; Structure(s)
  of workshop, (chapter), 77
Germany
  as setting for EuroPLoP, 75
"Gift and Commodity in Archaic Greece" by Ian Morris, 206
"The Gift: Imagination and the Erotic Life of Property" by Lewis Hyde, 206, 181, 182
Gift(s)
  See Also Benefits; Commodity economy; Work-in-progress[as gift of the author]; Writers' workshops[for role of gift economy]; Xenia
  -aspect, impact of piece's appearance on, 86
  as attribute of writers' workshop, 80
  of author
    in initial reading, 101
    of work-in-progress, 35
  to author, positive feedback as, 128
  -based community
    as consequence of work-in-progress attitude, 41
    failure to recognize as source of workshop failure, 41
    as writers' workshop salient characteristic, 39
  bond-forming role of, 49
  (chapter), 41
  of deepening, as benefit of writers' workshop, 39
  economy
    as code of ethics source, 80
    vs. commodity economy, 42
    experienced moderators and, 182
    as factor in lives of poets, 174
    failure to recognize, as source of workshop failure, 41
    group transformation through magic of, 49
    operations in parallel with commodity economy, 42

Gift(s), economy (*cont.*)
    vs. paid moderators, as writers' workshop paradox, xv
    (term description), 41
    as writers' workshop salient characteristic, 39
    xenia as spirit of, 43
  ethos, experience level impact on, 58
  experienced moderators, in creative writers' workshops, 182
  giving
    culture, shared experiences and common goals in, 77
    Pablo Neruda story, 49
    as PLoP custom, 79
    requirement for success of workshop, 110
    as salient characteristic of writers' workshop, 35
    surprise setting vs. ritual setting, 46
  of good suggestions for improvement sessions, multiple strategies for revision, 138
  magic of
    (chapter), 41
    focus on the work as, 35
  nature of workshop
    positive feedback reinforcement of, 133
    threats to in suggestions for improvement stage, 141
  of non-author expert leaders, 68
  resonance within workshop, as positive feedback consequence, 128
  shared, work-in-progress as essence of, 87
  in shepherding relationship, 45
  state of work, appropriate for a workshop, 42
  subversion
    by failure to observe safety rules, 57
    possibilities in suggestions for improvement stage, 141
  suggestions for improvement as, 145
  "The Gift: Imagination and the Erotic Life of Property" by Lewis Hyde, 182
  of work-in-progress
    ameliorating dangers of, 69
    trust encouragement by, 47
  wrapping up comments about the work, 152
Gilbert, Jack
  as creative writers' workshop leader, 65

"Is Jack Gilbert's Mind a Computer" by Richard Gabriel, discussion of, 83
  noise and voice, 164
Ginsberg, Allen
  reference to, 140
Global relationships
  See Also Relationships
Glossary
  See Term descriptions
Glosses
  See Content; Poetry
  need for, in two skinny dogs in plaza of Taos Pueblo story, 102
  role in poetry workshop initial readings, 104
Goals
  See Also Attitudes and attributes; Benefits; Improvement; Setting; Teaching
  of authors, 86
  of book, xv, xvii, 185
  in gift-exchange culture, 77
  of work summary, 117
  writers' workshops, 78, 92, 106, 110
Goldman, Ron
  interview with the author, 206
  software pattern workshopping example, 195
  suggestions for improvement, on "Sharing Feelings or Being Clear or Communicating Subtlety" pattern, 198
  summary and feedback, on "Sharing Feelings or Being Clear or Communicating Subtlety" pattern, 197
Good
  See Also Ethics; Positive; Safety
  complexity of, positive feedback highlighting of, 128
  power for, of positive feedback stage, 128
Graphics
  as source of quality, for positive feedback, 129
Greece
  gift economy operation in parallel with commodity economy, 42
Gregg, Linda
  writing poems every day, 160
Gross, Terry
  Walter Murch interview, 178
Ground rules
  See Also Guidelines; Responsibilities

importance for safe writers' workshop
environment, xvi
Grounding
participants, guidelines for, 76
Group(s)
See Also Communities; Culture; Shared
activities
See Also Collaboration
criticism, vs. private act of writing, xv
composition that mitigates moderator
weakness, 64
criticism, vs. private act of writing, as writers'
workshop paradox, xv
dynamics
inter-session rituals importance for
managing, 153
moderator balancing, 144
moderator impact on, 64
moderator sensitivity requirement, 63
of experienced writers, value of diversity for, 68
importance for success of risky making, 32
improvement process, positive deviance, 130
mind, as writers' workshop characteristic, 69
mismatched
effective methods of working with, 65
importance of authoritative leader for, 65
of novices, setting appropriate level for, 57
practices
that assist individual creation, 1, 12
that benefit writers, (chapter), 11
starting, guidelines for, 68
transformation into family, through gift
economy magic, 49
types of activities, See
brainstorming
charrettes
critiques
master class
open source
pair programming
Growth
writers' workshop facilitation of, 171
Guidelines
See Also Culture; Responsibilities; Ritual(s);
Rules
for criticism, experience level buffering by, 57
feedback, (appendix), 201

for grounding participants, guidelines for, 76
for handling equipment required for
workshop, 75
importance of same level of expertise among
writers, 68
for initial reading, 102, 104
for introductions of authors and participants,
75
moderator, 63
opening remarks, 75
for protecting tone of workshop, 76
for reviewing, 97
order, 75
for running a workshop, as goal of book, xvi
as safety mechanism, during suggestions for
improvement stage, 141
for shepherds, 97
reviewing level, 99
for starting a group, 68
for workshop participation, as goal of book, xvi
for writers' workshops, (appendix), 201
"gush"
See Also Culture
as shorthand for "I agree with the preceding
statement," 133

Habitual slog
See Also Creativity
breaking out of, games as stimulant for, 81
Hachiya, Kim
"Focus, Focus, Focus," 206, 178
Harrison, Neil
"Pattern Languages of Program Design 4," 206
Hass, Robert
as creative writers' workshop leader, 173
Hearing
difficulties in, during positive feedback, 132
Heart of the poem
See Also Poetry
as workshop expression, 78
Helm, Richard
as "Design Patterns" author, 78
"Design Patterns: Elements of Reusable
Object-Oriented Software," 206
Hendrix, Jimi
impromptus, 178

Herman, Gabriel
    "Ritualized Friendship and the Greek City," 206
        xenia definition in, 181
Hermetic poetry
    See Also Poetry
    triggers relationship to, in art making, 26
    understandings important to, 117
Hierarchy
    in creative writers' workshops, 64, 182
Hijacking
    See Also Actions; Attitudes and attributes; Guidelines; Moderator(s), responsibilities
    of author's work, statements that signal, 60
Hillman, Brenda
    as creative writers' workshop leader, 65
    revision advice, 81
Hillside Group
    See Also Communities; Group(s); Pattern(s)
    Boulder Creek meeting, 5
    creation of, as shared story culture component, 80
    evaluation of
        initial reading in, 105
        technical writers' workshop use for, 9
    goals vs. Christopher Alexander, 6
    history of, 5
    initial concerns about writers' workshops, 7
    technical writers' workshop rules design by, 8
Hirsch, Ed
    as creative writers' workshop leader, 65
    as workshop leader, in "Is Jack Gilbert's Mind a Computer" story, 83
Hirshfield, Jane
    as creative writers' workshop leader, 65
    writing assignment by, 83
History of writers' workshops
    See Also Creative writers' workshops; Culture; Technical writers' workshops; Writers' workshops
    1880, University of Iowa writers' workshops, 177
    1896, George Cook's "Verse Making" course, 177
    1994, as starting date of software pattern writers' workshop, xiv, 4

1998, technical writers' workshop used for product launch, 8
in creative writing community, xiv
    Clark Fishers short story course, 177
    Edwin Piper's "Poetics" course, 177
    F. R. Leavis' close reading practice, 2
    Iowa Writers' Workshop, 1
in software patterns community, xiv
    Hillside Group introduction to, 5, 7
    Writers' Workshop, (chapter), 1
Hospitality
    See Xenia
How to
    See Guidelines; Responsibilities
Hugo, Richard
    "The Triggering Town," 206
    (quotation), 27, 31
Humanization
    See Also Attitudes and attributes; Responsibilities
    as consequence of range of comment types, 133
    ritual setting encouragement of, 46
Humor
    See Also Creativity; Culture; Games
    as source of quality, 129
    in two skinny dogs in plaza of Taos Pueblo story, 102
Hyde, Lewis
    "The Gift: Imagination and the Erotic Life of Property," 206, 181, 182

"I Love You Sweatheart" by Tom Lux
    as shared story culture component, 80
    special meaning for Warren Wilson College alumni, 78
Idioms
    creative writers' workshop use, 78
    technical writers' workshops, 78
"The Idler" by Samuel Johnson, 206
    writing strategies, 169
Illustrations
    as source of quality, for positive feedback, 129
Imitation
    See Also "Stealing"
    as creative writer practice strategy, 164

Impromptu writing
  as one type of writers' workshop, 70
  as teaching strategy, 82
  value of, 84
Improvement
  See Also Creativity; Goals; Integrity[for appropriate attitudes towards the work-in-progress]; Respect[for appropriate attitudes towards the work-in-progress]; Suggestions for improvement; Teaching; Work-in-progress
  by contact with those more skilled, as workshop benefit, 130
  craft
    -based criticism importance for, 31
    examination of craft masters, 89
    suggestions for improvement stage, 135
    writing about craft elements, 84
  effective
    comments in suggestions for improvement stage, 138
    standard review vs. writers' workshop, 4
  in one's own work, as benefit of listening, 15
  practice and reflection as crucial tools for, 21
  as purpose of writers' workshop, 135
  question-asking tactics, 144
  reading inflections as aid to, 102
  of skills as writers' workshop benefit, 15, 39, 173
  speed, as writers' workshop advantage, xvii
  strategies
    for novices, 30
    positive deviance as, 130
  work
    as goal of writers' workshop, 110
    within its own frame of reference, not change into something else, as purpose of workshop, 135
  writing, clarification of thought as component of, xv
"Improvident Collision: Strategies of Expression and Formal Containment in the Work of Three Spanish/Spanish-American Poets—Federico Garcia Lorca, Cesar Vallejo, and Antonio Machado" by Ian Wilson, 207

"In Search of Duende" by Frederico Garcia Lorca, 206
  (quotation), 178
In situ
  See Also Setting
  (chapter), 77
Individual(s)
  See Also Communities
  collaboration practices that benefit, (chapter), 11
  creativity, group practices that aid, 1
"Inferno" by Dante
  moderator compared to the guide Virgil in, 72
Inflections in speech
  See Also Initial reading stage
  relationship to meaning of work, 102
Information transfer
  See Also Collaboration; Communication
  crucial importance in technical writing, 116
Initial reading stage
  See Also Stages of the writers' workshop
  alternatives to author as sole reader, 106
  (chapter), 101
  in Hillside Group evaluation, 105
Innovations
  See Also Creativity
  in conferences for technical writers' workshopping, 8
  as property of risky making, 25
Insight
  See Also Benefits; Creativity
  factors that deepen, 59
  as valuable characteristic in workshop members, 59
Insults
  See Also Attitudes and attributes; Responsibilities
  by author, during clarifications stage, 148
  protecting authors from
    during suggestions for improvement stage, 144
    as moderator responsibility, 112
Integration
  (term description), 17
Integrity
  See Also Attitudes and attributes; Gift(s)
  of work-in-progress, respecting, during suggestions for improvement stage, 135

Intended reading
    See Also Communication; Glosses
    author, notetaking about differences between reader perception and, 118
Inter-session rituals
    See Also Ritual(s)
    importance for managing dynamics of workshop, 153
Interaction(s)
    See Also Collaboration; Relationships
    as advantage in collaborative evaluation, 13
    during clarification stage, between author and reviewers, 147
    during comment process, 90
    of craft lectures and workshopping process, in pedagogical context, 62
    face-to-face
        absence in anonymous peer review, 44
        brainstorming, 14
        design charrettes, 14
        pair programming, 14
    with gift ethos, behavior boundaries, 58
    among roles in a workshop, 63
    rules, software community rule acceptance of, 47
    shepherd, 97, 99
    territoriality drawbacks to, 61
Internalization
    See Also Attitudes and attributes
    of another's work, in creative writing workshops, 14
Interpretation
    See Also Glosses; Semantics
    vs. literal meaning, 119
Interviews
    with Browning Porter, 206
    with Jutta Eckstein, 205
    with Linda Elkin, 206
    with Richard Schmitt, 207
    with Ron Goldman, 206
Intimacy
    See Also Context; Setting
    of creative writers' workshop, 35
    enhancement, by authors staying together for duration of workshop, 70
    of technical writers' workshop, as advantage and danger, 41

Introduction(s)
    of authors, guidelines for, 75
    (chapter), xiii
Investment
    See Also Attitudes and attributes
    in work being evaluated, in writers workshops, 15
Iowa Writers' Workshop
    as writers' workshop origin, 1
Irrelevant details
    detecting and handling of, 16
"Is Jack Gilbert's Mind a Computer" by Richard Gabriel
    discussion of, 83

Jargon
    See Also Culture
    creative writers' workshop use, 78
    technical writers' workshops, 78
Jealousy
    as anonymous peer review complication, 43
"Jimmy, Jimmy, O, Jimmy Mack" by Richrad Gabriel, 206
    as alternate spelling of title, 190
    background on poem, 182
    workshopping of, 64
"Jimmy, Jimmy, Oh Jimmy Mack" by Richard Gabriel, 206
"Jimmy, Jimmy, O Jimmy Mc" by Richard Gabriel (quotation), 191
    workshopping of, 144, 190
Johnson, Ollie
    "Disney Animation: The Illusion of Life," 207
Johnson, Ralph
    as "Design Patterns" author, 78
    "Design Patterns: Elements of Reusable Object-Oriented Software," 206
    support for trial of writers' workshop notion, 7
Johnson, Samuel
    Rick Bass use of dash compared with, 162
    "The Idler," 206
    "The Rambler," 206
    writing strategies, 169
Jokes
    inter-session ritual use, 153

Journals
  anonymous peer review process, 44
  review process as a shepherding process, 45
Judgmentalism
  See Also Dangers; Negative
  avoidance, importance in emotionally-disturbed children story, 19
  language that reflects, avoidance during work summary, 116

Keats, John
  letter to Benjamin Bailey, 185
  (quotation), 140, 171
Kindness
  See Also Attitudes and attributes
  importance in shepherd relationship, 99
King, Stephen
  "On Writing," (quotation), 19
"Kloster Hearsay" newsletter
  as EuroPLoP daily workshop newsletter, 79
Kloster Irsee
  See Also Conferences; Location
  as setting for EuroPLoP, 75
Knowledge
  See Also Culture; Experience(s)
  shared, as culture component, 77
Knuth, Donald
  craft elements, 89
KoalaPLoP (Australia) conference
  See Also Conferences
  as regional PLoP conference, 177
Kumin, Maxine
  effective leadership style, 65

Language
  See Also Craft
  deeply buried nature of, as source of discussion difficulties, 140
  judgmental, avoidance during work summary, 116
  poetry
    See Also Poetry
    moderator handling of comprehension issues, 123

"Sentences My Father Used" by Charles Bernstein, 120
  of summary, 116
Law of diminishing returns
  in commodity economy, 42, 181
Lazy reviewing
  See Also Review(s)
  damage of, 90
Leader
  See Moderator(s)
Learning
  See Also Notetaking; Practice(s); Teaching; Tools
  resources
    experienced writers as, 168
    writers' workshop as, 21
  theory
    bibliographic references, 183
    "The Writer as an Artist: A New Approach to Writing Alone and with Others" by Pat Schneider, 175
Leavis, F. R.
  close reading practice, as original idea behind writers' workshops, 2
Lectures on craft
  See Also Teaching
  as component of national workshops, 81
  in creative writers' workshops, 62
Length
  of initial author reading, 101
  of stay, importance for building community of trust, 70
  of workshopped pieces, as indicator of workshop style, 70
  of writers' workshop sessions, 4
Level(s)
  completion, determining when ready to be workshopped, 17
  meta
    guidelines for, in initial reading of work, 102
    shallow and broad review handling of, 91
  of review, for shepherd, guidelines, 99
  of reviewer preparation, 89
  as small step that measure specific progress, 83
Lexington avenue
  birthday gift surprise story, 46

Limitations
    See Also Benefits
    of author, in revising a piece, handling, 143
    of autonomous critic, 34
    of private making, 34
    of shepherding, 46
Lineation
    as craft term, 78
Lisp
    Common Lisp standards discussion, 177
    programmers, including in canon-building, 82
Listening
    See Also Attention; Readers/reading
    active, (term description), 63
    benefits of
        applying to one's own work, 15
        in creative writers workshop, 15
    difficulties in, 184
        during positive feedback, 132
    selective, as important author skill, 164
    strategies that enhance, 66
Literal meaning
    See also Semantics
    vs. connotations, 119
"Literary Theory: An Introduction" by Terry Eagleton, 205
Literature
    building
        as goal of writers' workshop communities, 78
        software pattern community difficulties and solutions, 6
        writers' workshop as ritual for, 80
    creating, establishing the significance of, 79
    form of, patterns and pattern languages viewed as, 6
    -review errors, handling, in suggestions for improvement stage, 135
    vocabulary, creative writers' workshop use, 78
    writers' workshops for, history of, xiv
Liu, Timothy
    as creative writers' workshop leader, 65
Local Variables pattern by Richard Gabriel, 177
Location
    See Also Culture; Setting
    of audience, impact on workshop, 73
    of author, importance for effectiveness of the workshop, 72

of moderator, 182
    (quotation), 182
workshop
    (chapter), 77
    remote, 80
    rural, 78
writing on
    as one type of writers' workshop, 70
    as teaching strategy, 82
Long
    pieces, written in advance, as one type of writers' workshop, 70
    -term efforts
        collaboration strategies, See Design charrettes
        collaboration strategies, See Open source; Pair programming
        frequent release possible in groups set up for, 18
    workshop sessions, need to accommodate materials for, 71
Lorca, Frederico Garcia
    duende, 33
    "In Search of Duende," 206
        (quotation), 178
    "Scream to Rome"
        (quotation), 190
        summarization example, 190
"Lorca's Poet in New York: The Fall into Consciousness" by Betty Jean Craige, 205
Lorde, Audre
    (quotation), 169
    "The Transformation of Silence into Language and Action," 206
Lux, Thomas
    "I Love You Sweatheart," special meaning for Warren Wilson College alumni, 78
    as shepherd for Richard Gabriel's "Jimmy, Jimmy, O Jimmy Mack," 182
    as "Time Leaves" advisor, 187

Magic
    See Also Gift(s); Mojo; Xenia
    of the gift
        (chapter), 41

economy, group transformation through, 49
  focus on the work as, 35
writers' workshop
  for experienced writers, 172
  mojo, pattern community additions, xiv
  of writing in flow, 181
  of xenia, initial reading stimulus for, 101
Making
  See Also Art; Craft; Work-in-progress; Writing
  art
    commonalities with software making, 28
    flexibility vs. creativity in, 26
    skill development, 39
    triggers role in, 26
  characteristics of the work involved in, 34
  private, limitations of emphasis on, 34
  repetitive
    risky making compared with, 29
    vs. risky making, semantics of, 178
    (term description), 25
  risky
    acceptance and approval seeking in, 29
    repetitive making compared with, 29
    vs. repetitive making, semantics of, 178
    reward for, in writers' workshop, 39
    (term description), 25
  software, commonalities with art making, 28
  technological, triggers role in, 27
  things
    creative process of, xvii
    the work of, coda, (chapter), 167
    work of, (part), 23
Marriage
  See Also Communities; Gift(s), economy
  gift economy embedded in, 42
Master class
  See Also Group(s), types of activities; Teaching
  as group activity that assists the individual, 13
  (term description), 13
Master classes
  as short-term collaboration, 14
Master of Fine Arts (MFA) programs
  See MFA (Master of Fine Arts) programs

Masterpieces
  teaching role in software patterns community, 6
Maturation cycle
  See Also Learning; Teaching; Work-in-progress
  changes in writers' workshop benefits, 170
  ordering of pieces consideration, 85
  in risky making, 161
  transitions characteristic of, 172
  uncertain course, 30
  writers' workshop role, 173
McCarthy, Cormac
  minimal punctuation, 162
McHugh, Heather
  puns in work of, 182
McPherson, Sandra
  as creative writers' workshop leader, 65
  door-to-door comments story, 102
Mean-spiritedness
  See Also Attitudes and attributes; Negative, attitudes and attributes
  moderator handling of, 59
Mechanisms
  See Also Strategies; Structure(s); Tactics; Tools
  for creating fly-on-the-wall illusion, 111
  genres as, in multi-workshop conference partitioning, 82
  learning
    more skilled writers as resource, 168
    writers' workshop as, 21
  for overcoming fear, writers' workshop as, 29
  releasing, focus on craft as, 20
  for reviewing, 43
  risk sharing, writers' workshop as, 32
  safety
    guidelines, 141
    in technical writers' workshops, 55
  summary of work, for detecting misunderstandings, 117
  writing
    within the brain, 18
    sources, 178
Melville, Herman
  "Moby Dick," transparency vs. meaning in, 122

238 ~ INDEX

Memories
  See Also Triggers
  accessing, through writing when not accessible to speech, 20
  muscle, role in writing revision practice, 158
Mensore PLoP (Japan) conference
  See Also Conferences
  as regional PLoP conference, 177
Merwin, W. S.
  "Berryman," (quotation), 167
  "Flower and Hand: Poems 1977-1983," 206
  minimal punctuation, 162
Meta level
  See Also Ritual(s); Structure(s); Tactics
  guidelines for, in initial reading of work, 102
  handling confusion and misunderstanding with, 122
  meta, handling confusion and misunderstanding with, 122
  shallow and broad review handling of, 91
Metaphors for writers' workshop
  See Also Gift(s); Process(es)
  crucible, xvii
  dance, xvi
  midwife, 20
MFA (Master of Fine Arts) programs
  creative writers' workshops as part of, 2
  Warren Wilson College
    culture of, 78, 79
    educational philosophy of, 84
    examples of workshop experiences, 187
    "MFA Program for Writers Handbook," 76, 207
    teaching tools, 181
    workshops, as established creative writers' workshops, 77
"MFA Program for Writers Handbook" by Warren Wilson College, 207, 76
Michelangelo
  Sistine Chapel frescoes, 179
  skills and "tricks" of, 178
Midwife
  See Also Gift(s); Metaphors for writers workshop
  as metaphor for writers' workshop, 20

Misunderstanding
  See Also Communication; Strategies; Tactics; Tools
  creative workshop handling of, 120
  eliciting reasons for, 165
  masking of, work summary as tool for avoiding, 123
  meta level as tool for handling, 122
  uncovering, as role of work summary, 120
  of work
    as moderator problem, 118
    summary of work as mechanism for detecting, 117
"Moby Dick" by Herman Melville
  transparency vs. meaning in, 122
Model(s)
  See Also Teaching
  other peoples work, use in one's own work, 161
  teaching role in software patterns community, 6
  of writing and writing process, as goal of Part 1-"The Work of Making Things," xvii
Moderator(s)
  See Also Attitudes and attributes; Responsibilities; Role(s); Setting; Strategies; Tactics; Teaching
  attributes
    needed, 67
    safe setting requirements, xvi
  clarification request, as exception to author silence rule, 111
  craft lectures by, in creative writers' workshops, 62
  creative writers' workshops
    effectiveness of, 61
    strategies for deflecting content discussion, 66
  destructive, hard judgmental poetry workshop leader story, 103
  dual, advantages, 64
  effective, methods of working, 65
  experience
    aid in starting a new workshop, 96
    benefits for novices, 32
    gift economy and, 182
    range, 61
    requirements relative to group, 58

hierarchy of, in creative writers' workshops, 64
location of, 182
novice, training of, 63
outside
  when needed, 67
  when to use, 112
paid, vs. gift economy, as writers' workshop paradox, xv
positioning of, 72
preparation by, 93
problems
  when boss is participant, 112
  failure to control negativity, 67
  handling an obstreperous author, 112
  handling confusion, 122
  maintaining control during suggestions for improvement stage, 141
  in work summary stage, 118
responsibilities, 54
  towards author during fly-on-the-wall role, 113
  for author protection from insults, 112
  damage control, 68
  ensuring honest praise, 132
  maintaining control, 141
  monitoring the state of the author, 131, 141
  vs. regular reviewer, 94
  during suggestions for improvement, 144
  teaching roles, 62
role
  in bridging diverse experience levels, 58
  teaching, 94
rotating, advantages, 82
tactics
  towards author during fly-on-the-wall role, 113
  dealing with confusion, 120, 122
  ensuring that praise is honest, 132
  incomplete work summaries, 118
  obstreperous author, 112
  well-explored subjects, 140
  when author is distressed, 132, 144
teaching role, 62
  in creative writers' workshops, 67
  value of, 94
(term description), 53

weakness
  as failure cause in creative writers' workshops, 48
  group composition that mitigates, 64
  as writers' workshop role, 2
Mojo
  See Also Magic
  writers' workshop, pattern community additions, xiv
"Mona Lisa" by Leonardo da Vinci
  poem about, illustration of author limitations issues, 143
Money
  See Commodity economy
Monticello, Illinois
  Allerton Park Conference Center, as setting for PLoP, 74, 79
Morris, Ian
  "Gift and Commodity in Archaic Greece," 206
Motivation(s)
  See Also Benefits; Gift(s)
  appropriate praise value, 83
  for collaborative involvement, "scratch your own itch," 15
  dependence on writers' workshop for, as danger, 185
  focus on, as failure cause in creative writers' workshops, 48
  joy as, in writers' workshops, 174
Mudball
  workshop pattern danger of becoming, 163
Multiple
  authors, initial reading when there are, 101
  pieces, workshopping order for, 107
  points-of-view, as advantage in collaborative evaluation, 13
  strategies, for handling suggestions for improvement, 138, 143
  workshop conferences
    genres as partitioning mechanism in, 82
    leader rotation in, 82
Murch, Walter, 206
  "Fresh Air" interview, 178
Music
  See Also Art
  impromptus in, 178

Music (*cont.*)
  -like qualities, as source of quality, 129
  workshopping of, 2
Myers, D. G.
  "The Elephants Teach: Creative Writing Since 1880," 206
    history of writers' workshops in, 177
Myths
  See also Culture
  shared, as culture component, 80

Napa Valley Writers's Conference
  See Also Conferences
  writing on location at, 82
Narrative
  See Also Craft; Poetry
  narrator position and stance, as creative writers' workshop subject, xvi
  structure
    as craft term, 78
    as creative writers' workshop subject, xvi
    as source of quality, 129
    as technical term from literature vocabulary, 78
  transformation of, workshop help with, 136
  transparency vs. meaning in, 122
National Geographic
  photographers, proportion of pictures used to pictures taken, 38
Natural voice
  (term description), 160
Negative
  See Also Attitudes and attributes; Feedback; Positive, attitudes and attributes
  actions, insults, protecting authors from, 112, 144
  attributes and attitudes
    author hijacking, 60
    competitiveness, 42, 58, 141
    defensiveness, 111, 112, 147, 185
    deleterious effects of "but" in positive feedback stage, 131
    generosity amelioration of, xv
    hard judgmental poetry workshop leader story, 103
    jealousy, 43

    mean-spiritedness, 59
    rivalry, 43
    territoriality as drawback, 45, 61
    trashing of work and/or author, 67
    vicious attacks on work and/or author, 142
  capability, (term description), 171
  comments, during positive feedback, deleterious impact on safety, 132
  criticism
    damage control importance, 68
    impact on novices, 32
    in suggestions for improvement stage, dangers of, 135
  effect of classroom-style organization, 71
Negotiation of roles
  as pedagogical tool, 84
  (term description), 84
Neil Harrison Shepherding Award, 184
Neruda, Pablo
  "Childhood and Poetry," 206, 182
  (quotation), 49
Neutrality
  See Also Separation of author from work
  as advantage of summary-only workshop, 124
  of language, importance in work summary, 116
New Critics
  philosophy of, 3
"New Princeton Encyclopedia of Poetry and Poetics" by Alex Preminger and T. V. F. Brogan, eds., 206
  topos definition in, (footnote), 117
Newsletters
  See Also Culture
  as writers' workshop culture component, 79
Noise
  as craft element, 140, 164
    Jack Gilbert, 164
    source of quality, 129
  environmental, author seating arrangement, 72
Normal distribution
  (term description), 179
Notes
  (chapter), 175
Notetaking
  See Also Learning
  accommodations for, 72

annotations as aid in use of comments, 156
on differences between reader perception and author's intended reading, 118
difficulties and recommendations, 88
revision use of, 155
strategies, (quotation), 88
Novice(s)
See Also Arc; Experienced writers; Improvement; Teaching
bad side-effects of uncritical constant praise, 141
benefits of, writers' workshops for, 170
experienced participant impact on, 55
group level setting for, 57
harsh criticism impact on, 32
moderators, training of, 63
review order guidelines, 75
revision tactics, 164
strategies
importance of experienced writer comments for, 164
for improvement, 30
teaching role importance in workshop comprised of, 56
types of comments useful for, 87
writers' workshop
dangers for, xvi
experience like that of an encouraging family, 39
NPR (National Public Radio)
"Fresh Air" program, 178

Object-oriented programming
See Also Programming; Software
vocabulary, technical writers' workshop use, 78
Objectification
See Separation of author from work
Obligation
mutual, gift economy bonds formed from, 41
Obstreperous author
moderator handling of, 112
"Of Mere Being" by Wallace Stevens (quotation), 121
"On Writing" by Stephen King (quotation), 19
On-location writing
as one type of writers' workshop, 70

as teaching strategy, 82
Open source
See Also Collaboration; Group(s), types of activities
collaborative evaluation advantages, 14
development, as group practice that aids individual creativity, 1
gift economy components, 42
as group activity that assists the individual, 12
"release early, release often" maxim, 17
software projects, writers' workshop compared with, xiv
(term description), 12
Openness to new approaches
See Also Attitudes and attributes; Positive, attitudes and attributes
creativity and, role in art making, 26
Order
See Also Ritual(s); Structure(s)
of comments, importance for maximizing authorial comfort, 70
emergence from chaos, writers' workshop compared with, xiv
pecking, deleterious effects of attempts to establish, 61
of pieces for review
classification by moderator, 93
guidelines, 75
as moderator responsibility, 93
when there are multiple pieces for same author, 107
of workshop stages, emotional impact of, 151
Organization(s)
See Also Communities; Culture; Structure(s)
classroom-style, deleterious effects on writers' workshops, 71
drawbacks in review process, 45
evaluation of
questions that might be asked, 9
writers' workshop use for, 9
Hillside Group, technical writers' workshop use for evaluation of, 9
initial reading in, 105
special workshop settings for, 74
of work, impact on revision practices, 160
writers' workshop approach applicable to, 2

Orland, Ted
  "Art and Fear: Observations on the Perils (and Rewards) of Art-making," 205
Overview
  writers' workshop, (chapter), 1
Ownership
  See Also Author(s); Co-ownership
  author vs. shepherd, 98
  as corporate culture problem, 185
  feelings, as drawback in organizational review process, 45
  spiritual, as aspect of work-in-progress gift, 86
  of work, reversion to author after workshop, 155
  in writing workshops, 14

Pacing
  See Also Setting; Time
  control, moderator responsibility, 62, 94
Pair
  See Also Group(s), types of activities; Interaction(s); Programming
  programming
    face-to-face interaction, 14
    as group practice that aids individual creativity, 1, 12
    (term description), 12
  writing, as activity that assists the individual writer, 12
Palate-cleansing
  inter-session ritual viewed as, 153
Paley, Grace
  revision practices, 158
Paradigms
  See Also Pattern(s)
  software patterns vs. formalist paradigm, 6
Paradoxes
  of crowd vs. individual, in risky making, 32
  of writers' workshop, xv
  paid moderator in gift economy, 182
Participant(s)
  See Also Role(s)
  audiences that are, 55
  (term description), 54
  benefits of being, in creative writers workshop, 15

difficulties when project leader is workshop participant, 67
experienced, impact on novices, 55
feedback guidelines, (appendix), 201
grounding, guidelines for, 76
introductions of, guidelines for, 75
moderator difficulties when boss is, 112
role, in writers' workshop, 2
shared culture as binding force, 78
writers' workshop
  (chapter), 53
  culture determination in advance by, 94
"A Pattern Language" by Christopher Alexander, 205
  canon component, 80
  Hillside Group influenced by, 5
  purpose and characteristics, 5
  (quotation), 176
"Pattern Languages of Program Design 4" by Neil Harrison, Brian Foote, and Hans Rohnert, eds., 206
Pattern(s)
  See Also Conferences; Structure(s); Technical writers' workshops; Writing
  characteristics, 175
  Christopher Alexander
    "A Pattern Language," as canon component, 80
    pattern example, 176
    work on discovering and defining patterns, 5
  community
    history of writers' workshops for, xiv
    mindset of, xiv
  examples
    Christopher Alexander, 176
    software, 177
  Hillside Group, introduction to writers' workshops, 5
  languages
    Christopher Alexander's work, 5
    skilled moderator handling of, 62
    (term description), 6, 175
    workshopping example, 195
  problem statements vs. solution statements, 136
  software
    example, 177

vs. formalist paradigm, 6
workshopping example, 195
suggestions for improvement tactics, examples of good approaches, 136
(term description), 6, 163, 175
as term used by technical writers' workshops, 78
user-visible, characteristics and aesthetics, 93
work summary recommendations, 118
workshop piece characteristics, 163
writers' workshops
examples of, 77
overview of the process, 3
where to find, 2
writing, belief that it is repetitive making, 26
Pecking order
See Also Negative
deleterious effects of attempts to establish, 61
People
arrangement of, importance for effectiveness of the workshop, 71
"The Perfection of Imperfection" by Christopher Alexander, 205
(quotation), 129
Performances
applause for, 152
attributes that contribute to quality, 129
grand, work-in-progress contrasted with, 35
workshopping, 2, 73
Perry, Susan K.
"Writing in Flow," 206
flow in writing, 178
Perseverance
role in art making, 28
Personal
See Also Communities; Separation of author from work
aspects of risky making, 28
selection of details, vs. needs of the piece, 15
Philips, Carl
as workshop leader for "Time Leaves," 187
Philosophy
Alexander, Christopher, user-visible patterns relationship to, 93
educational, of Warren Wilson College, 84
Feyerabend, Paul, (quotation), 91
handling philosophical conflicts, 116

postmodernism
relativism, deleterious impact on craft discussions, 140
as technical term from literature vocabulary, 78
of Russian formalists, 3
of technical writers' workshops, vs. traditional scientific conferences and workshops, 8
Photographers
bibliographic references for craft information, 178
craft mastery habits of, 37
preparation activities, 38
Piece(s)
See Also Drafts; Work
as a whole, as starting point for shepherding review, 99
author defense of, moderator handling, 112
completion of, 166
multiple, workshopping order for, 107
piece-as-fiction approach, fly-on-the-wall role compared with, 111
revising, (chapter), 155
short
initial reading for, 107
written on location, as one type of writers' workshop, 70
workshop, (term description), 163
"Pieta" by Michelangelo
skills and "tricks" used to create, 179
Pine cone
See Also Stories
in Pablo Neruda's story of gift-giving, 50
Pinneo, Joanna
"Working for National Geographic Magazine," 206, 178
Piper, Edwin
"Poetics" course, 177
Pitman, Kent
Common Lisp standards, 177
Planning
See Also Preparation(s)
role in making things, 168
Play
See Culture; Games; Ritual(s)
Players
See Participant(s); Role(s)

"The PLoP News" newsletter
   as PLoP daily workshop newsletter, 79
PLoP (Pattern Languages of Programs) conference
   See Also Conferences
   getting there, as part of the culture, 79
   as regional PLoP conference, 177
   setting for, 74
   as technical writers' workshop, 2, 77
   as workshop with relatively uniform expertise and expectation level, 61
Plot
   See Also Craft
   (term description), 137
"Poet in New York" by Fedèrico Garcia Lorca
   "Scream to Rome," (quotation), 190
Poetry
   See Also Art; Craft; Creative writers' workshops; Triggers; Writing
   advanced writers' workshop characteristics, 171
   "Berryman" by W. S. Merwin, (quotation), 167
   "Childhood and Poetry" by Pablo Neruda, 182
   contradictory reviewer comments, subjective nature of writing indicated by, 139
   explanatory notes, handling need for, 102
   form, value of viewing ritual setting as, 49
   gift economy role in lives of poets, 174
   glosses, in poetry workshop initial readings, 104
   heart of the poem, as workshop expression, 78
   hermetic
      triggers relationship to, in art making, 26
      understandings important to, 117
   "Is Jack Gilbert's Mind a Computer" by Richard Gabriel, discussion of, 83
   "Jimmy, Jimmy, O Jimmy Mc" by Richard Gabriel, (quotation), 191
   Keats, John, (quotation), 140
   language
      moderator handling of comprehension issues, 123
      "Sentences My Father Used" by Charles Bernstein, 120
   meaning vs. transparency in, 122
   misreading of, summary of work as mechanism for detecting, 117

"New Princeton Encyclopedia of Poetry and Poetics," topos definition in, (footnote), 117
"Of Mere Being" by Wallace Stevens, (quotation), 121
reading aloud, importance of, 102
revision options, story, 143
rewriting of poem, in creative poetry workshops, 14
Richard Gabriel's background in, xvi
"The Sacred Wood: Essays on Poetry and Criticism" essay by T. S. Eliot, (quotation), 162
"Scream to Rome" by Federico Garcia Lorca, (quotation), 190
"Sentences My Father Used" by Charles Bernstein, (quotation), 120
shepherding possibility limitations, 46
Squaw Valley Community of Writers Workshop in Poetry
   as established creative writers' workshop, 77
   writing on location at, 82
strangeness as virtue in, 81
"Time Leaves" by Richard Gabriel, (quotation), 189
transformation of initial triggers, workshop help with, 136
triggers in, 27
well-known creative writers' workshops for, examples of, 77
workshop piece characteristics, 163
workshops, craft topics, 164
writers' workshops for, history of, xiv
Points-of-view
   See Also Collaboration
   in context of specific work, as benefit of workshop, 16
   multiple, as advantage in collaborative evaluation, 13
Politeness
   See Also Attitudes and attributes; Positive, attitudes and attributes; Respect
   workshop success dependent on, 114
Porter, Browning
   interview with the author, 206
   (quotation), 104

Positive
    See Also Actions; Attitudes and attributes
    attributes and attitudes
        generosity, 80
        gentleness, 102
        gift-giving, 80
        kindness, 99
        xenia, 80
    comments, as tactic for providing emotional closure, 151
    deviance, (term description), 130
    feedback stage
        See Also Stages of the writers' workshop
        difficulties in hearing, 132, 184
        workshopping example, 197
        of writers' workshop, (chapter), 127
    suggestions, importance as companion to criticisms, 144
    things about the work, identifying, in positive feedback stage, 127
    tone, moderator responsibility to maintain, 63
Postmodernism
    See Also Philosophy
    relativism of, as barrier to effective craft discussions, 140
    as technical term from literature vocabulary, 78
Power
    See Also Safety
    for good, of positive feedback stage, 128
    of shepherd, balancing with effective review, 99
Practice(s)
    See Also Craft; Preparation(s); Revision; Writing
    close reading, as original idea behind writers' workshops, 2
    cross-fertilization of creative writing workshop and technical writing community, xvii
    as crucial improvement tool, 21
    daily, importance of, 160
    effective, selection as strategy for, 166
    group
        that assist individual creation, 1
        that benefit writers, (chapter), 11
    importance
        for improving skill in making things, 26, 168
        to Mark Strand, 159

as predictor of future success, 30
in quotation of "The Triggering Town," 31
requirements
    for craft mastery, 38
    for success in making things, 37, 167
revision
    as crucial tool for skill development, 158
    of Dickey, James, 157
    of Paley, Grace, 158
    of Richard Gabriel, 160
    of Richard Gabriel, changes in, 160
    of Schmitt, Richard, 158
shepherding, as practice different from traditional conferences, 8
sketching as, revisions compared to, 159
software pattern community, for author development, 6
successful, vs. analysis of how something works, xv
technical writers' workshop
    examples, 195
    games, 8
as tool for learning writing, 89
triggers and, (chapter), 25
as underlying learning theory in writers' workshops, 84
Praise
    See Also Feedback; Positive; Suggestions for improvement stage
    appropriate, motivational value of, 83
    faint, avoiding in positive feedback stage, 131
    honest, moderator responsibility to ensure, 132
    uncritical, bad side-effects of, 141
Preminger, Alex
    "New Princeton Encyclopedia of Poetry and Poetics," 206
Preparation(s)
    See Also Planning; Practice(s)
    audience, for writers' workshops, 85
    authors, for writers' workshops, 85
    of experienced photographer, 38
    moderator, 93, 94
    reviewers
        recommendations, 89
        for writers' workshops, 85
    for writers' workshop
        by attending as audience member, 96

Preparation(s), for writers' workshop (*cont.*)
    deciding the kinds of comments you want, 87
    reflection on desired experience, 92
    shepherd's role, 89

Presentation(s)
    appearance determination for work, 86
    attributes that contribute to quality, 129
    deciding the kinds of comments you want, 87
    initial reading in, 105
    by moderators, 93
    reflection
        on desired experience, 92
        on self-knowledge, 92
    reviewer preparations for, 92
    of reviewers, 89
    role in achieving perfection, 38
    shepherd role in, (chapter), 97
    value of, 96
    workshopping, setting for, 73
    writers' workshops
        as alternative to, xiv
        (chapter), 85

Pride
    writers' workshop uncovering of, 41

Prior works
    as best teacher for current work, 30

Privacy
    protection of, importance in emotionally-disturbed children story, 19

Private
    See Also Collaboration; Shared
    act of writing
        vs. group criticism, as writers' workshop paradox, xv
        vs. public evaluation in writers' workshop, xv
    making, limitations of emphasis on, 34

Problems
    See Also Dangers; Negative; Responsibilities; Setting
    creative writers' workshops, failure to observe safety rules, 57
    finding and fixing, as a purpose of the workshop, 127
    mean-spiritedness, moderator handling, 59
    moderator
        handling an obstreperous author, 112
        handling confusion, 122
        maintaining control during suggestions for improvement stage, 141
    readers lack of comprehension, 118
    termination of work summary stage, 118

Process(es)
    See Also Setting; Stages of the writers' workshop; Tools
    acceptance, shepherd's role, 97, 100
    creative, writer's workshop role in the cycle of, xv
    planning, writers' workshop applicability for, 2
    review
        journal and conference anonymous peer, 44
        journals, shepherding aspects of, 45
        organizational, attitudes that hinder, 45
    revision, post-workshop handling of workshop comments, 155
    writers' workshop
        comment dynamics, 90
        creative vs. technical community attitudes, 41
        in educational context, 62
        examination of, as goal of the book, xv
        technical writers' workshop overview, 3
    writing, xiii
        model, as goal of Part 1-"The Work of Making Things," xvii

Product launch
    collateral material, writers' workshops use for review of, 4
    technical writers' workshop
        as example, 8
        as example of nightmare scenario, 142
        failure of, 67

Professional
    See Also Experienced writers; Practice(s)
    vs. amateur, practice as differentiator, 37

Programming
    See Also Software
    extreme, "continuous integration" maxim, 17
    object-oriented, vocabulary, technical writers' workshop use, 78
    pair
        face-to-face interaction, 14
        as group activity that assists the individual, 12
        as group practice that aids individual creativity, 1
        (term description), 12

symbol definition in programming language
        specification story, 16
    vocabulary, technical writers' workshop use, 78
Prosody
    as craft language for poets, 141
Psychological
    See Also Attitudes and attributes; Emotions;
        Responsibilities; Safety; Setting
    benefit, of separation of author from work, 37
    dimension, importance for writers' workshop,
        xv
    effects, of writers' workshop-like work with
        emotionally disturbed children, 19
    safety, writers' workshop atmosphere geared
        towards, 2
Public
    evaluation in writers' workshop, vs. act of
        writing, xv
Publication
    See Also Literature
    software pattern community difficulties and
        solutions, 6
Punctuation
    dash
        Emily Dickinson use, 185
        semantic value of, 162
        minimal, of W. S. Merwin and Cormac
            McCarthy, 162

Quality
    See Also Arc, of maturation; Improvement
    combined with speed, as writers' workshop
        advantage, xvii
    distribution, within a piece, differentiating, 130
    ensuring, statistical distribution role in, 181
    identifying, in positive feedback stage, 127
    Michelangelo strategies for creating, 178
    QWAN (quality without a name), 78
    seeking for, in positive feedback stage, 129
    writing, technical writing attitude towards, 140
Questions
    See Also Strategies; Tactics; Tools
    by author, during clarifications stage, 147
    framing comments as, 100
    as moderator tactic, during work summary
        stage, 118

    for organization evaluation, 9
    in suggestions for improvement stage, fiction,
        137
    as tactic for effective improvement suggestions,
        144
    what-if type, as skilled moderator tool, 62
Quiet
    See Also Setting
    importance for effectiveness of the workshop, 74
Quotations
    See Also Examples; Stories
    advantages of reading a piece to an audience, 86
    Alexander, Christopher
        "179. Alcoves" pattern from "A Pattern
            Language," 176
        "The Perfection of Imperfection," 129
    anonymous, xiii
    authors
        benefit of writers' workshop, 35
        difficulties during fly-on-the-wall role, 114
        as initial reader in a poetry workshop, 106
        strategy for handling multiple suggestions,
            138
    Bernstein, Charles, "Sentences My Father
        Used," 120
    Christopher Alexander, "The Perfection of
        Imperfection," 129
    common seating arrangements, importance of,
        72
    confusion, creative workshop handling of, 120
    content vs. technique as workshop material,
        59
    contradictory reviewer comments, 139
    creativity, secret to, 27
    dumbing down dangers, 165
    educational value of reviewing, 90
    Einstein, Albert, 27
    Eliot, T. S., 171
        "The Sacred Wood: Essays on Poetry and
            Criticism," 162
    in emotionally disturbed children story, 19
    example of software pattern, 177
    experienced writers, benefits of workshop, 172
    Feyerabend, Paul, 91
    Gabriel, Richard
        "Jimmy, Jimmy, O Jimmy Mc," 191
        "'Time Leaves," 189

Quotations (*cont.*)
  gift effect of positive feedback, 128
  glosses in poetry workshop initial readings, 104
  healing qualities of writers' workshop, xiii
  Hugo, Richard, 27, 31
  impact
    on author of fly-on-the-wall role, 110
    of gift-giving on child's development, 49
    on workshop of author presence, 110
  Keats, John, 140, 171
  King, Stephen, 19
  leadership strategies, 66
  location of moderator, 182
  Lorca, Federico Garcia
    "In Search of Duende," 178
    "Scream to Rome," 190
  Lorde, Audre, 169
  magic of workshop for experienced writers, 172
  Maxine Kumin's leadership style, 65
  Merwin, W. S., "Berryman," 167
  MFA workshop failure, 48
  National Geographic photographer image volumes, 38
  Neruda, Pablo, 49
  notetaking strategies, 88
  Porter, Browning, 104
  post-workshop revisions, handling comments, 155
  protecting tone of workshop, guidelines for, 76
  Sartore, Joel, National Geographic photographer image volumes, 38
  shallow review advantages, 91
  "Sharing Feelings or Being Clear or Communicating Subtlety" pattern, 195
  Stafford, William, 26
  Stevens, Wallace, "Of Mere Being," 121
  summary-only workshop advantages, 124
  take what is food for you and leave the rest, as author strategy for handling revisions, 138
  value of
    craft seminar plus workshop, 62
    respect and insight, 59
    revisions and practicing, 159
  workshop
    benefits, 95
    experience, unexpected riches, 95
    writing poems every day, as effective practice, 160
Quux
  See Steele, Guy L. Jr.
QWAN (quality without a name)
  See Also Alexander, Christopher; Quality; Reasons why, writers' workshops work
  as term used by technical writers' workshops, 78
"The Rambler" by Samuel Johnson, 206
  writing strategies, 169

Range
  of comments
    balance as consequence of, 133
    in creative writers' workshops, 164
  of moderator experience, 61
  of writers, writers' workshop introduction to, as goal of book, xvii
Readers/reading
  See Also Listening; Speaking; Stages of the writers' workshop; Voice
  aloud, reinforcement of communication by, 102
  alternative
    to author as sole reader, 106
    interpretations by audience, 117
  to an audience, advantages, 86
  author's intentions, notetaking about differences between reader perception and, 118
  autonomous role, limitations, 34
  close
    pedagogical tool, 181
    writers' workshop as a form of, 2
  confusion, work summary uncovering of, 117
  as culture-building component of national workshops, 81
  feedback guidelines, (appendix), 201
  inflections as aid to improvement, 102
  initial
    guidelines for how much to say, 104
    in Hillside Group evaluation, 105
    in presentation(s), 105
    reaction to, 106

role in establishing context, 104
special workshopping instructions placed after, 130
as stage of the writers' workshop, (chapter), 101
writers' workshop, (chapter), 101
misunderstanding, summary of work as mechanism for detecting, 117, 120
Reasons why
  beautiful things are beautiful, as concern of pattern community, xiv
  comfortable things give comfort, as concern of pattern community, xiv
  writers' workshops work, See
    culture
    gift(s)
    ritual(s)
    safety
    work-in-progress
    xenia
Recording
  workshops, not recommended, 88
Recusion
  when appropriate, 116
References
  (chapter), 205
  "New Princeton Encyclopedia of Poetry and Poetics," (footnote), 118
Reflection
  See Also Craft; Improvement; Practice(s); Tools
  on craft issues, in context of specific work, 16
  as crucial improvement tool, 21
  on desired experience, as workshop preparation, 92
  on self-knowledge, 92
  as thorough review preparation component, 89
  on work results, as indicator of professional, 37
Reinforcement
  See Also Benefits; Gift(s); Positive
  of communication, reading aloud as, 102
  of gift nature of workshop, positive feedback as, 133
  for strong parts of the work, in positive feedback stage, 127
Relationships
  See Also Collaboration; Culture; Role(s)

email, style of, between shepherd and author, 99
global, shallow and broad review handling of, 91
shepherding
  interpersonal chemistry role in, 46
  nature of, 98
  working, impact on effective workshops, 67
Relativism
  postmodern, as barrier to effective craft discussions, 140
"release early, release often"
  as open source community maxim, 17
Release(ing)
  content, writing as tool for, 19
  frequent, workshops designed to handle, 18
  mechanism, focus on craft as, 20
  tension, during clarifications stage, 149
  (term description), 17
"Released Into Language: Options for Teaching Creative Writing" by Wendy Bishop, 205, 183
Religions
  gift economy in, 41
Repetitive making
  vs. risky making, semantics of, 178
  risky making emotional investment compared with, 29
  (term description), 25
Reprimands
  See Behavior; Rules
Requests
  for deep reviews, protocol for, 91
  by moderator, as exception to author silence rule, 111
  placing after the initial reading, 107
Requirements
  See Also Responsibilities
  criticism, possible fix be included along with, 4
  equipment, handling for workshop, 75
  excellent pattern writing, deep seeing, 136
  for moderator, 62
    experience relative to group, 58
  practice, for success in making things, 30, 37, 167
  preparation, 85
  for risky making, 26
  safe writers' workshop environment, xvi
  sensitivity, canon-building precautions, 82

Requirements (*cont.*)
   successful writers' workshop
      author safety and respect, 114
      politeness, 114
Resources
   See Also Attitudes and attributes; Creativity; Culture; Games; Structure(s)
   fresh thinking, 81
   learning
      experienced writers as, 168
      writers' workshop as, 21
   locating, 68
   of the mind, writing as way to tap into, 18
   review, 43
   technical writing skills, 138
   where to find writers' workshops, 2
Respect
   See Also Attitudes and attributes; Politeness; Positive, attitudes and attributes
   factors that deepen, 59
   as valuable characteristic in workshop members, 59
   as value of workshop preparation, 96
Response
   See Also Attitudes and attributes; Responsibilities
   complex, positive feed back aid to, 128
   connotations as, 119
   to gift of work-in-progress, 37
   of reader, work summary uncovering of, 117
   of workshop, to work-in-progress gift of the author, 152
Responsibilities
   See Also Attitudes and attributes; Ethics; Guidelines; Problems; Stages of the writers' workshop; Strategies; Tactics
   of audiences, 55
   of authors
      deciding if workshop with be of benefit or not, 95
      take what is food for you and leave the rest, 139
   of moderators, 54
      towards author during fly-on-the-wall role, 113
      for author protection from insults, 112
      damage control, 68

      maintenance of control, 141
      maintenance of positive tone, 63
      monitoring the state of the author, 131, 141
      vs. regular reviewer, 94
      review order of pieces, 93
      during suggestions for improvement, 144
      teaching roles, 62
      workshop pacing, 62
Revenge
   See Also Attitudes and attributes; Dangers; Negative; Responsibilities
   seeking by author, during clarifications stage, 148
Review(s)
   See Also Stages of the writers' workshop actions
   anonymous
      advantages and disadvantages, 43, 109
      as fly-on-the-wall strategy, 114
      peer review process, 44
      (term description), 43
   code, writers' workshop format use with, 18
   deep, request protocol, 91
   of documentation, writers' workshops as replacement for, 4
   guidelines, 97
   initial stage of, as initial review stage, 115
   journal, shepherding process in, 45
   literature-review errors, handling, in suggestions for improvement stage, 135
   order of pieces for
      classification by moderator, 93
      as moderator responsibility, 93
      when there are multiple pieces for same author, 107
   organizational, 45
   positive comments, bad effects of requiring reviewers to provide, 132
   presentations, 92
   resources, 43
   shallow
      advantages, 91
      as characteristic of workshop review, 91
   thorough
      advantages, 89
      strategies for presentation of, 90

Reviewers/reviewing
  See Also Actions; Attitudes and attributes;
      Shepherds; Stages of the writers'
      workshop; Tactics
  attitude, impact of appearance on, 87
  author as fly on the wall
      as alternative to anonymous peer review,
          110
      (chapter), 109
  contradictory comments, subjective nature of
      writing indicated by, 139
  face-to-face, disadvantages of, 109
  importance of obtaining summarization from
      all reviewers, 123
  lazy, damage of, 90
  level, for shepherd, guidelines, 99
  order, guidelines for, 75
  preparation
      recommendations, 89
      for writers' workshops, 85
  resources for, 43
  rewrite of author's work, dangerous and
      inappropriate nature, 93
  shepherd
      as kind of, 97
      role in, 45
  suggestions for improvement
      as pure gifts to the author, 145
      software patterns, 136
  type of work, feedback on, as initial review
      stage, 115
Revision
  See Also Drafts; Practice(s)
  multiple strategies for
      as outcome of good suggestions for
          improvement stage, 138
      in poem about Leonardo da Vinci, 143
  of piece
      (chapter), 155
      handling author limitations, 143
  of poem, in creative poetry workshops, 14
  practices
      Dickey, James, 157
      Paley, Grace, 158
      Richard Gabriel, 160
      Richard Gabriel, changes in, 160
      Schmitt, Richard, 158

role, in developing writing skills, 158
  writing without, 185
Rewriting of poem
  See Also Dangers
  in creative poetry workshops, 14
  dangerous and inappropriate nature, 93
  as failure cause in creative writers' workshops,
      48
Reynolds, Joshua H.
  John Keats letter to, (quotation), 140
Right-brain activities
  See Also Creativity; Games; Ritual(s)
  inter-session ritual use, 153
Risks
  See Also Failure(s); Safety
  of judgment, creating a context that reduces, 25
  making things under, as creative making's
      common denominator, 25
  sharing, as antidote to fear, 32
Risky making
  See Also Attitudes and attributes; Emotions;
      Failure(s); Safety; Setting
  acceptance and approval seeking in, 29
  vs. repetitive making, semantics of, 178
  repetitive making emotional investment
      compared with, 29
  reward for, in writers' workshop, 39
  (term description), 25
Ritual(s)
  See Also Safety; Setting
  as culture component, 79
  end-points of workshop, particular value for,
      108
  failures, in creative writers' workshops, 48
  formal initial reading, value of the, 102
  gift-giving nature of workshop enhanced by, 69
  inter-session, importance for managing
      dynamics of workshop, 153
  "Ritualized Friendship and the Greek City" by
      Gabriel Herman, xenia definition in, 181
  safe setting as primary purpose of, 69
  setting
      advantages of rules in, 46
      importance in gift giving, 46
  as shared culture component, in work-in-
      progress community, 37
  software vs. creative writing communities, 47

Ritual(s) (*cont.*)
　of workshop cultures, 69
　writers' workshop
　　impact on the experience, 2
　　importance for effectiveness of, 2
　　the author reads, (chapter), 101
　　viewed as, 80
"Ritualized Friendship and the Greek City" by Gabriel Herman, 206
　xenia definition in, 181
Rivalry
　See Also Reviewers/reviewing
　as anonymous peer review complication, 43
Rohnert, Hans
　"Pattern Languages of Program Design 4," 206
Role(s)
　See Also Audience(s); Author(s); Moderator(s); Participant(s); Reviewers/reviewing; Stages of the writers' workshop
　audience, types of, 54
　authors, as fundamental players in the workshop, 54
　autonomous readers, limitations, 34
　of circumstances, in art making, 28
　co-authors, treatment of, 54
　collaboration, in writers' workshop "midwife" job, 20
　competition, in commodity economy, 42
　distribution, in art making, 181
　fly-on-the-wall author
　　creative vs. technical writers' workshops, 72
　　importance, in suggestions for improvement stage, 143
　　origins, 3
　　role violations, 113
　　stage of writers' workshop, (chapter), 109
　　termination of, during clarifications stage, 147
　　workshop success dependent on, 114
　of games, in creating culture, 81
　gift economy
　　in forming bonds, 49
　　in lives of poets, 174
　Hillside Group, in development of "Design Patterns," 5
　interaction among, 63
　moderator, 54
　　in bridging diverse experience levels, 58
　　teaching, in creative vs. technical writers' workshops, 94
　negotiation of
　　as pedagogical tool, 84
　　(term description), 84
　in ritual setting, importance in gift giving, 46
　separation of author from work, in art making, 39
　shepherds, 97
　　in reviewing process, 45
　target audience, importance in assessing technical writing comprehensibility, 123
　teacher
　　in creative writers' workshops, 62
　　masterpieces as, in software patterns community, 6
　of triggers, in art making, 26, 28
　work summary, 120
　writers' workshop
　　audience, 53
　　author, 2
　　in creative process cycle, xv
　　in finding direction for an author, xv
　　games master, 80
　　in maturation cycle, 173
　　moderator, 2
　　participants, 2
　　participants, (chapter), 53
Rooms
　See Also Location; Ritual(s); Structure(s)
　layout, importance for effectiveness of the workshop, 71
　shared, as culture component, 79
Ropes course
　See Also Culture; Games
　software pattern community use as bonding exercise, 6
Rotation
　of workshop leaders, advantages, 82
Rules
　See Also Guidelines; Responsibilities; Ritual(s); Safety

of behavior
    importance in suggestions for improvement
        stage, 143
    shared culture component, 37
enforcing, as responsibility of moderator, 54
of engagement, absence as drawback of
    anonymous peer review, 44
ground, importance for safe writers' workshop
    environment, xvi
in ritual setting, advantages, 46
safe setting as primary purpose of, 69
software community rule acceptance of, 47
of technical writers' workshop, Hillside Group
    design of, 8
value for creative writers' workshop, 49
Rural location
    See Also Location
    as national writers' workshop culture
        component, 78
Russian formalists
    philosophy of, 3
Rut
    breaking out of, games as stimulant for, 81
"The Sacred Wood: Essays on Poetry and
    Criticism" by T. S. Eliot, 206
    (quotation), 162

Sacrifices
    gift economy component of, 41
Safety
    See Also Attitudes and attributes;
        Responsibilities; Ritual(s); Setting
    active listening as tool for protecting, 63
    author
        as consequence of work-in-progress
            attitude, 41
        importance for, 69
        protection from insults during workshop, 112
        requirement for success of workshop, 110
    deleterious impact on, of negative comments
        during positive feedback stage, 132
    failure to observe rules for, as workshop
        danger, 57
    mechanisms
        guidelines, 141
        in technical writers' workshops, 55

psychological, writers' workshop atmosphere
    geared towards, 2
setting, importance for authors, 69
Sanderson, David W.
    "Smileys," 207
    in Ron Goldman's pattern evaluation, 199
Sanderson, Doherty
    "Smileys," 207
    in Ron Goldman's pattern evaluation, 199
Sartore, Joel
    (quotation), National Geographic
        photographer image volumes, 38
Scarcity
    See Also Gift(s)
    commodity economy based on, 42
Schacter, Daniel L.
    "Searching for Memory," 207
    writing sources in the brain, 177
Schedule
    See Also Format; Pacing; Time
    priority of maintaining, in shepherd/author
        relationship, 99
Schmitt, Richard, 207
    interview with the author, 207
    revision practices, 158
Schneider, Pat
    "The Writer as an Artist: A New Approach to
        Writing Alone and with Others," 207,
        175
School
    See Teaching
Scientific
    See Also Technical writers' workshops
    basis, as technical writers' workshop subject, xvi
    writing, things to look for, in suggestions for
        improvement stage, 137
"scratch your own itch"
    as motivation for collaborative involvement, 15
"Scream to Rome" by Federico Garcia Lorca
    (quotation), 190
"Searching for Memory" by Daniel L. Schacter,
    207
    writing sources in the brain, 178
Secret
    See Also Benefits; Gift(s); Practice(s)
    to creativity, (quotation), 27
    to writing, revision as, 158

Index ~ 253

Seeing
　See Also Listening
　deep, as requirement for excellent pattern writing, 136
　problems with, trigger traces in work, 169
　writing relationship to, 170
Selection
　See Also Craft; Practice(s); Triggers
　of details, creative writing, personal vs. needs of the piece, 15
　in listening, as important author skill, 164
　role in achieving perfection, 38
　role in art making, 181
　skills in, role in art making, 39
　as strategy for practice, 166
Self
　See Also Separation of author from work
　-expression, limitations of emphasis on, 34
　-organized workshops
　　dangers of, 66
　　moderator less important, 61
　-organizing structures, games as resource for evolving, 81
"Self-Interviews" by James Dickey, 205
Semantics
　See Also Craft
　of creative writing, transparency vs. meaning, 122
　of duende, 178
　literal meaning vs. connotations, 119
　of punctuation, 162
　repetitive vs. risky making, 178
　of work, inflections in speech relationship to, 102
Sensitivity
　See Also Attitudes and attributes; Emotions
　to criticism, varying levels of, impact on writers' workshop, 57
　to group dynamics, as moderator requirement, 63
　requirements, canon-building precautions, 82
"Sentences My Father Used" by Charles Bernstein (quotation), 120
Separation of author from work
　See Also Attitudes and attributes; Fly-on-the-wall author role; Work-in-progress

　as benefit of writers' workshop, 37
　importance of, 114
　as key attitude, 145
　role in art making, 39
　as skill aided by working on other people's work, 16
Sestina
　See Also Poetry
　as technical term from literature vocabulary, 78
Setting
　See Also Context; Culture; Location; Ritual(s); Structure(s)
　audience impact on, 73
　contemplative, advantages, 74
　formal
　　creative vs. technical writers workshops, 57
　　software community acceptance, 47
　geographical, of workshop, (chapter), 77
　group level, for novices, 57
　guidelines for handling equipment, 75
　out-of-the-ordinary, as source of strength in writers' workshops, 81
　outdoors, potential distractions, 74
　pedagogical, as workshop context, 84
　for performance and presentation workshopping, 73
　physical, importance of people arrangement, 71
　ritual
　　advantages of rules in, 46
　　formality value, 49
　　importance in gift giving, 46
　safe, shared culture value for, 71
　special, requirements for, 74
　specialized, selecting for specific workshops, 74
　of writers' workshops, (chapter), 69
Sewanee Writers' Conference
　See Also Conferences
　as creative writers' workshop, 2
　workshop leader characteristics, 64
Shakespeare, William
　sonnets, 89
　as canon component, 80
Shallow review
　See Also Review(s)
　advantages of, 91
　as characteristic of workshop review, 91

Shapiro, Alan
  denotative gloss advocacy, 104
Shared
  See Also Collaboration; Communities;
      Culture
  accommodations
    as culture component, 79
    danger of not participating in, 183
  culture
    cliques as danger of, 183
    safe setting created by, 71
    of work-in-progress community, 37
  experiences, as binding force for workshop
      participants, 78
  gift, work-in-progress as essence of, 87
  history, as binding force for workshop
      participants, 78
  knowledge, as culture component, 77
  ownership, suggestions for improvement stage
      threat to, 141
  purpose, of work-in-progress community, 37
  risks, as antidote to fear, 32
  stories, as culture component, 80
  vocabulary, as binding force for workshop
      participants, 78
  world view, as binding force for workshop
      participants, 78
"Sharing Feelings or Being Clear or
    Communicating Subtlety" pattern
    (quotation), 195
Sheep
  See Also Stories
  in Pablo Neruda's story of gift-giving, 50
Shepherds
  See Also Reviewers/reviewing
  (chapter), 97
  comments, importance of establishing the
      right tone, 98
  in creative writing world, 183
  interactions with, 99
  in journal reviews, 45
  kindness importance in, 99
  Neil Harrison Shepherding Award, 184
  power of
    balancing with effective review, 99
    in determining conference acceptance for
        author, 100

preparation use of, 89
as representative of writers' workshop culture, 98
reviewing
  level guidelines, 99
  role, 45
technical writers' workshop
  development of, 8
  as practice different from traditional
      conferences, 8
  (term description), 45, 89, 97
Short
  pieces
    initial reading for, 107
    written on location, as one type of writers'
        workshop, 70
  -term efforts, See
    brainstorming
    critiques
    master classes
Shorthand comments
  See Also Emoticons
  for repeated phrases, 133
Sistine Chapel frescoes by Michelangelo
  skills and "tricks" used to create, 179
Size
  See Also Setting
  ideal, for writers' workshop, 53
Skill(s)
  See Also Attitudes and attributes; Craft;
      Listening; Practice(s); Teaching; Tools
  in criticism, role in art making, 39
  improvement
    as benefit of workshopping, 15
    as goal of writers' workshop, 110
    as writers' workshop benefit, 173
  in making things, attention and practice, 26
  moderator
    tools, active listening, 63
    tools, interrelated comments, 62
    tools, what-if type questions, 62
  separation of author from work, aided by
      working on other people's work, 16
  teaching, importance for creative writers'
      workshop leaders, 61
  writing
    revision role, 158
    teaching technologists the value of, 62

Smileys
  as emoticon name, 198
"Smileys" by Doherty Sanderson and David W. Sanderson, 207
  in Ron Goldman's pattern evaluation, 199
Snake Lake
  as shared story culture component, 80
  special meaning for Warren Wilson College alumni, 78
Snyder, Gary
  as creative writers' workshop leader, 65
  readings at the Art of the Wild conference, 82
Social mechanisms
  See Culture; Group(s); Ritual(s); Setting
Software
  See Also Creative writing; Technical, writing
  belief that it is repetitive making, 26
  code review, writers' workshop format use with, 18
  communities
    cross fertilization with creative writing community insights and practices, xvii
    Hillside Group introduction to writers' workshops, 5
    literature building efforts, 6
    writers' workshop history in, xiv
  community, formal setting acceptance by, 47
  development
    characteristics of the work, 34
    software patterns vs. formalist paradigm, 6
  extreme programming, "continuous integration" maxim, 17
  making, commonalities with art making, 28
  object-oriented programming, vocabulary, technical writers' workshop use, 78
  open-source projects, writers' workshop compared with, xiv
  pair programming
    face-to-face interaction, 14
    as group activity that assists the individual, 12
    as group practice that aids individual creativity, 1
  pattern community, conferences, 6
  patterns, vs. formalist paradigm, 6
  technical expertise, impact on writers' workshop, 56
  writers' workshop approach applicable to, 2f

Songs
  See Also Games; Music; Ritual(s)
  inter-session ritual use, 153
Sonnets of Shakespeare
  See Also Poetry
  as canon component, 80
  craft elements, 89
Sound
  See Also Setting
  as potential distraction, 74
Speaking
  See Also Listening; Voice
  brain mechanisms different from writing, illustrated by story of brain-damaged boy, 18
Special instructions
  placing after the initial reading, 107, 130
Speed
  See Also Practice(s)
  of improvement, as writers' workshop advantage, xvii
  writing, impact of overcoming fear on, 161
Spiritual
  See Also Attitudes and attributes; Culture
  components, of gift, 42
  leaders, of workshop culture, 80
  magic, writing in flow as, 181
  ownership, as aspect of work-in-progress gift, 86
Squaw Valley
  See Also Conferences
  Art of the Wild conference, Gary Snyder's readings, 82
  Community of Writers Workshop in Poetry
    as established creative writers' workshop, 77
    writing on location at, 82
Stafford, William
  "Writing the Australian Crawl," (quotation), 26
Stages of the writers' workshop
  See Also Creative writers' workshops; Technical writers' workshops; Writers' workshops
  author as fly on the wall, (chapter), 109
  clarifications, (chapter), 147
  as goal of Part 2-"Writers' Workshop," xviii
  initial reading, (chapter), 101
  positive feedback

(chapter), 127
        workshopping example, 197
    post-workshop revision, (chapter), 155
    suggestions for improvement
        (chapter), 135
        workshopping example, 198
    summarization of work
        (chapter), 115
        workshopping example, 197
    wrapping up, (chapter), 151
Standard deviation
    (term description), 179
Stanford University
    Computer Science department transfer to
        School of Engineering, significance of, 26
Start(ing)
    See Also Setting; Termination
    a group, guidelines for, 68
    point for shepherding review, piece as a whole,
        99
    of software pattern writers' workshop, xiv, 4
    of a work, beliefs about importance of, 33
    writers' workshops, 96
Statistical distribution
    quality assurance use of, 181
"stealing"
    See Also Actions; Craft; Voice
    aka hiding sources, as creativity secret,
        (quotation), 27
    as creative writer practice strategy, 164
    plagiarizing vs., 161
    T. E. Eliot recommendations, 162
    (term description), 161
Steele, Guy L. Jr.
    craft elements, 89
Stern, Gerald
    as creative writers' workshop leader, 65
Stevens, Wallace
    "Of Mere Being," (quotation), 121
    "The Palm at the End of the Mind," 207
Stories
    See Also Examples; Quotations
    Alan Shapiro denotative gloss advocacy, 104
    atheist poem with Christian reading, 117
    author who couldn't tolerate fly-on-the-wall
        role, 113
    benefit to author of writers' workshop, 35

brain damaged boy, writing vs. speaking brain
    mechanisms illustrated by, 18
contradictory reviewer comments in a poetry
    review, 139
creative workshop handling of confusion, 120
door-to-door comments, 102
dual workshop leaders who disagreed on poem
        interpretation, 64
    background on poem, 182
emotionally disturbed children
    importance of focus on writing, not content,
        60
    writers' workshop-like work with, 19
gift-giving impact on Pablo Neruda's
    development, 49
hard judgmental poetry workshop leader, 103
Hillside Group evaluation, initial reading in, 105
Hillside Group introduction to notion of
    technical writers' workshop, technical
    writers' workshop use, 4
Lexington avenue birthday gift surprise, 46
Maxine Kumin's leadership style, 65
MFA workshop failure, 48
moderator skill in workshopping a pattern
    language for software development, 62
organization evaluation in 2000, writers'
    workshop use, 9
product launch workshop
    in 1998, 8
    failure of, 67, 142
purpose of, xviii
revision of poem about Leonardo da Vinci, 143
shared, as culture component, 80
as source of quality, 129
sources of, topos as story-generating story,
    (footnote), 117
symbol definition in programming language
    specification, 16
take what is food for you and leave the rest, 138
    (term description), 137
two skinny dogs in plaza of Taos Pueblo, 102
    followup experience, 104
workshopping of "Jimmy, Jimmy, O, Jimmy
    Mc," 144
writing of "Is Jack Gilbert's Mind a Computer,"
    83
Strand, Mark

as creative writers' workshop leader, 65, 173
  importance of practice to, 159
Strangeness
  See Also Attitudes and attributes
  as source of quality, 129
  as virtue in poetry and writers' workshops, 81
Strategies
  See Also Guidelines; Responsibilities; Tactics
  author
    for handling multiple suggestions, 138
    multiple approaches, 138
    in poem about Leonardo da Vinci, 143
    practice, imitation use, 164
  content discussion deflection, 66
  for effective practice, selection as, 166
  fly-on-the-wall, anonymous peer review as, 114
  focus
    on work, 112
    on work-in-progress, 70
  improvement, novices, 30
  listening, enhancement, 66
  notetaking, (quotation), 88
  pedagogical
    bad side-effects of uncritical constant praise, 141
    writing on location, 82
  revision, in good suggestions for improvement sessions, 138
  thorough review presentation, 90
  writing, Samuel Johnson, 169
Strengths
  See Also Positive
  emphasizing, in effective leadership style, 66
  identifying, in positive feedback stage, 127
Structure(s)
  See Also Order; Pattern(s)
  of book, xvii
  narrative
    as creative writers' workshop subject, xvi
    as technical term from literature vocabulary, 78
  organizational reward, as drawback in organizational review process, 45
  outline and planning, role in making things, 168
  room layout format, importance for effectiveness of the workshop, 71

self-organizing, games as resource for evolving, 81
sentence, Samuel Johnson and Rick Bass, 162
summarization workshop, advantages and characteristics, 124
of technical writers' workshop, Hillside Group design of, 8
writers' workshop format
  code review use, 18
  overview, 3
  purpose of, 4
of writing, as source of quality, 129
Style
  See Also Appearance; Craft
  email relationship, between shepherd and author, 99
  of workshop
    culture, variations in, 69
    importance of determining in advance, 94
  writing, as source of quality, 129
"Style: Toward Clarity and Grace" by Joseph M. Williams, 207
Stylized behavior
  of writers' workshop, importance for effectiveness of, 2
Subjective components of writing
  See Also Comments; Writing
  reflected in contradictory reviewer comments, 138
Success(ful)
  See Also Benefits; Positive; Reasons why, writers' workshops work; Responsibilities
  making things, practice requirements, 30, 37, 167
  operation, how and why vs. doing it, xv
  practice, vs. analysis of how something works, xv
  risky making, groups importance for, 32
  writers' workshop
    author expectations and emotions impact on, 61
    author safety and respect requirement, 114
    fly-on-the-wall role crucial to, 114
    generosity importance, 8
    politeness requirement for, 114
    writing for target audience, obtaining feedback, 117

SugarLoafPLoP (Latin America) conference
   See Also Conferences
   as regional PLoP conference, 177
Suggestions for improvement
   See Also Feedback; Stages of the writers'
       workshop
   audience responsibilities, 144
   author strategies for handling, 138
   behavior rules importance for effective
       transmission of, 143
   competitive attitude dangers, 141
   concrete, value of, 135
   effective comment characteristics, 138
   handling confusion about, 184
   moderator control responsibilities and
       strategies, 141
   moderator responsibilities, 144
   reviewers, in software patterns community, 136
   in scientific and technical writing, things to
       look for, 137
   as stage of writers' workshop
       (chapter), 135
       effective comments in, 138
       workshopping example, 198
   tactics, creative writers' workshop, 136
   workshopping examples, 198
       creative writers' workshop, 187
   writers' workshop facilitation of, 2
Summarization
   See Also Stages of the writers' workshop
   in creative writers' workshops, workshopping
       example, 190
   crucial value of, 124
   importance of obtaining from all reviewers,
       123
   as opening interaction by shepherd, 99
   problems
       readers lack of comprehension, 118
       when to terminate, 118
   as source of acceptance, 124
   in technical writers' workshops
       author explanations after, 105
       workshopping example, 197
   value to author of, 125
   of work, as writers' workshop stage, (chapter),
       115
   workshop, advantages and characteristics, 124

"Summer of Deliverance" by Christopher Dickey,
   205
"The Sun Singer" statue
   as Allerton Park feature, 79
Supervisors
   impact on effective workshops, 67
Support group
   See Communities
Surrogate author
   situations where needed, 67
Swannanoa, North Carolina
   as Warren Wilson College location, 187
Swarming behavior
   writers' workshop compared with, xiv
Sweatheart
   See Also Culture
   as Warren Wilson College idiom, 78, 80
Symbol definition story
   See Also Stories
   as example of triggering situation handling, 16

Tact
   See Also Attitudes and attributes;
       Responsibilities; Tactics
   importance in helping students to listen, 66
   in two skinny dogs in plaza of Taos Pueblo
       story, 102
Tactics
   See Also Guidelines; Responsibilities;
       Strategies
   for emotional closure, in wrapping up stage, 151
   moderator
       towards author during fly-on-the-wall role,
          113
       ensuring that praise is honest, 132
       handling an obstreperous author, 112
       handling confusion, 122
       handling confusion about work, 120
       handling well-explored subjects, 140
       incomplete work summaries, 118
       when author is distressed, 132, 144
   question-asking, for effective improvement
       suggestions, 144
   revision, 163, 164
   software patterns, suggestions for
       improvement, 136

260　　INDEX

Tactics (cont.)
 suggestions for improvement
  creative writers' workshop, 136
  technical writers' workshop, 136
Take what is food for you and leave the rest
 as effective author strategy for handling multiple suggestions, 138
Taos Pueblo
 two skinny dogs story, 102
 followup experience, 104
Target audience
 See Also Goals
 of book, xvii
 crucial role in assessing technical writing comprehensibility, 123
 writing for, obtaining feedback on success, 117
Teaching
 See Also Craft; Learning; Tools; Writers' workshops
 context
  examples of, 84
  fly-on-the-wall strategy can work with anonymous review, 114
  impact on participant qualifications, 56
  interaction of craft lectures and workshopping process, 62
 feedback guidelines, (appendix), 201
 handling diverse experience levels, moderator as teacher role, 56, 58
 moderator as teacher, vs. moderator as author, 67
 opportunity, each piece potential for, 129
 skills of, importance for effective moderators, 61
 strategies
  bad side-effects of uncritical constant praise, 141
  imitation as, 164
 tools
  one-on-one conferences, 81
  Warren Wilson College MFA program, 181
  writing method books, 183
 workshop steps, as moderator responsibility, 62
 writers' workshops, bibliographic references, 183

writing
 creative writers' workshop role, 62
 "The Elephants Teach: Creative Writing Since 1880" by D. G. Myers, 206
 as gift of non-author leaders, 68
 practice as tool for, 84
 "Released Into Language: Options for Teaching Creative Writing" by Wendy Bishop, 205
 role of masterpieces and exemplars, 6
 role of moderator, 54, 94, 182
 role of work itself, 30
 software pattern community practices for, 6
 value of close reading, 181
 value of confusion and misunderstanding, 122
 value of identifying good parts of a piece, 130
 value of on-location writing, 82
 value of workshop preparation, 96
Technical
 See Also Creative writing
 basis, as technical writers' workshop subject, xvi
 content, handling of, 59
 people, teaching the value of writing to, 62
 review, vs. writers' workshop, 60
 work
  triggers relationship to, 16
  triggers role in, 27
 writing
  benefits of book, xvii
  comprehensibility assessment dependent on target audience, 123
  content privileged over writing quality, 140
  vs. creative writing, Richard Gabriel's experience, 185
  examining for quality, 130
  information transfer importance in, 116
  (term description), xviii
  things to look for in suggestions for improvement stage, 137
  transparency and understandability in, 119
Technical writers' workshops
 See Also Creative writers' workshops; Pattern(s); Teaching; Writers' workshops; Writing

audience safety mechanisms in, 55
canon, 80
conference innovations, 8
vs. creative writers' workshops
   aggressiveness in, 185
   attitudes towards workshop process, 41
   audience, 53, 55
   benefits of workshop, 170
   clarity and understanding of work, 119
   comparison, xvi
   content as subject for comments, 139
   craft expertise of workshop moderators, 64
   craft topics, 165
   expert writers as moderators, 173
   explanations in initial reading of work, 105
   family-like behavior in, 58
   fly-on-the-wall role, 72
   formal setting adherence differences, 57
   game types, 81
   handling confusion in, 121, 122
   initial reading, 101
   shallow review advantages, 92
   suggestions for improvement tactics, 136
   summarization of piece as area of greatest difference, 3
   summary of work, 115, 116
   teaching role of moderator, 94
   things to look for in suggestions for improvement stage, 137
   transparency and understandability in, 119
   types of comments appropriate to, 87
   types of feedback from, 87
   value of good writing in its own right, 90
domain area expertise issues, 56
examples
   of well-known, 77
   of workshopping practice, 195
importance of summary of work for, 116
knowledgeable leadership value for, 62
overview of the process, 3
strategies for maintaining focus on work, 70
subjects and concerns of, xvi
technical content handling, 59
(term description), xviii
vs. traditional scientific conferences and workshops, 8

vocabulary of, 78
where to find, 2
work summary recommendations, 118
Tension
   See Also Attitudes and attributes; Emotions
   around content as appropriate topic for discussion, 139
   release, during clarifications stage, 149
Term descriptions
   acceptance, 29, 124
   active listening, 63
   amphitheater, natural, 73
   annotation, 182
   anonymous peer review, 43
   approval, 29, 124
   audiences, 53
      non-participatory, 54
      participatory, 54
   brainstorming, 11
   charrette(s), 12
   commodity economy, 42
   contributors, 182
   courage, 167
   creative
      writers' workshops, xiv, xviii
      writing, xiv, xviii
   critiques, 11
   culture, 77
   deviance, positive, 130
   distribution, normal, 179
   duende, 178
   economy
      commodity, 42
      gift, 41
   essay, 168
   fly-on-the-wall author role, 113
   formalist paradigm, 6
   gift(s), economy, 41
   integration, 17
   listening, active, 63
   making
      repetitive, 25
      risky, 25
   master class, 13
   moderator(s), 53
   natural voice, 159
   negative, capability, 171

Term descriptions (*cont.*)
  normal distribution, 179
  open source, 12
  pair, programming, 12
  participant(s), audiences that are, 54
  pattern, 6, 163, 175
    languages, 6, 175
  piece(s), workshop, 163
  plot, 137
  positive, deviance, 130
  programming, pair, 12
  release(ing), 17
  repetitive making, 25
  review(s), anonymous, 43
  risky making, 25
  role negotiation, 84
  shepherds, 45, 89, 97
  standard deviation, 179
  "stealing," 161
  stories, 137
  technical
    writers' workshops, xviii
    writing, xviii
  topos, 117
  transparency, 119
  triggers, 26
  understandability, 119
  voice, natural, 159
  waitstaff, 182
  workshop, piece, 163
  writers' workshops, 1, 35, 39, 80
  writing
    creative, xiv, xviii
    technical, xviii
  xenia, 42
Termination
  See Also Stages of the writers' workshop
  of fly-on-the-wall role, during clarifications stage, 147
  of session
    when author is distressed, 144
    when author is obstreperous, 113
    when reviewers are obnoxious, 142
    with the summary, when needed and appropriate, 123
  of work summary stage, as moderator problem, 118

Territoriality as drawback
  See Also Attitudes and attributes; Negative
  in organizational review process, 45
  in writers' workshop interactions, 61
Thanks
  See Also Gift(s); Xenia
  by author, during clarifications stage, 148
"The Palm at the End of the Mind" by Wallace Stevens, 207
"The Passion of Emily Dickinson" by Judith Farr, 206
Themes
  See Also Content; Culture
  of book, See
    gift(s)
    role(s)
    teaching
    work-in-progress
    writers' workshops, creative vs. technical
  as unifying focus for mixed groups, 65
  in work, focus on, as failure cause in creative writers' workshops, 48
Thomas, Frank
  "Disney Animation: The Illusion of Life," 207
Thorough review
  See Also Review(s)
  advantages of, 89
  strategies for presentation of, 90
Time
  See Also Pacing; Setting
  of writers' workshop sessions, 4
"Time Leaves" by Richard Gabriel
  (quotation), 189
  as workshopping example, 187
"The Timeless Way of Building" by Christopher Alexander, 205
  as canon component, 80
Tone
  See Also Attitudes and attributes; Ritual(s); Setting
  negative, warding against in positive feedback stage, 131
  positive, moderator responsibility to maintain, 63
  of shepherd relationship, 98
  of workshop
    guidelines for protecting, 76

helper or owner attitude impact on, 60
putdowns effect on, 61
Tools
   See Also Attitudes and attributes; Craft;
      Culture; Responsibilities; Strategies;
      Structure(s); Tactics; Teaching
   close reading
      as pedagogical tool, 181
      writers' workshop as a form of, 2
   for craft improvement
      examination of craft masters, 89
      practice as, 21, 89
      reflection as, 21
      suggestions for improvement stage, 135
      writing about craft elements, 84
   for discovery, writing as, 19, 168
   pedagogical
      confusion and misunderstanding as, 122
      Warren Wilson College MFA program, 181
   of skilled moderator
      active listening, 63
      interrelated comments, 62
      what-if questions, 62
   teaching, writing method books, 183
   trust, for overcoming fear, 169
   work summary, for unmasking of confusion
      and misunderstanding, 123
   for writing, writing method books, 183
Topos
   See Also Craft; Meta level
   (term description), (footnote), 117
Training
   See Also Responsibilities; Teaching
   of novice moderators, 63
      in creative writers' workshops, 64
Transformation
   See Also Benefits; Improvement
   in emotionally disturbed children story, 20
   of group, through magic of gift economy, 49
   of initial triggers into craft, workshop help
      with, 136
"The Transformation of Silence into Language
   and Action" by Audre Lorde, 206
Transparency
   See Also Attitudes and attributes;
      Clarification/clarity
   in creative writing, 120

vs. meaning, in poetry, 122
(term description), 119
"The Triggering Town" by Richard Hugo, 206
(quotation), 27, 31
Triggers
   See Also Craft; Creativity
   characteristics of, 27
   external nature, relationship to writers'
      workshop, 28
   practices and, (chapter), 25
   problems with residue traces of, 169
   relationship to work product, 16
   residue remaining of, possible confusions
      resulting from, 117
   role in
      art making, 26, 28
      technological making, 27
   separation from autobiography, 182
   (term description), 26
   transformation of, workshop help with, 136
Trust
   See Also Attitudes and attributes; Emotions;
      Tools
   courage relationship to, 169
   development, reasons for, in a writers'
      workshop, 47
   enhancement, by authors staying together for
      duration of workshop, 70
   as gift of the author, 35
Tufte, Edward R.
   "Envisioning Information," 207
   "The Visual Display of Quantitative
      Information," 207
   "Visual Explanations: Images and Quantities,
      Evidence and Narrative," 207
"Twenty Poems" by Pablo Neruda, 206, 182
Two skinny dogs story, 102
   See Also Stories
   followup experience, 104
Types of
   See Also Structure(s)
   audience, 54
   comments
      draft level impact on, 86
      in suggestions for improvement stage, 138
   experience, 56, 57
   fear, 29

Types of (*cont.*)
  feedback from
    creative writers' workshops, 88
    technical writers' workshops, 87
  games, creative vs. technical writers workshops, 81
  pieces, moderator classification, 93
  questions, as skilled moderator tool, 62
  work, feedback on, as initial review stage, 115
  writers' workshops
    See Also Writers' workshops, creative vs. technical
    prepared vs. on-location writing, 70

Understandability
  See Also Clarification/clarity
  (term description), 119
Uniform seating arrangements
  See Also Setting
  importance for effectiveness of the workshop, 72
University of Iowa
  See Also Conferences
  history of, bibliographic reference, 177
  as writers' workshop origin, 1
UP (Using Patterns) conference
  See Also Conferences
  as regional PLoP conference, 177
User-visible patterns
  See Also Pattern(s)
  characteristics and aesthetics, 93
  workshopping example, 195

Validation
  See Also Acceptance; Approval
  need for, deleterious impact on success of workshop, 61
Variables (software)
  Local Variables pattern example, 177
Venues and vehicles
  See Also Reviewers/reviewing
  for reviewing, 43
Viereck, George Sylvester
  "What Life Means to Einstein: An Interview by George Sylvester Viereck," 206

"The Visual Display of Quantitative Information" by Edward R. Tufte, 207
"Visual Explanations: Images and Quantities, Evidence and Narrative" by Edward R. Tufte, 207
Vlissides, John
  as "Design Patterns" author, 78
  "Design Patterns: Elements of Reusable Object-Oriented Software," 206
Vocabulary
  See Also Craft
  literature, creative writers' workshop use, 78
  technical writers' workshops, 78
  understanding, as benefit of workshopping, 15
Voice
  See Also Listening; Readers/reading
  importance in reading of poetry, 102
  natural
    as consequence of growth as writer, 171
    (term description), 160
    as writing and revision aid, 160
Voigt, Ellen Bryant
  as outstanding creative writers' workshop leader, 65, 187
Vulnerabilities
  See Also Attitudes and attributes
  of creative writers vs. software writers, 48
  fear of exposure, in risky making, 29

Waitstaff
  See Also Conferences
  in creative writers' workshops, (term description), 182
Wally(s)
  See Also Culture
  creation myth, as shared myth culture component, 80
  as Warren Wilson College idiom, 78
Warmth
  See Also Attitudes and attributes
  in two skinny dogs in plaza of Taos Pueblo story, 102
Warren Wilson College MFA program
  See Also Conferences; Creative writers' workshops
  culture of, 78, 79

educational philosophy of, 84
examples of workshop experiences, 187
"MFA Program for Writers Handbook," 207 (quotation), 76
teaching tools, 181

Weakness
See Also Dangers; Responsibilities
moderator, as failure cause in creative writers' workshops, 48

"What Life Means to Einstein: An Interview by George Sylvester Viereck," 206

What-if questions
See Also Tactics; Tools
as skilled moderator tool, 62

Whitman, Walt
as canon member, 80

Williams, Joseph M.
"Style: Toward Clarity and Grace," 207

Wilson, Ian
summary analysis of "Scream to Rome," 190
thesis, 207

Women
positive feedback difficulties, 132
writers, including in canon-building, 82

Words
See Also Semantics
denotation vs. connotation of, 119

Work
See Also Piece(s); Work-in-progress
attributes that contribute to quality, 129
completion of, 166
defensiveness about, disadvantages of, 111
focus on
as antidote to focusing on fear, 31
author reference strategies for maintaining, 112
in comments, as goal, 92
as magic of the gift, 35
good parts, pedagogical value, 130
of making things
coda, (chapter), 167
(part), 23
objectification of, as benefit of writers' workshop, 37
revising the, (chapter), 155
separation of self from
as benefit of writers' workshop, 37

importance of, 114
as key attitude, 145
role in art making, 39
as skill aided by working on other people's work, 16
state of, appropriate for a workshop, 42
summarization of, (chapter), 115
type of, feedback on, as initial review stage, 115

Work-in-progress
See Also Collaboration; Drafts; Gift(s); Improvement; Writers' workshops
accurate reaction to, as goal of writers' workshop, 106
attitude, consequences, 41
(chapter), 33
collaborative help with, 34
community, shared purpose and culture of, 37
dangers, ameliorating, 69
gift
of the author, 35
of the author, workshop response, 152
as essence of shared gift, 87
trust encouragement by, 47
in writers' workshop community, 42
grand performance contrasted with, 35
impact of piece's appearance on expectations of, 86
improvement, as goal of writers' workshop, 110
integrity, respecting, during suggestions for improvement stage, 135
as state of mind, appropriate for a workshop, 43
as strategy for maintaining focus on work in technical writers' workshops, 70
writers' workshop viewed as, 37

"Working for National Geographic Magazine" by Joanna Pinneo, 206, 178

Working relationships
impact on effective workshops, 67

Wrapping up stage
See Also Stages of the writers' workshop
of writers' workshop, (chapter), 151

Wright, James
influence on Richard Gabriel's "Time Leaves," 187
translation of Pablo Neruda's "Twenty Poems," 182

"The Writer as an Artist: A New Approach to Writing Alone and with Others" by Pat Schneider, 207, 175
Writerly fingerprints
　See Also Reviewers/reviewing
　as anonymous review inhibitor, 114
Writers
　See Author(s); Experienced writers; Novice(s); Writers' workshops
Writers' workshops
　See Also Creative writers' workshops; History of writers' workshops; Technical writers' workshops
　benefits of, experience level changes in, 170
　bibliographic references, 183
　(chapter), 1
　characteristics summary, 174
　creative, See Creative writers' workshop
　creative vs. technical
　　aggressiveness in, 185
　　attitudes towards workshop process, 41
　　audience, 53, 55
　　benefits of workshop, 170
　　clarity and understanding of work, 119
　　comment range, 164
　　comparison, xvi
　　content as subject for comments, 139
　　craft expertise of workshop moderators, 64
　　expert writers as moderators, 173
　　explanations in initial reading of work, 105
　　family-like behavior in, 58
　　fly-on-the-wall role, 72
　　formal setting adherence differences, 57
　　game types, 81
　　handling confusion in, 121, 122
　　initial reading, 101
　　shallow review advantages, 92
　　suggestions for improvement tactics, 136
　　summarization of piece as area of greatest difference, 3
　　summary of work, 115, 116
　　teaching role of moderator, 94
　　things to look for in suggestions for improvement stage, 137
　　transparency and understandability in, 119
　　types of feedback from, 87, 88
　　value of good writing in its own right, 90

culture
　ascertaining in advance, 94
　shepherd as representative of, 98
dynamics, variations dependent on moderator skills, 64
effective, hallmarks of, 149
essential characteristics, 2
experienced moderators, gift economy and, 182
external nature of process, 28
failure, explosive possibilities, 41
feedback guidelines, (appendix), 201
finding, 68
format
　code review use, 18
　overview, 3
　purpose of, 4
gift
　acceptance and approval as, 39
　exchange in, 35, 42
　work-in-progress as, 42
gift economy
　as characteristic of, 80
　experienced moderators and, 182
　vs. paid moderators, as paradox, xv
　xenia as spirit of, 43
goals, See Goals, writers' workshops
healing qualities of, (quotation), xiii
history of
　as binding force for workshop participants, 78
　in creative writing, xiv, 1, 2, 177
　in software patterns community, xiv, 4, 7
　hopping, as bad practice for building trust, 70
　how it works, examination of, as goal of the book, xvi
leader, See Moderator(s)
location and setting of, (chapter), 77
moving from one to another, vs. staying with one over a long period of time, 18
as object of study to patterns community, xiv
pacing
　moderator management, 94
　as moderator responsibility, 62
(part), 51
preparing for, (chapter), 85
as presentation and science workshop alternative, xiv

process, examination of, as goal of the book, xv
purpose
    avenues of improvement, not criticism, 135
    making piece best it can be, 135
as release early phenomenon, 17
as risk sharing mechanism, 32
roles, (chapter), 53
science, writers' workshop as alternative to, xiv
self-organized
    dangers of, 66
    moderator less important, 61
session
    length, 4
    length, for on-going workshops, 4
    termination, when author is distressed, 144
    termination, when author is obstreperous, 113
    termination, when reviewers are obnoxious, 142
    termination with the summary, 123
setting, (chapter), 69
stages
    author as fly on the wall, (chapter), 109
    clarifications, (chapter), 147
    as goal of Part 2-"Writers' Workshop," xviii
    initial reading, (chapter), 101
    positive feedback, (chapter), 127
    positive feedback, workshopping example, 197
    suggestions for improvement, (chapter), 135
    suggestions for improvement, workshopping example, 198
    summarization of work, (chapter), 115
    summarization of work, workshopping example, 197
    the author reads, (chapter), 101
    wrapping up, (chapter), 151
starting, 96
strangeness as virtue in, 81
success
    fly-on-the-wall role crucial to, 114
    politeness crucial to, 114
summary-only, advantages and characteristics, 124
technical, See Technical writers' workshop
(term description), 1, 35, 39, 80
types of, 70

what it is not, xvi
where to find, 2
why they work, See
    gift(s)
    responsibilities
    ritual(s)
    safety
    work-in-progress
    xenia
as work-in-progress, 37
workshop piece
    See Also Dumbing down as danger
    (term description), 163
Writers's Conference (Napa Valley)
    See Also Conferences
    writing on location at, 82
Writing
    See Also Craft; Teaching; Tools; Writers' workshops
    brain mechanisms
        different from speaking, illustrated by story of brain-damaged boy, 18
        writing sources, 178
    as content releaser, 19
    creative
        community, informality preferences, 47
        craft expertise, impact on writers' workshop, 56
        detail selection, personal vs. needs of the piece, 15
        (term description), xiv, xviii
        transparency and understandability in, 119
    deeply buried nature of, as source of discussion difficulties, 140
    difficulties and process, xiii
    as discovery tool, 19, 168
    family, writers' workshop as, 35
    flow in
        magic of, 181
        "Writing in Flow" description of, 178
    group practices that benefit, (chapter), 11
    on-location
        as one type of writers' workshop, 70
        in pattern conferences, 83
        as teaching strategy, 82
    pair, as activity that assists the individual writer, 12

268 INDEX

Writing (cont.)
   as pervasive atmosphere and them, of national workshops, 81
   prepared vs. on-location, as classifier for writers' workshops, 70
   process, model, as goal of Part 1-"The Work of Making Things," xvii
   as release vehicle for emotionally disturbed child, 20
   without revising, 185
   skills
      learning from experienced writers, 168
      practice role, 168
      revision, (chapter), 155
      revision role, 158
      teaching technologists the value of, 62
   speed, impact of overcoming fear on, 161
   strategies, Samuel Johnson, 169
   structure of, as source of quality, 129
   style, as source of quality, 129
   subjective components, reflected in contradictory reviewer comments, 138
   teaching
      creative writers' workshop role, 62
      as gift of non-author leaders, 68
      role of masterpieces and exemplars, 6
      role of moderator, 54, 94, 182
      role of work itself, 30
      software pattern community practices for, 6
      value of close reading, 181
      value of confusion and misunderstanding, 122
      value of identifying good parts of a piece, 130
      value of on-location writing, 82
      value of workshop preparation, 96
   technical
      benefits of book, xvii
      comprehensibility assessment dependent on target audience, 123
      content privileged over writing quality, 140
      examining for quality, 130
      information transfer importance in, 116
      (term description), xviii
      things to look for in suggestions for improvement stage, 137
      transparency and understandability in, 119
   tools
      practice, 89
      study of masters' craft, 89
      writing method books, 183
   at the workshop
      as one type of writers' workshop, 70
      as teaching strategy, 82
"Writing and Sense of Self: Identity Negotiation in Writing Workshops" by Robert E. Brooke, 205, 183
"Writing in Flow" by Susan K. Perry, 206
   flow in writing, 178
"Writing the Australian Crawl" by William Stafford
   (quotation), 26
"Writing Workshops: Guidelines for Feedback" by Linda Elkin
   (appendix), 201

Xenia
   See Also Attitudes and attributes; Culture; Generosity; Gift(s); Relationships
   in advanced workshop characteristics, 171
   attributes, 80
   bibliographic references for definitions of, 181
   deleterious impact of money on, 46
   destructive effect of a bad workshop leader on, 103
   gift economy embedded in, 42
   importance during suggestions for improvement stage, 145
   magic of, initial reading stimulus for, 101
   as spirit of gift-giving in writers' workshop, 43
   (term description), 42

Yeats, William Butler
   craft elements, 89
Young, Dean
   craft elements, 89
   in "Jimmy, Jimmy, O Jimmy Mc" notes, 191

About the Author

Richard P. Gabriel holds a Ph.D. in computer science from Stanford University and an MFA in Writing (Poetry) from Warren Wilson College. His research areas include programming languages, design techniques, development environments and methodologies, software patterns, and the nature of poetic beauty. He is the author of two prior books, *Performance and Evaluation of Lisp Systems* (MIT Press) and *Patterns of Software: Tales from the Software Community* (Oxford University Press). He has published more than a hundred scientific, technical, and semipopular papers, articles, and essays on computing, and numerous poems in literary magazines. His manuscript *Leaf of My Puzzled Desire* was a finalist for the National Poetry Series and won Honorable Mention in the Sawtooth Poetry Prize Competition. Throughout his twenty-five-year career in academia and industry he has endeavored to bring together art and science, artists and scientists. He lives in California.

Register Your Book

at www.aw.com/cseng/register

You may be eligible to receive:
- Advance notice of forthcoming editions of the book
- Related book recommendations
- Chapter excerpts and supplements of forthcoming titles
- Information about special contests and promotions throughout the year
- Notices and reminders about author appearances, tradeshows, and online chats with special guests

Contact us

If you are interested in writing a book or reviewing manuscripts prior to publication, please write to us at:

Editorial Department
Addison-Wesley Professional
75 Arlington Street, Suite 300
Boston, MA 02116 USA
Email: AWPro@aw.com

Visit us on the Web: http://www.aw.com/cseng